WAGONS OF THE FINAL BRITISH RAIL ERA

A Pictorial Study of the 1983 to 1995 Period

WAGONS OF THE FINAL BRITISH RAIL ERA

A Pictorial Study of the 1983 to 1995 Period

David Larkin

Kestrel Railway Books
PO Box 269
SOUTHAMPTON
SO30 4XR

www.kestrelrailwaybooks.co.uk

Printed by the Amadeus Press.

ISBN 978-1-905505-17-3

Front Cover (Top Left): 110051, OBA, Exp. red/white livery at Scunthorpe in November 1980. (Author's Ref No W9041/DL)
Front Cover (Bottom Left): 110709, OBA as RRA, at Cardiff in June 1992. (Author's Ref No W17235/DL)
Front Cover (Top Right): 230008, VEA, as new in maroon, at Battersea in April 1978. (Author's Ref No W6885/DL)
Front Cover (Bottom Right): 361859, HEA, red/grey, at London Bridge in August 1982. (Author's Ref No W11621/DL)

Back Cover (Top Left): B927769, BDW, at Southampton in February 1989. (Author's Ref No W14911/DL)
Back Cover (Top Right): 361460, HEA, at Bow, East London in February 1989. (Author's Ref No W14994/DL)
Back Cover (Bottom Left): B745000, FVA, at Southampton in February 1989. (Author's Ref No W14927/DL)
Back Cover (Bottom Right): B955163, CAR, at Hither Green in July 1992. (Author's Ref No W17274/DL)

Contents

Introduction

B ritish Rail continued in existence until the early 1990s, gradually being broken up into privatised companies. As far as wagons were concerned, three train operating companies, Loadhaul, Mainline Freight and Transrail, were created and this series will stop at the point that the wagon fleet was disposed of to these companies. The subsequent fortunes of the fleet and the fairly rapid merging into one company, English, Welsh & Scottish, will not be covered and will be left to another author.

There were certain new types introduced after 1983 and these will be covered in depth; they were all part of the air braked fleet. There were far more conversions to this fleet and this will also be dealt with. The reallocation of many to the departmental fleet will be touched on but will be fully covered in a more appropriate volume in this series. It should be noted, however, that I ceased to have access to wagon records in the mid-1980s. I have tried, with the aid of books published in 1991 and 2008, to keep up with later modifications but I may have got the dates of introduction of modifications wrong, for which I apologise.

A major livery change was being implemented in 1983 and this was followed by another one in 1987, after it was decided that Railfreight's image was very poor. This will be covered in depth.

The TOPS computerised wagon record system was modified in 1983 to allow for more codes to be available for privately owned wagons and two ranges formerly allocated to BR-owned stock were merged with existing ranges. This will also be covered in detail.

Finally, many vacuum-braked wagons were given air through-pipes to make them compatible with the air-braked fleet, this representing the last fling of the traditional fleet.

The disposal of each class to the new owners in 1994 will be recorded, although individual numbers are not known.

The acknowledgements from the earlier volumes are repeated, especially to Jean.

David Larkin,
January 2010

910000, taken at Tinsley Yard, Sheffield in May 1992. Right up until privatisation, individual wagons were still being converted for possible new traffics. This is the prototype BBA with box bodywork for carrying hot metal. The new bodywork is black and the remainder flame red/black with double arrow and Railfreight symbol. Code BUA, it passed to LOADHAUL Ltd on 1st January 1994, although in store. (Author's Ref No W16997/DL)

Wagon Diagram Numbers and TOPS Codes

Private Owner wagons had been allocated only the P range for other than railtanks and T for all railtanks. After 1st October 1983 the K range for four-wheeled coil wagons became part of the S range for four-wheeled steel-carrying wagons, the J range for bogie coil wagons became part of the B range for bogie steel-carrying wagons and the U range for bulk materials and X ranges for special wagons were merged into existing series. Details are as follows:

JAV: None surviving.

JEV: Vacuum-braked Bogie Strip Coil wagons (W16xxxx series) became BJV.

JGV: Vacuum-braked Bogie Strip Coil wagons (W16xxxx series) became BGV.

JKX: Dual-braked Bogie Strip Coil wagons (26 70 428 8 xxx-x series) became BNX.

JMV: Converted BDV wagons for strip coil became BUV.

JPV: Converted BEV wagons for strip coil became BWV.

JRV: None surviving.

JSV: None surviving.

JTV: Vacuum-braked Bogie Strip Coil wagon (B9495xx series) became BYV.

JUV: None surviving.

JVV: Vacuum-braked Bogie Strip Coil wagons (B949050 – B949089) became BVV.

JWV: None surviving.

JXO: None surviving.

JYV: None surviving.

JZV: Vacuum-braked Bogie Strip Coil wagons (B949551 – B949608) became BFV.

KAV: Vacuum-braked Strip Coil wagons (B949130 – B949179) became SFV.

KBV: Vacuum-braked Strip Coil wagons (B949180 – B949219) became SGV.

KCO: Non-fitted Pig Iron wagons for strip coil became SCO.

KEV: Converted SPV wagons for rod coil became SEV.

KGO: None surviving.

KHO: None surviving.

KJO: Converted MSO wagons for strip coil became SJO.

KLV: None surviving.

KOA: Converted SAA or SPA wagons for rod coil became SKA.

KRV: Converted SPV wagons for rod coil became SRV.

KSV: None surviving.

KTA: Converted SAA or SPA wagons for strip coil became SHA.

KYV: None surviving.

UCV: Vacuum-braked 13T China Clay wagons (B743000 – B743874) became OOV.

UYV: Vacuum-braked 25T Anhydrite wagons (B747000 – B747149) became HYV.

XKB: Dual-braked Nuclear Flask wagons became FNA (now air-braked only).

XVA: Air-braked 990000 – 990049 became BXA.

XYV: Vacuum-braked BOILER EB wagon (B902805 – B902808) became FRV.

There may have been a few other X-coded vehicles but survival is uncertain.

B949537, taken at Hamworthy, Dorset in March 1989. This former JKX has now received the new code BNX. Little paintwork survives and the effect is pure rust. The sheets are grey nylon. (Author's Ref No W15806/DL)

550012, taken at Hither Green, South East London in July 1992. The rebuilt Nuclear Flask wagons are a buff colour with white hood and black bogies. Lettering, including the later FNA code, is black on white. (Author's Ref No W17273/DL)

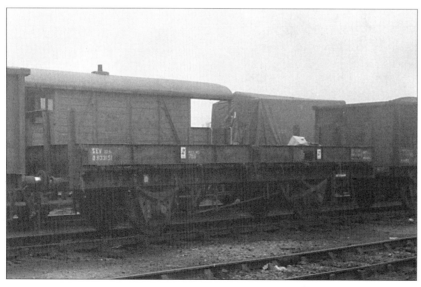

B933151, taken at Cardiff, Tidal Sidings in November 1983. This wagon has also received a coat of freight brown paint, along with the new SEV code. This is one of the earlier former Plate wagons with LNE pattern brakegear.
(Author's Ref No W13589/DL)

460722, taken at March, Cambridgeshire in March 1984. This SPA conversion retains the flame red livery that it was delivered in and has merely had the code changed to SHA. The sheets are grey translucent plastic. (Author's Ref No W13779/DL)

460654, taken at Cardiff, Tidal Sidings in June 1992. The SPA conversion to KOA, which became SKA after 1983, retained the flame red ends and the side supports were also painted the same colour to match. (Author's Ref No W17049/DL)

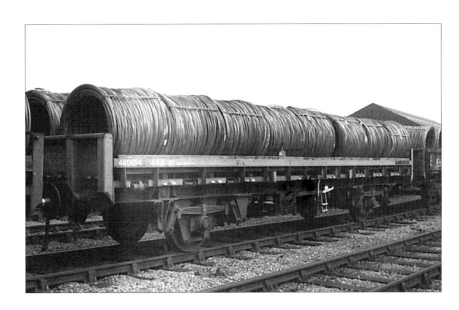

B934880, taken at Cardiff, Cathays in November 1983. There was more wood involved with the KRV Plate conversion and this retained the freight brown livery. The chalked lines for the new code and the number can plainly be seen. (Author's Ref No W13587/DL)

RAILFREIGHT and TRAINLOAD FREIGHT Liveries

There were basically two revised liveries to consider and all classes covered in the previous volume (1969–1982) will also be illustrated in this volume with later liveries. New vehicles delivered after 1983 will also be fully dealt with.

1979/1981 Experimental Liveries

The OBA 110264 was repainted yellow/grey (the so-called "Dutch" livery that was later used on civil engineer's wagons). Subsequently, it was further repainted flame red overall with white symbols and white lettering on a black panel. The VDA 210197 was painted with rail grey sides and flame red ends, with white lettering and symbols. Both these were photographed in 1979 and differed considerably from the standard flame red/ rail grey RAILFREIGHT livery.

The OBA 110044 was painted flame red/off white with white symbols and white lettering on black panels. Similarly, the VDA 201021 was given flame red ends and upper side panels and white lower side panels with white symbols and black lettering. Both these were photographed in 1981 and, apart from the substitution of rail grey for white, were of the standard final RAILFREIGHT livery.

110264, taken at Temple Mills Yard, East London in April 1979. This vehicle has recently emerged from Stratford works and represents the yellow/grey livery, which was not used for revenue-earning stock. (Author's Ref No W7925A/DL)

210197, taken at Temple Mills Yard, East London in April 1979. This van is seen next to the OBA illustrated above and was in a livery that was not proceeded with. (Author's Ref No W7485A/DL)

110264, taken at Temple Mills Yard, East London in August 1979. The OBA with yellow/grey livery appeared in all flame red livery a few months later and appeared to be in traffic. (Author's Ref No W7787/DL)

110044, taken at Rochester, Kent in April 1981. Certainly in traffic was this OBA with white lower sides. The new livery really stands out between the maroon liveried wagons on either side. (Author's Ref No W9040A/ DL)

201021, taken at Hoo Junction, near Rochester in April 1981. Similarly, this Taperlite suspension VDA stands out well against the maroon van to the right. (Author's Ref No W9020/DL)

Flame red/rail grey livery

The last vehicles to appear in maroon were the first 50 VEA vans, built in late 1978, and the next batch, built in early 1981, received the new livery. Some types, such as the OCA wagons of late 1981/early 1982 and the SPA wagons built from 1979 to 1981, did not lend themselves to two-toned liveries and were flame red only. The ODA wagons of 1983 were two-tone. Specialist wagons, such as the HDA hoppers, had flame red framing, as did the later CBA batch. The last batches of BDA and the BPA, BRA and XVA wagons were flame red with black. The VGA sliding-wall vans had flame red ends and symbol panels.

Most groups of RAILFREIGHT wagons did receive repaints and examples can be seen below. The grey specified was rail grey but certain wagon works appear to have used a much darker shade, possibly executive grey when it became available. This makes it rather difficult, in some cases, to see the different colour in a black and white photograph; my records show all the vehicles below as red/grey livery.

OAA class (freight brown from new)

Note: None of these appear to have been repainted in maroon RAILFREIGHT livery.

Vehicles known to have been repainted in flame red/rail grey livery:
100004/5/9/11/2/4/21/30/2/55/6/62/72/6/90/5/6/9.

100004, taken at Warrington, Arpley in May 1984. Depending on the plank size, the RAILFREIGHT symbol box did vary according to type. Under certain lighting conditions, it was sometimes difficult to determine where the flame red/rail grey dividing line was. (Author's Ref No W13906/DL)

100005, taken at Peterborough, in October 1982. The bottom four planks of the OAA class were the ones painted rail grey although, again, it is not that easy to tell. (Author's Ref No W12301/DL)

OBA class (maroon from new)

Note: The early wagons of this class, which retained original springs, were transferred to the civil engineer's department and did <u>not</u> receive flame red/rail grey livery. Only vehicles numbered above 110500 were so treated and my earliest numbered vehicle is in fact 110600.

Vehicles known to have been repainted in flame red/rail grey livery:
110600/35/7/8/49/58/68/81/7-9/91/7, 110712/24/6/38/40/69/98, 110800.

110635, taken at Plumstead, South East London in December 1988. As with the OAA class, it was sometimes difficult to work out the point where the flame red ended and the rail grey started. The top two planks, and the ends, are flame red. (Author's Ref No W14347/DL)

110649, taken at Chichester, Sussex in February 1989. The main vehicle here has an unusually placed symbol and very scruffy livery, although with definite demarcation of colours. The vehicle on the right is even more marked. (Author's Ref No W14898/DL)

110740, taken at Dumfries, Scotland in October 1988. This is another wagon with clearly marked livery change but it lacks a RAILFREIGHT symbol. It also retains the original springs. (Author's Ref No W14210/DL)

OCA Class (None maroon; flame red only from new)

ODA Class (None maroon; flame red/rail grey only from new)

VAA/VBA/VCA Classes (excluding 200550 – 200649) (freight brown from new)
Vehicles known to have been repainted in maroon livery: 200017/53/6/98, 200103/11/7/48, 200211//6/25/43/50/1/63/72/9/85/7/8/99, 200307/21/37/46/51/2/6/89, 200439.

Vehicles known to have been repainted in flame red/rail grey livery (including 200550–200649, which were delivered in maroon livery): 200006/15/6/21/5/6/33/72/82/6/95, 200100–2/5/714–7/21/5/8/32/3/43/59/73/5/96, 200211/22/39/45/63/81, 200302/11/2/25/31/4/8/9/41/3/4/50/3/9/63/5/6/97, 200407/13/50/1/3/7/9/61/72/6/7/80/8/95, 200504/11/27/52/75/6/84/8/98, 200601/4/9/13/28/32.

*200021, taken at Toton Yard, Nottinghamshire in February 1983. As was the case with the open wagons, the rail grey sides did not show up well when newly repainted. The flame red came down to the second rib under the roof.
(Author's Ref No W12654/DL)*

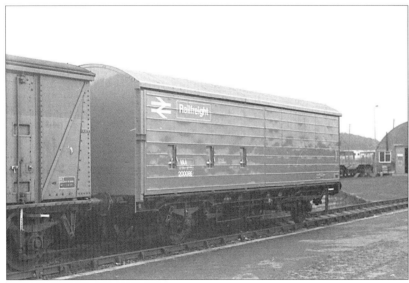

200086, taken at Ludgershall, Wiltshire in March 1989. The vacuum through-pipe has now been removed from this van and it has been recoded VAA, probably at the same time it was repainted flame red/rail grey. (Author's Ref No W15495/DL)

200105, taken at Warrington, Arpley in February 1982. Even after repainting in flame red/rail grey livery, which is very obvious here, the code is still the incorrect VBB instead of VAB. (Author's Ref No W11288/DL)

200576, taken at Crawley, Surrey in June 1983. The sides of the early vans were ribbed and this must have made application of the RAILFREIGHT and double arrow symbols a bit tricky, as seen here. (Author's Ref No W13093/DL)

200211, taken at Southampton, Hampshire in February 1989. The rendition of the livery, and the way the camera interpreted it on film, produced some bizarre results. The centre vehicle and the one on the left are both flame red/rail grey but the colours appear to be reversed on the latter van. (Author's Ref No W14940/DL)

200222, taken at Dinton, Wiltshire in June 1983. The vans with experimental suspension worked with all the others and were presumably monitored by the design department. Although repainted flame red/rail grey, this van has retained the vacuum through-pipe. (Author's Ref No W13087/DL)

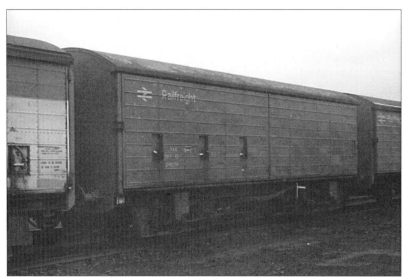

200239, taken at Dumfries, Scotland in October 1988. This van has had the vacuum through-pipe removed and been recoded VAA. The work seems to have been done at Carlisle Currock wagon shops, hence the small fox symbol. This was where the unusual RAILFREIGHT and double arrow symbols were applied when the livery was changed to flame red/rail grey. (Author's Ref No W14206/DL)

200281, taken at Swindon, Wiltshire in March 1989. From memory, the grey shade used on the lower part of the sides was not always rail grey, which would explain the wide variation of effects in these views. (Author's Ref No W15723/DL)

200302, taken at Mossend Yard, Scotland in March 1984. The middle 1980s period was the last when the early vans could be seen in any numbers, as they were soon to be replaced by more modern vehicles and, in certain cases, converted to other forms or transferred. (Author's Ref No W13828/DL)

200339, taken at Ebbw Vale, South Wales in November 1983. Showing signs of damage to the door runners, this wagon was withdrawn without repair but had lasted long enough to receive flame red/dark grey livery. (Author's Ref No W13674/DL)

200527, taken at York, Dringhouses Yard in April 1983. This van became part of the CM&EE department fleet in due course, which may have been imminent as others on the same day were photographed with new numbers and codes but remained in flame red/ grey livery. (Author's Ref No W13028/DL)

VDA Class (maroon from new)

Vehicles known to have been repainted in flame red/rail grey livery: 200688, 200718/29/91/6, 200811/26/9/60/86, 200926/8/32/4/55/65/79/94, 201005/7/10/2/5/32/42/6/56/62/7/82, 210110/8, 210267, 210330/7/54/9/90.

200729, taken at Manchester, Dewsnap Yard in November 1983. This is one of the variants with a darker grey shade and non-standard symbols, probably done at Carlisle. (Author's Ref No W13425/DL)

201010, taken at Three Bridges Yard in May 1983. This is a much more standard variant with obvious red/grey demarcation and correct symbols. (Author's Ref No W13068/DL)

210354, taken at Carlisle, Kingmoor Yard in October 1988. This appears to be another Carlisle Currock quirky livery with dark grey and another set of non-standard symbols. (Author's Ref No W14198/DL)

200791, taken at York, Dringhouses Yard in November 1983. A small number of the white-roofed VDA vans on Rowntree's chocolate traffic were repainted. This is one of the first batch and has clearly recognizable red/grey livery. (Author's Ref No W13703/DL)

200994, taken at Doncaster, South Yorkshire in May 1992. This is the only lot 3890 van to receive red/grey livery and it was photographed stored out of use with many other VDA vans. (Author's Ref No W17025/DL)

210359, taken at Doncaster, South Yorkshire in May 1992. Seen on the same occasion as the van above, this VDA carries the Carlisle Currock version of flame red/ dark grey livery and is also lettered BARRIER. (Author's Ref No W17022/DL)

The opens and the vans so far dealt with were the chief groups of vehicles to receive the full flame red/grey livery. The HEA, ODA and VEA classes will be dealt with later in this volume and the other classes had red as the main colour only, with black as the second colour.

The 1987 RAILFREIGHT SECTOR Liveries

This was a new livery scheme commissioned because it was felt that trade was being lost because of the perception of RAILFREIGHT as a tatty organisation with scruffy rolling stock. It chiefly involved locomotive liveries but some wagons were also repainted; at this time, of course, the emphasis was very much on private companies owning, or leasing, the wagons, which would be in their own livery and hauled by suitably liveried locomotives of the appropriate sector.

Three wagons, an FBA, an HAA and a VDA, the last being illustrated below, formed part of a livery demonstration at Ripple Lane Yard, East London, on 15th October 1987.

200706, taken at Doncaster, South Yorkshire in May 1992. This shows one side of the experimental van livery. The main body colour is probably rail grey with yellow ends. The symbol, for the RAILFREIGHT DISTRIBUTION sector is red diamonds on a yellow background with red surround. (Author's Ref No W17006/DL)

200706, taken at Doncaster, South Yorkshire in May 1992. The opposite side of the experimental van does not have the sector symbol but it does have the Carlisle Currock wagon shops fox symbol, which is probably were the van was regularly serviced. (Author's Ref No W17009/DL)

From these beginnings, locomotives began to appear in liveries with symbols applicable to a number of sectors, that is: RAILFREIGHT COAL, RAILFREIGHT CONSTRUCTION, RAILFREIGHT DISTRIBUTION, RAILFREIGHT GENERAL, RAILFREIGHT METALS and RAILFREIGHT PETROLEUM.

It appears to have been the intention to also have the wagons painted in a new livery and given the appropriate sector symbol. However, political change overtook events with the production of a Government White Paper on the Privatisation of Railways, which appeared in June 1992.

By then, there had been no deliveries of new wagons, and only a small batch of rebuilt vehicles to appear in the new livery. A small proportion of existing stock had also been repainted.

In view of this, the air braked fleet will be covered in the same numerical order as the previous volume, giving details of livery changes, conversions and, where appropriate, new designs.

After 1992, RAILFREIGHT was split up, in preparation for privatisation, into three regional areas, that is: TRAINLOAD FREIGHT – NORTH EAST (which covered the area specified up to the Scottish Border), TRAINLOAD FREIGHT – SOUTH EAST (which covered approximately the old Network South East area) and TRAINLOAD FREIGHT – WEST (which covered the rest of the country, including Scotland and Wales). There is some evidence of identity, for example, TLF-W painted on a flame red SPA wagon, but this was after the end of my wagon photography, which coincided with the publication of the White Paper.

This period, the period after 1994, when TRAINLOAD FREIGHT – NORTH EAST became LOADHAUL Ltd, TRAINLOAD FREIGHT – SOUTH EAST became MAINLINE FREIGHT Ltd, and TRAINLOAD FREIGHT – WEST became TRANSRAIL Ltd, and the later period when these three companies became ENGLISH, WELSH & SCOTTISH Ltd are not photographed.

I have listed, however, the totals of wagons of each type at 1st January 1994 and to which company they were allocated. I have no record of individual numbers.

There were a number of "traditional" wagons modified to work with the air braked fleet, mostly Bogie Bolster wagons, and these will be duly recorded in this volume.

351923, taken at York, North Sidings in July 1992. The "merry-go-round" hoppers were given large Coal Sector symbols initially but these were found to be rendered unreadable by the automatic rubber wheels at the unloading points and the smaller ones were substituted. This is a rebodied HAA originally built in 1966. (Author's Ref No W17283/DL)

Wagon Descriptions

OAA Class (100000 - 100099)

After the conversions noted in the previous volume and the red/grey livery changes noted on Page 6, there were relatively few changes to this class.

SECTOR LIVERY (yellow ends/executive grey sides/red and yellow DISTRIBUTION symbol)
The following vehicles are known to have carried this livery: 100025/93.

DC100025, taken at Hither Green, South East London in April 1992. This wagon has been transferred to the civil engineer's department and has lost the DISTRIBUTION sector symbols. It has, however, received the SQUID fishknd code name. (Author's Ref No W16814/DL)

Transfers to departmental stock without modification
Note: List does include the REDLAND modifications covered in the previous volume

The following were listed in 1991 as being transferred to the CCE department and coded ZDA SQUID (Design Code ZD 155A) in 4/1991:
DC100001–4/6–11/3/4/7–22/4–8/30–3/5–7/41/4/5/7–51/3/4/6–9/62/4/5/7–9/71/2/4/5/7/8/80/1/3/5/7/9/93/7/8

These were split between LOADHAUL Ltd, MAINLINE FREIGHT Ltd and TRANSRAIL Ltd at 1st January 1994 but totals cannot be given as they were included in the ex-OBA and -ODA fleets similarly transferred.

Eight OAA wagons remained in service with MAINLINE FREIGHT Ltd, with a ninth already listed as withdrawn.

OBA Class (110000 - 100800)

After the red/grey livery changes noted on Page 6, there were significant changes to this class.

<u>SECTOR LIVERY (yellow ends/executive grey sides/red and yellow RAILFREIGHT DISTRIBUTION symbol)</u>
The following vehicles are known to have carried this livery: 110637/56/84, 110797.

110656, taken at Hoo Junction, Rochester in April 1991. This has the full yellow/executive grey livery with the Carlisle Currock "Fox" symbol prominent and the DISTRIBUTION sector symbol rather worn at the right-hand end. (Author's Ref No W6561/DL)

<u>Wagons fitted with BRUNNINGHAUS suspension</u>
Note: 110501 – 110800 had this from new and the vehicles listed may <u>not</u> all have received it before transfer to the CCE.

110001/4/5/8/21/68/70, 110105/9/13/8/9/22/39/58/74/91/4/6, 110210/29/38/9/50/82, 110324/9/34/49/56/73/84/91, 110401/3/9/18/21/8/32/42/6/9/64/75/7/84.

At 1st January 1994, LOADHAUL Ltd received 42 OBA wagons and MAINLINE FREIGHT Ltd received 5 OBA wagons. None went to TRANSRAIL Ltd.

<u>Transfers to departmental stock without modification</u>

The following were transferred to the Chief Civil Engineer's department in 1983 for conveying ancillary equipment on engineering trains and coded ZDA BASS (design code ZD 143A/B/C) in April 1991:

DC110000–4/8–15/7–35/7–45/7–63/5–99, DC110100–18/20–31/3–47/9–56/8–93/5–9, DC110200–2/4–32/4/6–49/51–6/8–62/4–7/9–99, DC110300/2–11/5–22/4–31/3–9/41–7/9/50/2– 61/5/6/8/70/2–91/4/5/7–9, DC110400–3/5–9/11–4/7–24/6–31/3–5/7/40/2/4/5/7/9/51/3–65/7–71/3/–5/ 7–82/4, DC110529/30/91/6, DC110661/9/84, DC110780/82/99.

The following were transferred to the CCE at the same time and were subsequently moved to the Signal and Telegraph department and coded ZDA SATLINK (design code ZD 143A/B/C) in April 1991:

KDC110005–7/16/36/46/64, KDC110119/32/48/57/94, KDC110203/35/50/63/8, KDC110301/12–4/23/32/40/8/51/62–4/9/71/96, KDC110404/10/5/6/25/32/6/8/9/41/3/8/52/66/72/83, KDC110588, KDC110612/36/89, KDC110703/57.

OBA Class (continued)

<u>Transfers to departmental stock without modification (continued)</u>

The following were transferred to the Chief Mechanical and Electrical Engineers department in 1983 for conveying HST spares and coded ZDA BASS (design code ZD 145A/B) in April 1991:

ADC110233/57, ADC110392/3, ADC110446/76.

To these were added at a later date the following:

ADC110515/6/8–28, ADC110630.

<u>Transfers to departmental stock with modification</u>

DC110517 was converted to a ZVA wheel/bogie - carrying wagon (design code ZV 228A) and DC110534 and DC110786 were converted to ZEA BREAM runner wagons (design code ZE 009A).

DC110257, DC110389, DC110619/30/77, DC110728 (and probably others) were converted to ZCA SEA URCHIN with new steel bodywork.

<u>OTA Timber Wagon conversion</u>

Only one OBA, **110793 (Design Code OT 001A)** was converted, probably prior 1987, and no photograph is available. The vehicle was recorded in October 1988 with red peaked ends and a grey plastic shroud over a framework lettered SPEEDLINK DISTRIBUTION and double arrow in red. Intended for bagged china clay, it was coded **OEA** and was in departmental use as a ZRA by July 1998.

<u>RRA Runner Wagon Conversions</u>

The following vehicles were converted to runner wagons from the late 1980s onwards to design code RR 046A:

110532/38/40/2/53/67/70/2/6, 110601–3/13/22/32/4/40/75/9/95/8/9, 110707/9/17/35/6/42/4/5/7 /9/51/64/74/6/9/85/9/6.

110602, taken at Middlesborough, Teesside in June 1992. The whole body was removed for this conversion and a small inward-turning lip fixed to the top of the solebar. The floor was covered by mesh. In this case, the load on each BDA overhangs towards the RRA. (Author's Ref No 17093/DL)

110613, taken at Southampton, Hampshire in February 1989. This example does not have the mesh floor and, as this was taken earlier than the others photographed by me, it may have been a retrospective feature. (Author's Ref No W14934/DL)

OBA wagons modified for PLASMOR traffic

These were OBA wagons given raised ends and dedicated to breeze block traffic from Heck, near Doncaster to locations in the south, such as Biggleswade, Bow and Willesden. Most, but not all, were painted in PLASMOR livery, worked with custom-built stock on VCA van chassis (qv) and were coded OBA (design code OB 001E).

Numbers were as follows:
110531/5/7/41/3/5/50/62/8/78/82/4/6/7/98, 110604/8/9/14/5/8/21/5/6/9/33/42/7/51/2/4/7 /60/2/3/5/6/85, 110701/18/9/25/30/7/46/54/60/3/77/95.

110737 was repainted in executive grey/yellow sector livery with RAILFREIGHT DISTRIBUTION symbols. The ultimate fate of these vehicles seems to have varied.

110531, taken in Biggleswade, Huntingdonshire in February 1989. This example carries the PLASMOR BLOCKFREIGHT legend with appropriate symbols; livery is green/white/orange. The altered ends are clearly visible. (Author's Ref No W15099/DL)

110633, taken at Biggleswade, Huntingdonshire in February 1989. At least two, this example and 110754, operated in maroon livery with only the usual RAILFREIGHT symbols. (Author's Ref No W15105/DL)

One final OBA transfer to record were 110486–110514 and 110624, which were sold to British Nuclear Fuels Ltd in 1983 and became BNFL91000–BNFL91029, PFA skip wagons operating between Sellafield and Drigg. 110624 became BNFL91000 and the others followed in numerical sequence.

OCA Class (112000 - 112399)

The OCA class were all steel general merchandise open wagons and were effectively a taller version of the standard SPA air-braked Plate wagon, with three-part dropsides, fixed ends and turnover bolsters in the floor. If sheeting was required, two 17ft 6in wagon sheets tied over the ends and secured haphazardly at the centre were used. One batch only was built and building details were as follows:

112000 to 112399	45T OCA (OC 001A)	10/1981 to 3/1982	4014	BR (SHILDON)

Suspension fitted was Brunninghaus pattern and there were no alterations to this. Full flame red livery was applied from new.

112039, taken at Rochester, Kent in March 1982. This brand-new wagon shows the plain, but smart, original appearance of the class. They operated regularly with OBA wagons but not, apparently, with the OAA wagons. (Author's Ref No W10307/DL)

112224, taken at Hoo Junction, Rochester in August 1989. By 1989, the OCA wagons were due for repainting and a freshly repainted example is seen here. The load is also typical of the use of the class. (Author's Ref No W16438/DL)

SECTOR LIVERY (yellow ends/executive grey sides/red and yellow DISTRIBUTION symbol)
(Both wagons actually carrying wagon parts to and from Carlisle Currock)
The following vehicles are known to have carried this livery: 112230/44.

112244, taken at Cardiff, Tidal Sidings in June 1992. This SECTOR liveried OCA is conveying wagon wheels to and from Carlisle Currock wagon works. (Author's Ref No W17076/DL)

OCA Class (112000 - 112399) (continued)

On 1ˢᵗ January 1994, LOADHAUL Ltd received 6 OCA wagons, MAINLINE FREIGHT Ltd received 8 OCA wagons and TRANSRAIL Ltd received 52 OCA wagons.

Transfers to departmental stock without modification

The following were transferred to the Chief Civil Engineers department from 1984 for conveying ancillary equipment on engineering trains and coded ZDA BASS (design code ZD 148B) in April 1991:

DC112000/3/20/1/26–8/30–7/41/3–9/51–8/60–2/5/6/8/71/2/4/5/7/9/81/3/5–93/6/7/9, DC112101/3–7/9/11/2/4–6/8–28/30/1/3–9/41/4–6/8/50/2/3/5/6/8.

The following were transferred to the Chief Mechanical and Electrical Engineers department from 1984 for conveying ancillary equipment on engineering trains and coded ZDA (design code ZD 148A) in April 1991:

ADC112001/4–19/22–5.

Transfers to departmental stock later modified

The following wagons transferred to the CCE department's fleet were subsequently rebuilt, from about 1988 onwards, with fixed sides for carrying ballast. These wagons were coded ZCA SEAHORSE (design code ZC 515A) and were numbered as follows:

DC112029/39/40/2/50/9/68/73/6/8/80/2/4/94/5/8, DC112100/2/8/10/3/32/40/2/3/7/9/51/4/7.

OTA Timber Wagon conversions

This group of vehicles were the only significant OCA conversion but the story is more complex than the records available to me indicate. Three design codes are listed (OT 001A, OT 001B and OT 001C) but the first of these was the one previously given to the OBA, 110793, and there are two distinct end variations amongst the OCA conversions.

The following list gives the numbers of all former OCA wagons converted to OTA:

112160–2/6/7/70/5/8/80/2–90/4/6, 112204/7/8/10/2/6/20/5/6/31/4–7/9/41/3/6–8/51/3/5/7 /63/4/6–8/71/2/5/8/80–3/6/8–92/4/9, 112301–4/8/10/2/3/6–9/22–4/7–30/32–4/6/8–42 /5/7/9/51–3/5/8/64–6/9–72/6/8/80–8/91/6/9. (Note: It is possible that some had been withdrawn before the list was compiled; 112388 certainly had been).

The following groups are confirmed by photographs.

High, angled end extensions, red painted ends with grey stanchions

112175/80/2/7/8, 112251/7/90, 112317/47/64/88.

Low, rectangular end extensions, red painted ends with grey stanchions

112185/6, 112225, 112324/47/65.

OCA Class (112000 - 112399) (continued)

<u>OTA Timber Wagon conversions (continued)</u>

<u>High, angled end extensions, blue painted ends with white stanchions, THAMES BOARD labelling</u>

112184/90, 112204/26/82/6, 112304/12/22.

<u>High, angled end extensions, light green painted ends with white stanchions, SHOTTON PAPER labelling</u>

112182, 112247/68, 112317.

112364, taken at Southampton, Hampshire in February 1989. This partly-loaded OTA shows the high, angled end most of these vehicles had very well. Being partly loaded, the nylon security straps are also prominent. Livery is red with white stanchions. (Author's Ref No W14945/DL)

112185, taken at Inverness, Scotland in June 1992. The difference in height between the high, angled type end and the much less common rectangular type can be seen in this view. Livery is red with white stanchions. (Author's Ref No W17154/DL)

OCA Class (112000 - 112399) (continued)

OTA Timber Wagon conversions (continued)

112312, taken at Workington, Cumbria in October 1988. This wagon is in the pale blue livery with white stanchions and has the Thames Board Ltd brand on the end. (Author's Ref No W14194/DL)

112268, taken at Cardiff, Tidal Sidings, in June 1992. The OTA trains in later years were quite a colourful mixture. There were two different classes (ex-OCA and ex-VDA), sub-classes amongst the OCA conversions and at least four liveries. The vehicle on the immediate left is an ex-VDA in dark blue KRONOSPAN livery and the main vehicle, 112268, is in green/white SHOTTON PAPER livery. (Author's Ref No W17063/DL)

On 1st January 1994, all 165 OTA timber wagons, of whatever design, went to TRANSRAIL Ltd, which suggests that they were all working in Scotland and Wales by then.

ODA Class (113000–113049)

The ODA class were traditional 12T dropside Pipe wagons which were fitted with air brakes and roller bearings. They, along with the VEA class (qv), were necessary because the longer standard air-braked could not work round the sharp curves found in Ministry of Defence establishments. One batch only was built and building details were as follows:

113000 to 113049   12T ODA (OD 001A)   3/1983 to 5/1983   4030   BR (SHILDON)

Full flame red/dark grey livery was applied from new.

<u>SECTOR LIVERY (yellow ends/executive grey sides/red and yellow DISTRIBUTION symbol)</u>
(This may have been a prototype, to test out the new livery.)
The following vehicles are known to have carried this livery: 113017.

113024, taken at Shildon Works in April 1983. Slightly obscured by the works fence, this brand-new wagon has just emerged from the paint shops, along with another vehicle of the same class on the left. (Author's Ref No W4826/DL)

113036, taken at Dinton, Wiltshire in June 1983. This location was one that the ODA class were needed, as there was, at that time, a large rail-served MOD establishment at this locality. (Author's Ref No W13086/DL)

None survived in revenue earning traffic to be passed to LOADHAUL, MAINLINE FREIGHT or TRANSRAIL. It is believed that they all passed to the Signal and Telegraph Department as ZDA wagons (design code ZD 117G) and were numbered KDC113000 to KDC113049.

VAA/VBA/VBB Classes (200000–208, 200210–324, 200550–649)

Although they were by far the oldest air-braked vans, this group of vehicles did not feature in any rebuilding programmes. This was probably due to the fact that the brakegear was of a very early type and many of the vans had experimental suspension.

SECTOR LIVERY (yellow ends/executive grey sides/red and yellow DISTRIBUTION symbol)
The following vehicles are known to have carried this livery: 200029/41, 200138/48/90, 200207/53, 200301/12.

Certain vans were transferred to the various departmental fleets as follows:

ADC200064, ADC 200102/8/46/7, KDC200070/7, KDC200104/65, KDC200288, KDC200567, KDC200626.

83 vans coded VAA were passed over on 1st January 1994 (9 to LOADHAUL Ltd, 3 to MAINLINE FREIGHT Ltd and 71 to TRANSRAIL Ltd). 103 vans coded VBA were passed over on 1st January 1994 (63 to LOADHAUL Ltd, 16 to MAINLINE FREIGHT Ltd and 7 to TRANSRAIL Ltd). None of these lasted very long in all probability as most were stored.

200029, taken at Basingstoke, Hampshire in March 1992. This van is probably in store when photographed but it had received full yellow/executive grey SECTOR livery with appropriate symbols. In fact a chalked code of ZDA can be seen, suggesting imminent transfer to the departmental fleet. (Author's Ref No W16655/DL)

200207, taken at Doncaster, South Yorkshire in May 1992. Also in full yellow/executive grey SECTOR livery, this van still carries the incorrect VBA painted code, which should be VAA. (Author's Ref No W17007/DL)

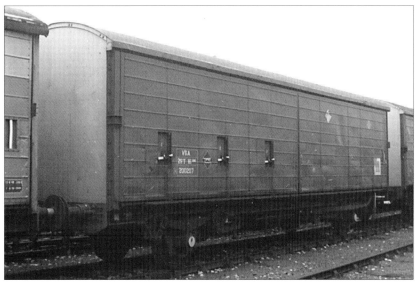

200253, taken at Cardiff, Tidal Sidings in June 1992. This van, in full SECTOR livery, was probably still in revenue-earning traffic, carrying South Wales tinplate. (Author's Ref No W17051/DL)

200301, taken at Cardiff, Tidal Sidings in June 1992. The rather complicated brakegear on the early air-braked designs is seen here and seems to have ruled them out for conversion, except for the ill-fated STEEL AB class (qv) (Author's Ref No W17052/DL)

200312, taken at Eastleigh, Hampshire in March 1992. The opposite side of the brakegear was very plain, as can be seen here. Full SECTOR livery on this group of vans does seem to have been more common than most classes. (Author's Ref No W16637/DL)

VCA Class (200325–200549)

This group of vans did not survive in revenue-earning traffic much beyond the late 1980s and the only 1989 view recorded by me was of a vehicle probably in store. Although large numbers received flame red/grey livery, only 200364 got yellow/executive grey livery, but without symbols, because it was a support vehicle in an exhibition train promoting the new image.

Comparatively few were converted, however, as almost the whole fleet was transferred to the various departments.

200341, taken at Dumfries, Scotland in October 1988. This van in flame red/dark grey livery appears to still be in traffic and was in company with other vans. (Author's Ref No W14205/DL)

200350, taken at Hoo Junction, Rochester in March 1989. The curse of graffiti was not quite so bad when this van in flame red/dark grey livery was recorded but it does suggest a van that has stood about a lot out of use. (Author's Ref No W15426/DL)

200364, taken at Harlow, Essex in February 1989. With brake pinned down to prevent any movement, this van was the generator vehicle for the SECTOR exhibition train and had received yellow end and executive grey sides to blend in. (Author's Ref No W15084/DL)

VCA Class (200325–200549) (continued)

There were a small number of conversions.

<u>RRA Runner wagons</u>

Two VCA vans had badly damaged bodywork and this was removed in late 1982 to leave just the chassis. Numbers were 200470 and 200478. Both were subsequently transferred to the Chief Civil Engineer as ZEA BREAM.

200478, taken at Bescot Yard, Walsall in February 1983. The floor remained unpainted but the sides and solebar were painted black and the buffer beam was red. (Author's Ref No W12670/DL)

<u>FPA Container Wagons</u>

These were VCA vans converted to carry a large open container of coal owned by J.G. RUSSELL and could be seen in Scotland and West London. They operated with converted SAA wagons from late 1984. Numbers were as follows:
200325/7/8/30/1/4/7/42/4/6/8/9/51/2/4/9/61/3/6, 200458/65, 200501/20

200337, taken at West Drayton, West London in June 1992. As with the RRA above, these vehicles were also painted black with a red buffer beam. The container is unpainted metal with a black on orange name. (Author's Ref No W17033/DL)

One final conversion to note was PNA breeze block wagons for PLASMOR. These were private owner wagons but the chassis came from VCA vans, all but one from the departmental fleet. For the record, these were as follows:
200367/71/5/7/81/6/90/2/3/5/6, 200409/11/3/6/7/9/21/4–7/34/7/9/44/5/7/9/50–2/5/8/60/9/79/82/5/7/90/1, 200502/7/10/3/6–8/21/2/6/33/41/9.

VDA Class (200650–201099, 210100–210399)

This group of vans remained in revenue-earning use until the early 1990s, by which time a fair proportion had been converted for other duties and a smaller proportion had been transferred into the departmental fleet.

SECTOR LIVERY (yellow ends/executive grey sides/red and yellow DISTRIBUTION symbol)
200706, covered on page 14, was one of the original SECTOR demonstration vehicles. 200882 and 200992 had flame red ends, rail grey sides and large DISTRIBUTION sector symbols.

The following vehicles are known to have carried the standard livery: 200723/5/60/73/85/94, 200805/27/34/73, 201084, 210303/74.

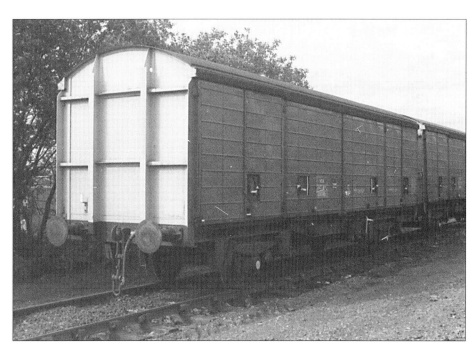

200785, taken at Carlisle Currock in June 1992. It is not thought that the yellow ends on the SECTOR vehicles were operationally inspired like the ends of locomotives and multi-units, but it could have been a safety feature. (Author's Ref No W17174/DL)

210374, taken at Doncaster, South Yorkshire in May 1992. The executive grey sides of the SECTOR vans, with just the symbol and data code, were quite distinctive provided they were kept clean. (Author's Ref No W17005/DL)

VDA Class (200650–201099, 210100–210399) (continued)

The following vans had been transferred to the departmental fleet by 1st January 1991:

ADC200651/2/4/6–8/61/4/6/7/9/75/7, ADC200715, ADC200815/79, ADC210271, KDC200655/60/2/3/5/8/70/1/
3/4/6/8–80/2/6/8/9/95/6/9, KDC200700/3/9/22/38/51/4/81/92/6, KDC200800/1/7/21/6/30/1/6/8/46/7/50/3/5/66/
70/91/3/6/8/9, KDC200900/3/4/12/7/9/21/6/37/9/71/7/83/4/92/5–7, DC201003/11/2/5/8/22/3/7/33/9/46/63/4/6/90,
KDC210107/25 /39/64/78/95/6/8, KDC210206/9/30/50/61/72/80/6/93, KDC210310/4/24/8/47/54/66/70/92.

98 vans coded VDA were passed over on 1st January 1994, 53 to LOADHAUL Ltd, 7 to MAINLINE FREIGHT
Ltd and 11 to Transrail Ltd. Most were already stored and few would have seen much further revenue-earning
traffic.

VDA 201070
This van was used as a test vehicle for new types of van bodywork. This was recorded in March 1984 as a VHA
with differing sides. One side was fully nylon and the other had nylon upper side with corrugated steel lower side
(the latter is thought to be a retrospective modification as it was originally reported as being fully nylon curtain).
This vehicle eventually became an OTA Timber wagon, with the VHA ends but without operating levers, and was
a CCE ZRA wagon by March 1992.

201070, taken at Mossend Yard, Scotland in March 1984. This would have been the original form of the VHA. The curtain was dark blue with red VHA code and white lettering. (Author's Ref No W13802A/DL)

201070, taken at Mossend Yard, Scotland in March 1984. This shows the opposite side of the van, with half curtain and half aluminium movable side. (Author's Ref No W13802B/DL)

VDA Class (200650–201099, 210100–210399) (continued)

OTA Timber Wagons

As with the OCA conversions (see page 21), this was an involved conversion, although not quite as complex as the OCA story was.

VDA vans from all three types were converted and they retained the original ends. This included 201070, which had been altered to VHA; this retained the altered ends. Some were later transferred to the CCE as sleeper wagons. Numbers were as follows:
200679, 200708/20/1/8/32/6/40/6/70, 200814/7/22/3/7/9/48/9/58/60/1/92, 200930/45/53/65/6/8/74/80–2/5, 201029/40/61/70/93, 210144/93, 210219, 210352/7/63.

It is believed that all these were in the flame red end/grey stanchion livery.

Certain wagons were subsequently repainted in the blue livery of KRONOSPAN Ltd and operated to Chirk, North Wales. Known examples were as follows:

200720/8/70, 200817/22, 200948/68, 201040/70/93, 210144/93, 210363.

210219, taken at Hexham, in October 1988. In the red/grey livery, this OTA has number and data plates attached to the sides, a feature not found on the OCA conversions. (Author's Ref No W14287/DL)

201040, taken at Hoo Junction, Rochester in June 1989. This partly-loaded OTA is converted from the VDA batch with Taperlite suspension. Livery is KRONOSPAN blue with white lettering. (Author's Ref No W16291/DL)

VDA Class (200650–201099, 210100–210399) (continued)

<u>RRA Runner Wagons</u>
Following the successful conversion of the two VCA chassis (see page 28), a number of VDA vans were also converted, to design code RR 038A, from 1983 onwards. Many subsequently were transferred to the CCE as ZEA BREAM wagons (design code ZE 001A) and given DC prefixes. Numbers were as follows:

200659/72, 200717/27/9/34/55/61/4/74/5/7/82/4/95/8, 200828/33/52/9/63/74/81/94/7, 200901/5/6/14–6/23/7/38 /43/6/9–52/4/61–3/72/6/8, 210103/4/6/10/4/6/7/9/28/34/5/7/40/7/55/7/60/8/80/9/92/4, 210204/10/4/20/3–5/7/8/ 31/7/42/4/7/51/7/73/95, 210333.

200915, taken at Cardiff, Tidal Sidings in June 1992. This wagon was the only one actually coded RRA, and thus in revenue-earning use, in 1991 and even this one had an overpainted BREAM code. Livery was black with red buffer beam. (Author's Ref No W17239/DL)

Two other conversions need to be recorded.

<u>REA Vans (RE 002A)</u>
These were Adaptor vans for use with LUL surface stock. Livery was brick red ends and upper sides and white lower sides with a narrow blue band. Numbers were as follows:
200756, 200808, 210142/52, 210309/67.

<u>RLA Vans (RL 001A/B/C)</u>
These were Adaptor vans for the transfer of London Underground tube stock. Livery was dark blue and one end had normal couplings and the other had low-height LUL stock couplings. Numbers were as follows:
200759/91, 200857, 201045/9/91, 210145/9/75/91, 210348.

165 OTA wagons of all types were transferred on 1st January 1994 and all went to TRANSRAIL Ltd.

88 RRA wagons of all types were transferred on 1st January 1994, 75 going to LOADHAUL Ltd and 13 to TRANSRAIL Ltd.

14 REA Adaptor vehicles were transferred on 1st January 1994, 6 going to MAINLINE FREIGHT Ltd and 8 to TRANSRAIL Ltd. (Note: These may actually have been B902601 – B902614 which were former BR passenger CCT chassis converted under lot 4041 in 1983.)

8 RLA Adaptor vans were transferred on 1st January 1994 and all went to MAINLINE FREIGHT Ltd.

VEA Class (230000–230549)

These vans were converted from VEV vans, which were themselves standard 12T Vanwide vans fitted with roller bearings. Those eventually classified VEA had received new running gear and suspension and were intended for use in tightly-curved Ministry of Defence establishments. They operated with the ODA class (see page 24) but predated them; in fact, the first fifty VEA vans were converted in 1978 but have been included here for convenience. Building details were as follows:

230000 to 230049	12T VAN (VE 001B)	4/1978 to 11/1978	3918	BR (ASHFORD)
230050 to 230109	12T VAN (VE 001B)	2/1981 to 5/1981	3982	BR (HORWICH)
230110 to 230399	12T VAN (VE 001B)	5/1982 to 1/1983	4017	BR (SHILDON)
230400 to 230549	12T VAN (VE 001B)	2/1983 to 6/1983	4028	BR (SHILDON)

The first batch, lot 3918, were delivered in maroon livery. The following subsequently received flame red/grey livery: 230013/22/37/40.

SECTOR LIVERY (yellow ends/executive grey sides/red and yellow DISTRIBUTION symbol)
The following vehicles are known to have carried this livery: 230142, 230326, 230414/69/98, 230523.

31 VEA vans were transferred on 1st January 1994, 2 going to MAINLINE FREIGHT Ltd and 27 going to TRANSRAIL Ltd; none were actually in traffic. The rest of the fleet had been transferred to the departmental fleet, the S&T department getting many, which were given KDC prefixes

230002, taken at Battersea, South West London in April 1978. Seen on delivery from Ashford Works, this was the third VEA van to be converted. (Author's Ref No W6884/DL)

230093, taken at Hoo Junction, Kent in May 1989. With the flame red/dark grey livery clearly visible, this Lot 3982 has an interesting set of warning posters, indicating military use. (Author's Ref No W16198/DL)

230332, taken at Bury St. Edmunds in February 1983. There were quite a few livery and lettering variations amongst these vans. The grey, not obvious here, aligns with the second end corrugation above the join. (Author's Ref No W12682/DL)

230163, taken at Hoo Junction, Kent in December 1988. Another livery/ lettering variation is shown here. This van also has the end vent blanked off, the only one recorded by me. (Author's Ref No W14459/ DL)

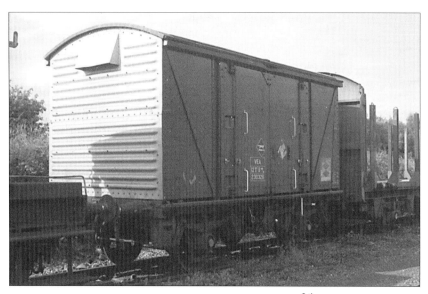

230326, taken at Carlisle Currock Wagon Works in June 1992. This van is one of six known to have been repainted in full SECTOR livery and is seen at the Carlisle Currock depot. (Author's Ref No W17176/DL)

VGA Class (210400–210650)

With the exception of the VEA class, all air-braked vans had been based on the early prototypes covered in the previous volume. The VGA class was the last BR van design and was very much based on contemporary European design. The design was described as "Sliding-wall" and this was a very accurate term. The sides in fact moved on runners to allow access. The ends were inset to allow the walls to slide out and also had the door-operating levers. The roof was slightly raised over the centre to cover the upper wall runners. Building details were as follows:

210400	24T VAN (VG 001A)	10/1981	4007	BR (SHILDON)
210401 to 210650	24T VAN (VG 001B)	2/1983 to 6/1983	4023	BR (SHILDON)

The first van, 210400, had flame red ends and unpainted metal sides and roof. Red double arrow and RAILFREIGHT transfers were applied to the left upper side. The production batch was given nameplates at the same height, double arrow and RAILFREIGHT on the left and SPEEDLINK on the right. There were a lot of variations over the years and the final vans were probably delivered without plates.

 SECTOR LIVERY (yellow ends/executive grey sides/red and yellow DISTRIBUTION symbol)
The following vehicles are known to have carried this livery: 210408/93, 210527/38/61, 210602/31/6/44. 210418 was painted in a special livery for an exhibition train.

160 VGA vans were transferred on 1st January 1994 and all went to TRANSRAIL Ltd. Some were recoded VKA but this variation has not been recorded and does not feature in the 1994 totals.

210400, taken at Rochester, Kent in October 1981. The prototype VGA van is seen here in company with contemporary European stock. (Author's Ref No W9029/DL)

210402, taken at Margam Yard, South Wales in February 1983. The second production VGA van, this was in use for South Wales metals traffic and is in as-new condition. (Author's Ref No W12825/DL)

210495, taken at Margam Yard, South Wales in March 1983. Also in as-new condition, this VGA van shows the ends and the levers to operate the sliding wall doors. Note the pulling handles. (Author's Ref No W12817/DL)

210650, taken at Mossend Yard, Scotland in October 1988. This view shows the last VGA van to be built but there is no evidence that nameplates were ever carried. (Author's Ref No W14231/DL)

210402, taken at Southampton, Hampshire in February 1989. This view shows the second production van some six years after the shot on page 35. Both nameplates have been removed and a small RAILFREIGHT transfer substituted in the upper left side. (Author's Ref No W14941/DL)

210464, taken at Avonmouth Docks in March 1989. This VGA van also has the small transfer but in this case it has been blanked out. It is uncertain if this is accidental or the result of wear. (Author's Ref No W15690/DL)

210418, taken at Harlow, Essex in February 1989. This VGA van formed part of an exhibition train promoting the SECTOR image and, although it has the yellow ends, the nameplates are non-standard. Both are lettered RAILFREIGHT with the double arrow symbol on the left and the General Sector symbol on the right. (Author's Ref No W15066/DL)

210527, taken at Carlisle Currock Wagon Works, in 1992. The standard SECTOR livery had the yellow ends and the Distribution Sector symbol on the lower right side. The RAILFREIGHT transfer was on the upper left side. (Author's Ref No W17168/DL)

CBA Class (250000–250056)

This class was not added to and details may be found on page 60 of the previous volume. Some began to appear with flame red framing in the late 1980s but none appeared with SECTOR livery. 35 vehicles were transferred on 1st January 1994 and all went to TRANSRAIL Ltd.

250001, taken at Burton-upon-Trent in February 1989. This was the second of the CBA class to be built and shows the plain end. The framing is flame red and the CBA code is in a normal number box. (Author's Ref No W15290/DL)

250035, taken at Burton-upon-Trent in February 1989. This CBA wagon, also with flame red framing but with the CBA code separate from the number box, shows the opposite end of this design. (Author's Ref No W15289/DL)

250056, taken at Burton-upon-Trent in February 1989. This CBA wagon is one of the later replacement batch from Lot 3922. Note the rivet line on the upper side, evidence that these vehicles had the later merry-go-round bodywork. Framing was probably flame red from new. (Author's Ref No W15280/DL)

HAA Class (Rebodying programme)

The last vehicles from Lot 3869 (at least from 358852) through to 359571 and 365000 to 366129 were built with slightly different bodywork, identified by a line of rivets on the upper sides and no internal cross bracing (although this was often missing anyway). Subsequently many HAA class vehicles were rebodied with this style. Known examples were as follows:

350004/54, 350303, 350408/42, 350638, 350915/55, 351060, 351199, 351214/59, 351334/50/67, 351691, 351704, 351811/39/79, 351902, 352169, 352274, 352334, 352454, 352602/3/81/3, 352821, 352926, 353030, 353230, 353343, 353529, 353615/9/54/63, 353791, 353823/40, 353955, 354027, 354256, 354309/16/7/71, 354430/48, 354618/62, 354779, 355009/44, 355203/80, 355763, 356129/63, 356322/44. 356595.

These were all in flame red bracing livery.

Un-rebodied vehicles known to be repainted in flame red bracing livery were as follows:
350005, 350297, 350379, 350537, 351111/69, 351673, 351902/76/88/92, 352537, 352668/75, 352877, 353006, 353143, 353201, 353334/90, 353448, 353535, 353635, 353728, 353935/95, 354104/32, 354214, 354312, 354504/23/33/68, 354738, 354939/89, 355098, 355324/9/95, 355411, 355617, 355841/77, 356041, 356473, 356650/78, 356893, 357027/34, 357155, 357399, 357635, 357735, 357828, 358225/99, 358328, 358524, 358616.

The following were painted in Coal SECTOR livery. Two variants were recorded.

LARGE SECTOR SYMBOL
351923, 356318.

SMALL SECTOR SYMBOL
351936, 352808, 353533, 353738, 354515, 354645, 354921, 355012/72, 355148, 355327, 355422, 355587, 355855, 356133, 356245, 356455, 356624, 357501, 357912, 358227, 358816.

4841 HAA wagons were transferred on 1st January 1994, 1897 going to LOADHAUL Ltd, 1569 going to MAINLINE FREIGHT Ltd and 1202 going to TRANSRAIL Ltd.

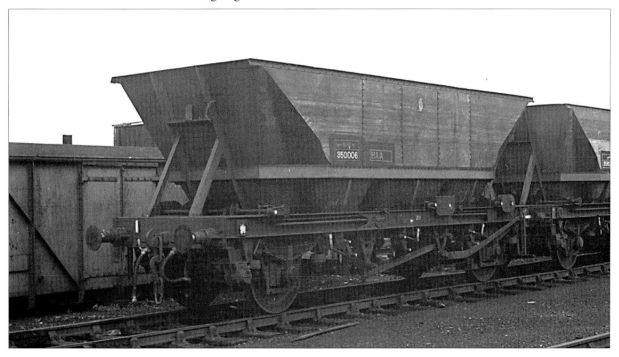

350006, taken at Hoo Junction, Rochester in October 1981. This early HAA has been given flame red bracing but is otherwise in the generally dirty condition of the un-rebodied fleet. (Author's Ref No W11192/DL)

359539, taken at Northwich, Cheshire in November 1983. This late HAA has the new bodywork with rivet line but is work-stained and has freight brown bracing. (Author's Ref No W13461/DL)

365000, taken at Warrington, Arpley in February 1982. All the HAA class in the new number range had flame red framing and the first of these has seen enough use to be marked by the rubber tires at discharge points along the sides. (Author's Ref No W11283/DL)

366068, taken at West Hartlepool in October 1981. This is a brand-new HAA with flame red bracing and natural metal bodywork with no work stains. (Author's Ref No W8983/DL)

350004, taken at Hither Green, South East London in March 1989. This early HAA has recently been rebodied and has flame red bracing and natural metal bodywork. (Author's Ref No W15944/DL)

356344, taken at Hither Green, South East London in March 1989. Taken a few days later, eight years separate the ages of this and the vehicle above but, with rebodying, they were indistinguishable from one another. (Author's Ref No W16020/DL)

351936, taken at Hither Green, South East London in March 1989. HAA wagons with Coal SECTOR livery, with yellow bracing, were working alongside those with flame red bracing. This example has the small Sector symbol. (Author's Ref No W16011/DL)

HCA Class (HAA wagons with canopy)

It had not been found necessary to have a special code for the HOP 32 AB class, which had canopies, when the TOPS codes were introduced. These wagons, although fairly widespread at first, eventually gravitated towards the collieries in the Edinburgh area.

By the early 1990s, HAA class wagons were operating over much longer distances at higher speeds, particularly on the West Coast Main Line, and, to alleviate complaints of coal dust being blown from loaded HAA class wagons, it was decided to use only those with canopies on the services affected. The initial fleet were recoded HCA to identify them and further vehicles were given canopies to add to the numbers of wagons available. (Note: See also the HDA class section (qv). Numbers for the HCA class were as follows:
350001, 350941/63/87, 351010/56/63/77/9/94/6, 351112/3/5/7–9/21/3/4/7/8/31/43/7/56/67/8/71/5/83/5/90/6, 351214/7/24/5/8/35/9, 351509/32/40/50/6/60/2–4/83/93, 351601/17/38/63/8/78, 351848/56/7/67/70, 352330, 352694–6/8, 352702/4–12/5/6/8/23–5/7/8/30–3/6–8/40–6, 353518, 354124, 354247/8/50/4/5/8/9/62–7/9/71/4/5/7/8/80–3/5–7/9/92/4–6, 354420/82, 355144/55, 356200, 357916.

113 HCA class wagons were transferred on 1st January 1994, 15 going to LOADHAUL Ltd, 4 going to MAINLINE FREIGHT Ltd and 91 going to TRANSRAIL Ltd.

350001, taken at Millerhill Yard, Scotland in March 1984. The first of the class is seen here with HAA code and in dirty livery with freight brown bracing. (Author's Ref No W13842/DL)

351117, taken at Northfleet, Kent in March 1989. This vehicle was recorded at Millerhill on the same occasion as the vehicle above. Here it is seen, some five years later, at the other end of the country. Livery was again freight brown framing and HAA code. (Author's Ref No W15867/DL)

351224, taken at Northfleet, Kent in March 1989. Also working into the APCM cement works (soon to close), this is another of the original canopy fitted vehicles with HAA code but with flame red framing. (Author's Ref No W15875/DL)

354248, taken at Millerhill Yard, Scotland in March 1984. Vehicles with flame red framing were also operating in Scotland in 1984. This one has retained the old HOP 32 AB code as well as the HAA code. (Author's Ref No W13836/DL)

354482, taken at York, North Yard in July 1992. This is an HAA wagon that has been rebodied, then retrospectively fitted with a canopy. At that stage it has received the HCA code. Livery is flame red bracing with a crudely overpainted code. (Author's Ref No W17286/DL)

HDA and HBA Classes (without and with canopies)

The HDA class were a derivative of the HAA class permitted to run at 60 mph and with prominent operating pistons on the corner of one buffer beam. Only one batch was built, details as follows:

368000 to 368459   32.5T HOP (HD 001A)   2/1982 to 10/1982   4008   BR (SHILDON)

Livery was natural metal with flame red framing. Only 32 remained unmodified (see below) to be transferred on 1st January 1994 and all went to TRANSRAIL Ltd.

Almost the whole fleet were subsequently given canopies, as per the HCA class. These were coded HBA, as the original use of this code (on domestic coal hoppers) had lapsed. Numbers were as follows:
368001/8/9/14–6/24/6/32/40/5/58/73/6/7/81/5/6/8/93/4/7/8, 368102/4/8/9/15/25/7/31/2/6/51/64/6/71/3/
4/85/6/90/6–8, 368203/8/11/3–5/21/3/6/8/9/33/5/7/9/46/57/60/2/5–8/76/7/9–81/6/96/9,
368301/9/11/2/7/22/4/6/9/32/5/7/8/46/52/4–6/9/70/5–7/89/91/8, 368405/9/10/8/25–7/9/31/2/44/6/55/9.

381 were transferred on 1st January 1994, 99 going to LOADHAUL Ltd, 182 going to MAINLINE FREIGHT Ltd and 99 going to TRANSRAIL Ltd.

368106, taken at Hoo Junction, Rochester in August 1982. The equipment that separated the HDA class from the earlier HAA class can be prominently seen on the far side of the right-hand buffer beam. Livery is natural metal with flame red bracing. (Author's Ref No W11611/DL)

368129, taken at Burton-upon-Trent in July 1992. The addition of the canopy might have been carried out here, as this location has a designated wagon works for merry-go-round hoppers. Livery remains flame red bracing but the HBA code has been applied. (Author's Ref No W17281/DL)

HAA Class (derivatives)

These were very few and far between. The final HAA of the original number range, 359571, was fitted with pneumatic doors but this vehicle subsequently became an RBA Barrier wagon by 1985.

A relatively small number of wagons were given box bodywork rather similar to that given to a larger number of HEA wagons (qv). Intended for coal, they were originally given vacuum through-pipes and coded MAB. Livery was SECTOR yellow/executive grey with small Coal SECTOR symbol. Numbers were as follows:
351749, 353237, 353458, 353700, 356725.

All five were transferred to TRANSRAIL Ltd on 1st January 1994.

In June 1992, three vehicles numbered 392000 to 392002 were recorded coded MAA. It is presumed these were three of the MAB conversions but details are not known as to which vehicle became which.

392001, taken at Swansea Docks, South Wales in June 1992. These box-bodied conversions always operated with the similar former HEA MEA conversions. (Author's Ref No W17206/DL)

392002, taken at Swansea Docks, South Wales in June 1992. The opposite side of the brakegear is shown here on this MAA conversion. No more were ever done and HAA wagons were cut up rather than re-used. (Author's Ref No W17205/ DL)

HEA Class (HBA domestic-coal with new springs)

The domestic coal hopper wagons of the original HBA class, this code being later used a second time for an HAA variant, had traditional springs. From the early 1980s, these wagons were given replacement Brunninghaus suspension and, in due course, were coded HEA.

In 1979, one vehicle, 361552, had appeared in an exhibition train in flame red/rail grey livery. This was slightly different to later applications of this livery in that the red extended all the way to the end floor on the end support and the struts; in the later vehicles, the lower half was grey. The double arrow/Railfreight symbol was also on the right; it was on the left on later repaints.

The following is a breakdown of flame red/grey combinations recorded.
Original springs; HBA code; Large symbols
360204/69/83, 360325, 360439, 360560, 360712/50
Original springs; HBA code; Small symbols
360320, 360522, 360667, 360708, 360838, 361537, 361726/71
Brunninghaus springs; HEA code; Large symbols
360001/34/54, 360100, 360201/75, 360672, 360719/51/6, 361338, 361534/55, 361817/97, 361910.
Brunninghaus springs; HEA code; Small symbols
360010/78, 360503/55, 360757, 361783, 361825/59/71/81/5, 361903/41/5/82/94/6.

Note: The following became HEA with new springs but retained freight brown livery:
360008/11/48/56/79/80/99, 360101, 360374, 360440, 360744, 360824/56, 360967, 361066, 361211/41/54, 361366, 361418/60/98, 361685.

360269, taken at West Hartlepool in October 1981. Repainting in flame red/grey livery came before conversion to HEA with new springs. This is an early example with one variation of new symbols. (Author's Ref No W8984/DL)

360320, taken at Birkenhead, Wirral in November 1979. This HBA has been repainted in flame red/grey livery but has a much smaller variation of new symbols in a different position. (Author's Ref No W8685/DL)

360011, taken at Aylesbury, Bucks. in May 1982. This wagon is one of the very early batch with end ladder in the central position. Although now converted to HEA, it has retained the freight brown livery. (Author's Ref No W11527/DL)

360275, taken at Avonmouth Docks in March 1989. This HEA is in flame red/grey livery and was loaded with coke when recorded, this being a long standing destination for such traffic. (Author's Ref No W15707/DL)

361996, taken at Strood, Kent in March 1983. It is possible that the last examples of the HBA were actually delivered in flame red/grey livery. This vehicle, in domestic coal duties, was third from last and is now an HEA. (Author's Ref No W12706/DL)

HEA Class (SECTOR Livery and derivatives)

Only two wagons have been recorded as being painted in SECTOR livery. These were 360853 and 361870. Livery was standard executive grey with yellow framing and top edge. The SECTOR symbol was the red/yellow DISTRIBUTION rather than the black/yellow COAL and probably reflected the domestic coal classification.

361870, taken at Basingstoke, Hampshire in March 1992. This wagon, and the similarly-liveried 360853, appeared to operate together and might have been demonstration wagons. (Author's Ref No W16656/DL)

1109 HEA class wagons were transferred on 1st January 1994, 206 going to LOADHAUL Ltd, 264 going to MAINLINE FREIGHT Ltd and 576 going to TRANSRAIL Ltd.

HSA Scrap Hopper Wagons (ex HEA)

This was a fairly simple conversion of the standard HEA. The hopper doors were welded shut and the load was removed from the hopper by electro-magnet or grab. This conversion appears to have been carried out in the mid-1980s. 148 HAS class wagons were transferred on 1st January 1994, 77 going to LOADHAUL Ltd, 40 stored going to MAINLINE FREIGHT Ltd and 8 to Derby Test Centre. Numbers of known examples were as follows:

360008/19/23/40/71/3/5/8/87/97, 360122–4/7/35/9/43/5/9/63/9/73/7/9/83/92, 360215/26/8/36/51/2/60/5/7/87, 360311/2/20/5/9/33/9/51/3/7/8/71/91, 360422/4/51/4/7/8/60/6/77, 360500/2/11/27/32/7/9/41/2/4/8/72/95, 360600/3/13/5/6/27/39/49/52/64/5, 360702/7/13/28/9/31/7/43/8/61/6/81/5/8/94, 360802/16/7/20/6/9/40/7/50/ 63/5/74, 360902/4/13/4/24/9/48/59/69/73/82/92–4, 361038/46/57/61/82–4/92/4/9, 361103/31–3/44/55/8/65/72/ 86/7/94/9, 361200/9/10/26/7/37/52/7/69/78/84/6/8, 361304/9–12/9/24/33/44/54/68/84/5/9/95/9, 361414/21/6/32– 4/7/9/82/3/6/93, 361509/25/6/38/44/5/9/83/92, 361618/22/4/34/46/8/59/61/84/9/93, 361702/14/7/26/31/41/9/ 50/8/66/73/7/85/92/6, 361800/4/34/45/54/5/9/64/71/80/95, 361901/12/9/35/9/41/63/5/98.

360040, taken at Manchester, Ardwick in October 1988. This is another early example with centre end ladder. The livery is freight brown with only the code changed to HSA. (Author's Ref No W14168/DL)

HEA Class (SECTOR Livery and derivatives) (continued)

361998, taken at Mossend Yard, Scotland in October 1988. This was the final HBA built and is in flame red/rail grey livery with HSA code. (Author's Ref No W14222/DL)

360162, taken at Tinsley Yard, Sheffield in May 1992. By 1992, the HSA class had received a blue and white St. Andrew's Cross symbol to help identification. This is yet another early centre ladder wagon in freight brown livery. (Author's Ref No W17001/DL)

Four HSA class wagons, 360040, 360761, 361468 and 361486, were rebuilt in the late 1980s with box bodies and recoded SJA. Intended for scrap traffic, they were not repeated, it being preferred to purchase second-hand stock (the SSA class (see page 59)). Three passed to LOADHAUL Ltd in 1994.

360761, taken at Tinsley Yard, Sheffield in May 1992. All the SJA conversions were delivered in flame red livery without rail grey and resembled contemporary private owner stock rather than the MFA wagons covered in the previous volume in this series, which were also of HBA origin. (Author's Ref No W16994/DL)

HEA Class (SECTOR Livery and derivatives) (continued)

Another box-bodied conversion was the MEA class. These were intended for coal traffic and all were delivered in yellow/executive grey livery with Coal SECTOR symbol. Three prototypes, 360610 (?), 360810 and 360821, were delivered with vacuum through-pipes, were not renumbered and were classed MEB; livery is uncertain for these. The main batch was air-braked only. They were converted at Doncaster in 1990 and at Crewe in 1993 and were renumbered as follows:

391000 (360744); 391001 (360688); 391002 (360900); 391003 (361349); 391004 (360206); 391005 (360440); 391006 (360854); 391007 (360152); 391008 (360370); 391009 (361239); 391010 (360409); 391011 (361117); 391012 (361463); 391013 (360463); 391014 (360550); 391015 (360172); 391016 (361454); 391017 (360081); 391018 (361119); 391019 (360911); 391020 (360378); 391021 (360033); 391022 (360670); 391023 (360680); 391024 (360327); 391025 (360624); 391026 (361230); 391027 (360876); 391028 (361037); 391029 (360974); 391030 (360806); 391031 (360782); 391032 (360427); 391033 (361231); 391034 (360983); 391035 (361097); 391036 (360113); 391037 (360588); 391038 (360066); 391039 (361241); 391040 (360694); 391041 (360795); 391042 (360963); 391043 (360990); 391044 (360554); 391045 (361608); 391046 (360938); 391047 (360835); 391048 (361244); 391049 (361727); 391050 (360531); 391051 (360234); 391052 (361818); 391053 (360555); 391054 (361134); 391055 (360605); 391056 (360618); 391057 (361287); 391058 (360754); 391059 (360257); 391060 (360405); 391061 (361934); 391062 (361953); 391063 (361071); 391064 (360059); 391065 (360379); 391066 (361727); 391067 (361222); 391068 (361153); 391069 (360001); 391070 (360611); 391071 (360727); 391072 (361636); 391073 (361345); 391074 (360498); 391075 (361377); 391076 (360661); 391077 (360082); 391078 (360635); 391079 (361138); 391080 (361769); 391081 (360106); 391082 (360184).

This was probably not the whole fleet as 127 MEA class wagons, plus the 3 MEB Class wagons, were transferred on 1st January 1994. Further batches of MEA class wagons were converted from 1995 until 2004; conversely 43 of the above were reduced in height as MFA class wagons.

Note: 360610 was recorded in 1992 as a RNB Nuclear Barrier wagon and it retained hopper bodywork, which throws doubt on it ever having been an MEB.

391007, taken at Swansea, South Wales in June 1992. The MEA class were serviced at Barry wagon works and had the sailing ship symbol as well as the full SECTOR livery with Coal Sector symbol. (Author's Ref No W17212/ DL)

The final HEA conversion was the RNA Nuclear Barrier wagons. Initially, these vehicles retained HEA configuration but the hoppers were cut down in due course. Numbers were as follows:
360046/69, 360211/54, 360492, 360592, 360630, 360718/68, 360808, 361001, 361105/12/84, 361253/74, 361394, 361484, 361522/61/81, 361627, 361738/9/74/98, 361867, 361900/10/68.

In 1992, 360323 (freight brown livery), 360610 (SECTOR livery) and 360254, 361990 (flame red/rail grey livery) retained hopper bodywork. 360592 (freight brown livery) and 360089, 360492, 361001, 361164, 361484, 361561, 361739/98, 361900 (SECTOR livery) had been cut down.

31 RNA class wagons were transferred on 1st January 1994, all going to TRANSRAIL Ltd.

HEA Class (SECTOR Livery and derivatives) (continued)

361990, taken at Hither Green, South East London in June 1992. This RNA is still in full HEA configuration and retains the flame red/rail grey livery it was probably delivered in. Only the code has been changed. (Author's Ref No W17257/ DL)

360610, taken at Hither Green. South East London in July 1992. This wagon is something of a mystery. It was listed in 1990 as an MEB (see page 50) but, apart from the removal of the door handles, it remains in HEA configuration. Livery is yellow/executive grey Coal SECTOR and code is BARRIER RNB. (Author's Ref No W17294/DL)

360592, taken at Grove Park, South East London in June 1992. The RNA fleet was eventually converted to this cut-down form to enable the guard to observe the nuclear flask wagon, as is demonstrated here. This example retains freight brown livery. (Author's Ref No W17195/DL)

CDA Class (Lot 4062 and conversions)

China clay traffic within Cornwall was still an important traffic and the elderly vacuum-braked open fleet, although given permanent sheets, was becoming time expired. In 1987, a new covered version of the HAA design was introduced. Numbers for these were as follows:

375000 to 375123   31.5T COVHOP (CD 001A)   1987/8   4062   BREL (DONCASTER)

These were supplemented in 1989 by fourteen converted HAA wagons numbered as follows:
353224 (Prototype); 375124 (350766); 375125 (355503); 375126 (356667); 375127 (356414); 375128 (351219); 375129 (353542); 375130 (353869); 375131 (356105); 375132 (351303); 375133 (355088); 375134 (356859); 375135 (353283); 375136 (350245); 375137 (354721).

A total of 139 vehicles were transferred to TRANSRAIL Ltd on 1st January 1994.

375001, taken at Par, Cornwall in June 1992. This is the second CDA built. When new, these wagons had natural metal bodywork with blue framing and a white on blue ECC symbol, which has been obliterated here. (Author's Ref No W17243/DL)

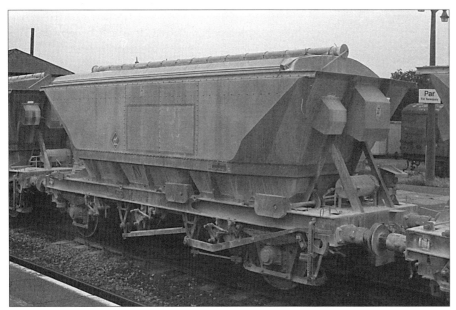

375100, taken at Par, Cornwall in June 1992. Viewed from the opposite angle, this CDA is in similar condition. The white on black Lizard symbol was a later addition, indicating servicing at St. Blazey. (Author's Ref No W17240/DL)

375131, taken at Par, Cornwall in June 1992. This was the former HAA 356105 but, when rebuilt to CDA configuration, they were indistinguishable from the Lot 4062 wagons. (Author's Ref No W17246/ DL)

375136, taken at Par, Cornwall in June 1992. The normal HAA brakegear was used on the CDA class but there was additional roof operating equipment. This was formerly HAA 350245. (Author's Ref No W17253/ DL)

375105, taken at Par, Cornwall in June 1992. This view shows the roof of the CDA, the movable portion of which was blue. These wagons appear to have operated with all the opening roof portions on the same side of the train. (Author's Ref No W17297/DL)

SAA Class (all conversions)

The STEEL AB (SAA) class were something of a problem. Designed to carry steel in the fashion of a Double Bolster wagon, there were rarely so used. It appears that there was a serious accident with the type, possibly with such a load, and 400043/61/74/84, 400108/22/7/8/72 and 400213/45/51/76/96 were all scrapped between 1971 and 1974.

The remainder were used for other traffic (see the previous volume in this series) and, by 1983, this became formalised.

FBA (Mini-Link Container Flat)
These were briefly operated by FREIGHTLINER Ltd as demonstration vehicles to try and attract short-haul traffic. Up to four yellow/red containers were carried. These conversions were still to be seen as late as April 1989. One was shown as being transferred to RAILFREIGHT DISTRIBUTION Ltd on 1st January 1994. Numbers were: 400042, 400120, 400244, 400297.

FPA (Coal/Dolophines Container Flat)
The bulk of the SAA fleet were converted during late 1984 to carry single containers owned by JG RUSSELL Ltd (see also page 28). Numbers were as follows:
400046/7/9/51/4/5/7/9/60/2–6/8/9/71/2/5–9/81/2/5/6/8–91/3–5/7–9, 400101–5/9/10/2–9/21/3–6/9/31/2/ 4–41/3/ 4/6–50/2–67/9/71/4–9/82–8/90/2–6/9, 400200–12/4–8/20–4/6–9/31–5/7–40/2/3/6–50/ 2–4/6–60/2–4/6–71/3/4/ 8–82/5/6/8–95/8.

216 FPA wagons were transferred to TRANSRAIL Ltd on 1st January 1994.

400082, taken at Aberdeen, Scotland in June 1992. This FPA is carrying a silver container. As can be seen, the standard ISO–sized container did not reach the full length of the chassis. (Author's Ref No W17125/DL)

400086, taken at West Drayton, London in June 1992. This FPA has a red buffer beam, as some of these vehicles did. The container is orange with purple RUSSELL on white panels. (Author's Ref No W17028/DL)

RBA/RRA (Barrier/Runner Wagons)

This has always been a regular use of this class and the following vehicles were formally coded RRA from 1984 onwards, some later going to the CCE department with DC-prefixed numbers:
400000–3/5/6/8–16/8–35/7–40/4/5, 400173/91/7, 400236/65/72/7/83.

400024, taken at Stoke-on-Trent in August 1983. This wagon has been in use as a barrier wagon and has a plate lettered ON HIRE TO I.C.I. TO WORK BETWEEN GRANGEMOUTH and HAVERTON HILL. In freight brown livery, it is being used as an RRA runner wagon. (Authors Ref No W13112/DL)

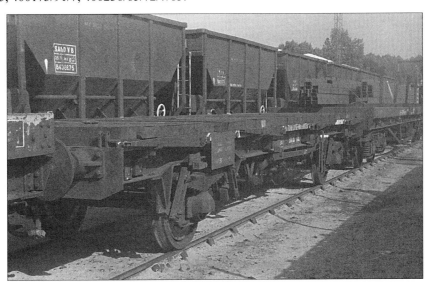

400191, taken at Southampton, Hampshire in February 1989. This wagon has received the full RRA conversion and is painted black with red bufferbeam. It is seen here marshalled between two BDA wagons with overhanging loads. (Author's Ref No W14931/DL)

SPA Class (originals)

Despite quite a large number of the SPA class being transferred to the CCE and other being converted, as listed below, a significant number remained in original condition, although designated SPA Coil/Dolophine. In 1990, the following wagons were still classified SPA:

460118/23/37, 460211/21/66, 460332–43/6–61/4–78/80/3/4/6–9/92–9, 460401–6/8–13/5/7/8/20/2–8/30/ 2–40/3/6/7/9–53/5–62/5–71/3–81/3/5/7–9/91/3–6/8/9, 460500–13/5/6/21/3–8/31–6/8/40/3–5/7/9/51–8/60/2/4–6/8–70/3/4/6–82/4–9/94/5/7–9,460600–5/7/9–11/5–8/20/2–5/8/30–6/8/9/41–53/6/8/60–2/4/7–9/71–3/5–7/80–2/4/6/7/9–93/5/6/8/9, 460701–3/5/8/10/1/3–5/7/9–21/5/7/30–41/5–9/52/5/6/9/62–5/7–9/72/4/7/8/80/2–91/4/7/8, 460800–8/12/4/7–9/24/8–31/3–5/7–41/3–5/8/50/1/3–5/7–60/2–4/6–71/3/4/6–8/80–2/4–8/90–5/7/9, 460900–3/5/7/8/10–5/8/9/21–34/6/8/40/3–8/50/1/4–6/8–65/7–72/4–82/4/5/7/8/90/1/3–9, 461001–3/6–10/3–23/5–7/9–34/6–44/6/8–51/3–5/60–4/6/7/9–71/3–5/8/80/1/3/5/6/8–91/4/5/7/8, 461101.

460433 was repainted into yellow/executive grey livery with Metals SECTOR symbol.

249 SPA wagons were transferred on 1st January 1994, 66 going to LOADHAUL Ltd, 10 going to MAINLINE FREIGHT Ltd and 167 going to TRANSRAIL Ltd.

460639, taken at Cardiff, Tidal Sidings in June 1992. This wagon shows the typical condition of the class in the 1990s before privatisation. The flame red livery is very rusty. Note the CARDIFF RODMILL symbol and the load of rod coil, which has not been sheeted. (Author's Ref No W17045/DL)

461101, taken at Hoo Junction, Rochester in December 1988. Taken a few years earlier, this is the final SPA, at this time carrying wire coil from Sheerness Steel Ltd. (Author's Ref No W14385/DL)

SPA Class (SDA and SEA conversions)

SDA Steel Bolster 2-axle

These wagons operated in the Rotherham area and were converted during the mid-1980s. The original sides were removed and three fixed bolsters, of the type used on the BDA class, were fitted onto the floor. Known numbers were as follows:
460563, 460612/3/26/7/74/83, 460706/9/18/23/54/8/71/5, 460813/21/2/5/6/56/79/89, 460906/16/20/73, 461000/28/58/76.

461000, taken at Rotherham, South Yorkshire in October 1988. This appears to have been the normal loading point for these wagons, Scunthorpe and Immingham Docks being other locations where SDAs have been recorded. (Author's Ref No W14118/ DL)

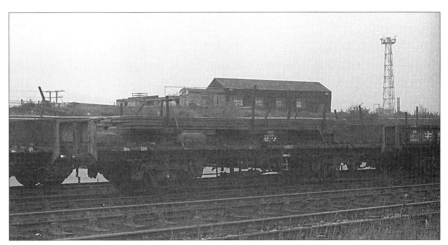

SEA Rod coil sideflex hood

These wagons operated from Cardiff Rod Mill and were converted during the late-1980s. The original sides and ends were retained and the whole bodywork was covered by a tall, rectangular nylon hood. Main colour of this was dark blue and there was white and yellow lettering, blue/yellow Metals SECTOR symbol and blue/red/white wire symbol. Most wagons retained flame red livery but 461100 received yellow/executive grey SECTOR livery. The whole fleet was transferred to TRANSRAIL Ltd on 1st January 1994. Known numbers were as follows:

460385, 460454, 460514/46/83, 460608/19/70/8/97, 460724/44/60/73/9/83/93, 460816/32/65/72/96, 460904/17/41/52/7/66/83/6/9/92, 461005/12/57, 461100.

461100, taken at Cardiff, Tidal Sidings in June 1992. As far as is known, this was the only SEA wagon to receive full yellow/executive grey SECTOR livery, all the others remaining in flame red. (Author's Ref No W17080/DL)

SPA Class (SHA and SKA conversions)

SHA Strip Coil (ex-Plate)(formerly KTA)

These wagons were converted in 1982 and were originally coded KTA, receiving the code SHA after 1984. The vehicles resembled SPA wagons when viewed from the normal angle; however, spigots were mounted on the floor to carry rolls of strip coil "eye-to-sky" fashion. 6 wagons were transferred to LOADHAUL Ltd on 1st January 1994. Known numbers were as follows:
460390, 460492, 460522/42, 460707/22/6/9/53/61/81/92/9, 460811/42/7/98.

460542, taken at Whitemoor Yard, Cambridgeshire in March 1984. This wagon is an SHA still carrying the old KTA code. It is loaded with three coils, which are covered by blue clear plastic sheet. (Author's Ref No W13778/DL)

SKA Rod Coil (ex-Plate)(formerly KOA)

These wagons were converted circa 1980 and were originally coded KOA, receiving the code SKA after 1984. The ends were retained, wooden floor supports were fitted to carry the coil longitudinally and new metal sides were provided to hold the load. 53 wagons were transferred on 1st January 1994, 31 going to MAINLINE FREIGHT Ltd and 8 going to TRANSRAIL Ltd; none were actually in traffic. Known numbers were as follows:

460344/62/79/82, 460416/21/9/31/41/4/8/63/4/82/4/6/97, 460517/9/20/37/61/7/72/5/90/2/6, 460601/6/14/21/9/40/54/9/66/85/8/94, 460700/4/12/6/28/42/3/57/66/70/96, 460809/15/27/36 /46/9/75, 460909/37/53, 461004/11/24/35/45/7/52/6/68/77/9/84/7/92/3.

460679, taken at Warrington, Arpley in August 1983. This view shows a normally loaded wagon still carrying the KOA code; such vehicles were regularly sheeted. The ends were the original flame red but the new sides appear to have been freight brown. (Author's Ref No W13282/DL)

SSA Class (acquired 4-wheeled scrap wagons)

After rebuilding three HEA hoppers as SJA Scrap wagons (see page 49), it was decided to acquire presumably surplus wagons from RAILEASE Ltd rather than convert any others. This unusual step was taken by the semi-privatised Railfreight Metals Sector. Batch details are as below:

470000 to 470099	16.5T BOX (SS 002A)	Acquired 1990	4070	Bt 1984 as RLS5000 to 99
470100	16.5T BOX (SS 001A)	Acquired 1990	4070	Bt 1978 as RLS5100
470101 to 470119	16.5T BOX (SS 001B)	Acquired 1990	4070	Bt 1984 as RLS5900 to 19
470120 to 470149	16.5T BOX (SS 001C)	Acquired 1990	4070	Bt 1984 as RLS5920 to 49
470150 to 470180	16.5T BOX (SS 001D)	Acquired 1990	4070	Bt 1984 as RLS5950 to 79

There were significant differences between the different batches, hence the number of design codes. All had originally been rebuilt from other types of wagon by Standard Wagon Co, Heywood. They appear to have been short-haul vehicles into the South Yorkshire steel works. 175 wagons were transferred on 1st January 1994, 101 going to LOADHAUL Ltd and 72 to TRANSRAIL Ltd, the remaining two being withdrawn. It should be noted that at least one was rebodied in the late 1990s by EWS Ltd.

470017, taken at Kingsbury, Warwickshire in July 1992. The diagram shown here is SS 002A and this was the most common variant of the SSA class. All these vehicles were pale blue with yellow ends originally. (Author's Ref No W17277/DL)

470075, taken at Tinsley Yard, Sheffield in May 1992. The diagram SS 002A wagons used the chassis from private owner hopper wagons which had operated from Ravenscraig steelworks in Scotland. (Author's Ref No W7509/DL)

470120, taken at Tinsley Yard, Sheffield in May 1992. This SSA variant was design code SS 001B, was not a conversion, and was a modification of the prototype design that became 470100 (not illustrated). (Author's Ref No W16993/DL)

470131, taken at Kingsbury, Warwickshire in July 1992. This is the SS 001C design code variant and differs from the vehicle above in having an access ladder. (Author's Ref No W17276/DL)

470169, taken at Tinsley Yard, Sheffield in May 1992. As far as is known, this design code variant, SS 001D, was virtually identical to the one seen above, SS 001C. (Author's Ref No W16985/DL)

FNA Class (Nuclear Flask wagons)

Having created the new nuclear flask design with shield and sliding cover, as seen in the previous volume, further batches were built to this design. One wagon, 550019, was deliberately destroyed in a staged accident for publicity purposes and 51 wagons were transferred to TRANSRAIL Ltd on 1st January 1994. Building details of the final batches were as follows:

550017 to 550018	50T XKB FLASK (XK 003A)	4/1982	4004	BR (SHILDON)
550019	50T FNA FLASK (FN 002A)	1984	4040	BR (SWINDON)
550020	50T FNA FLASK (FN 003A)	1984	4040	BR (SWINDON)
550021 to 550026	50T FNA FLASK (FN 003A)	1986	4057	BR (SWINDON)
550027 to 550050	50T FNA FLASK (FN 003A)	1988	4049	PROCOR (UK) Ltd
550051 to 550060	50T FNA FLASK (FN 003A)	1989	4063	PROCOR (UK) Ltd

550026, taken at Hither Green, South East London in July 1992. With the closure of Shildon works, Swindon works built the batch illustrated here. The livery was buff with white cover and black bogies. (Author's Ref No W17268/DL)

550042, taken at Hither Green, South East London in July 1992. By the time the next batches were ordered, Swindon works had also closed and the Lot 4049 vehicles illustrated here were built by PROCOR Ltd at Wakefield, as were the final Lot 4063 batch. (Author's Ref No W17295/DL)

BAA Class (originals and BKA, FOA)

The history of this class remained very complex. 99 wagons under the code BAA were transferred on 1st January 1994, 70 going to LOADHAUL Ltd and 29 to TRANSRAIL Ltd. One of these, 900205, is known to have been in yellow/executive grey livery with Metals SECTOR symbol; the others seem to have been generally repainted in flame red and black. Known numbers are as follows:

900000/2–4/8/9/11/4/6–22/5/7–31/4/8/40/1/3/4/7/9/50/8/79–81/3/5/7/8/93–6, 900112/8/21/4–32/4/5/7/9/41/4/7–55/9/61/3/70–2/4–6/8/80/2/4/6–9/91/3/5/7, 900201/4/6/7/9/11/2/4/6/22/4/5/31/4–9/41/4/5/7/9–51/4/6/9–63/6/9/71/4/5/8/9/88/92/7, 900300/1/4/5.

900095, taken at Carlisle, Cumbria in June 1992. The basic BAA wagon still saw use in the early 1990s. By this time, most has been painted with flame red ends and black solebar and bogies. The number was applied to the end and some had red/white RAILFREIGHT and double arrow symbols, as seen here. (Author's Ref No W17181/DL)

BKA Bogie Steel cradle and hood

Three wagons were transferred on 1st January 1994, two to LOADHAUL Ltd. and one, stored, to TRANSRAIL Ltd. This code had been re-used, having been previously applied to BAA wagons with longitudinal coil carrying beams; these latter vehicles became BZA.

Of the three designated BKA, 900160 had a blue hood with SPEEDLINK – STRUCTURE-FLEX and a double arrow and retained the original ends (this had been converted by 1986). The original wagon initially remained freight brown but had been painted flame red/black by 1989, still coded BAA; 900219 had new yellow ends and a grey Slidaflex hood with TRAINLOAD METALS in yellow; the identity of the other BKA transferred cannot be established.

FOA Atomic Flask Carrier (Winfrith)

Two other vehicles unrecorded photographically came from the BAA class. These were numbered 900115 and 900230 and they operated between Winfrith nuclear establishment, Dorset and Sellafield, Cumbria. Both were transferred on 1st January 1994 to TRANSRAIL Ltd.

BAA Class (BZA and BYA)

BZA Cradle Fitted (Gunshot, ex BAA)

These were the BAA class wagons with the so-called "Kinky Beams" to carry strip coil longitudinally and had previously been coded BKA. 118 wagons were transferred on 1st January 1994 to LOADHAUL Ltd. Most vehicles appear to have been in the flame red/black livery, sometimes with double arrow and RAILFREIGHT transfers. Known numbers were as follows:
900001/5/6/12/3/33/5/9/42/5/6/8/51–3/6/7/9–69/71–8/82/4/6/9/92/7/9, 900101/3–11/3/4/6/7/9/20/2/3/33/6/8 /40/2/3/5/6/56/8/62–9/73/7/9/81/3/5/90/2/4/8, 900200/2/3/5/8/10/5/7/8/20/1/3/6–9/32/3/40/2/3/6/8/52/3/5/ 8/64/5/7/8/70/3/6/7/81–5/7/9–91/4–6/8/9, 900302/3.

900051, taken at Cardiff, Tidal Sidings in June 1992. This view shows the BZA variant with a full load; normally this would be sheeted. The coil-supporting beams in this livery were flame red. (Author's Ref No W17060/DL)

BYA (ex BAA)

These were the BAA class wagons with the four custom-built cradles to carry strip coil laterally, and had previously been coded BAA. Most vehicles appear to have been in the flame red/black livery, sometimes with double arrow and RAILFREIGHT transfers. Known numbers were as follows:
900007/10/5/23/4/6/32/6/54/5/70, 900157/96, 900213/86.

900286, taken at Grimsby Docks in July 1992. This view shows the BYA variant in unloaded condition. The livery is flame red, including the cradles, and the solebar and bogies are black. (Author's Ref No W17292/ DL)

Accurate assessment of these vehicles, and the BBA conversions, is complicated by the apparent confusion of codes issued and re-issued after 1st January 1994 and this volume will not attempt to sort it out as most of the vehicles referred to were converted later.

BBA Class (originals and BLA, BRA, BUA)

The later history of this class of vehicles is awkward to follow, due to many of the modifications being temporary. Accurate assessment of these vehicles, and the BAA conversions, is complicated by the apparent confusion of codes issued and re-issued after 1st January 994 and this volume will not attempt to sort it out as most of the vehicles referred to were converted later.

Taking the prototype BBA, 910000, first, this was converted to a BUA Hot Metal Carrier and was transferred to LOADHAUL Ltd on 1st January 1994; it is illustrated on page vi.

Livery of the fleet generally followed the same pattern as the BAA class and most vehicles were repainted in flame red/black livery, sometimes with double arrow and RAILFREIGHT symbols. One vehicle, 910333, was repainted in 1990 in yellow/executive grey livery with Metals SECTOR symbols.

910172, taken at Carlisle, Cumbria in June 1992. This view shows the standard BBA in the early 1990s. Livery is flame red/black and the appropriate symbols have been applied. (Author's Ref No W17184/DL)

910378, taken at Mossend Yard, Scotland in October 1988. The BBA class were frequently used to carry strip coil and this was frequently load "eye-to-sky" style, as seen here. These were not conversions as such but probably had floor spigots to locate the load. Livery is weathered flame red/ black. (Author's Ref No W14260/DL)

BBA Class (originals and BLA, BRA, BUA) (continued)

The only significant conversion on the class was done in the early 1980s. The ends were removed and had six lateral coil cradles fitted. Confusingly, they remained coded BBA (Design Code BB 001E). Numbers for these vehicles were as follows:
910003/6/71, 910112/63/70/5/9, 910216/23/34/5/52/8/64/9/75/92, 910307, 910413/20–7/40/1/7/50/7/61/5/9/84/7/9.

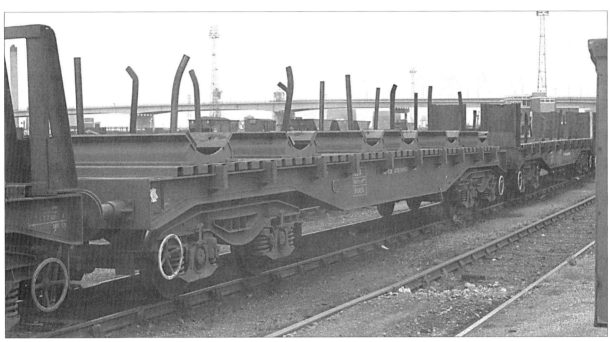

910428, taken at Tees Yard, Middlesborough in May 1981. The livery remained freight brown on this example of the coil cradle conversion, but later repaints had flame red cradles and black solebars and bogies. (Author's Ref No W9093/DL)

Of these, only 910071, 910112/63/70/9, 910223/52/8/64, 910307, 910420/3/7/41/57/65/9/87, remained in the condition shown above, re-coded BXA. These were all transferred to LOADHAUL Ltd on 1st January 1994.

Other conversions, for which I do not have photographs, were:

BIA (Bogie Strip Coil) (transferred to LOADHAUL Ltd):
910024/76/8, 910105/94, 910239, 910303/40/57, 910494, 910504/35.
BLA (Bogie Steel Cradle) (transferred to TRANSRAIL Ltd):
910005/11/8/20/2/5/9/30/5–8/41/3/52/3/9/74/86/93, 910106/14/8/9/62/4/7/72/6–8/80/2/6/7/9/95/7/8,
910202/3/10/3/7/9/20/5/6/8–30/2/6/42/7/50/1/3/4/9/63/6/8/70/1/3/9/80/7/90/4/6, 910301/4/9/12/4/5/7–
9/22/3/5/32/3/5/49/53/4/6/61/3/4/8/73/4/9–82/4/5/8/90, 910400–2/6/8/19/31/42/4/9/52/5/9/63/71/3/5/
6/8/9/81/3/6/8/90–3/9, 910500/11/3/6–9/21/4/7/9/32/6/7/9/51/5/8/60/2/6/8/72/3/6/9/82/6/8.
BSA (Bogie Steel Slab/Coil (Rollblock)) (code not in use on 1st January 1994):
910003/6/13/56/63/81, 910174/5/96, 910216/8/27/35/72/5/89/92, 910300/2/38/55/77/87/9, 910411/24/47/58/61,
910538/87.
BWA (Bogie Bolster Coil Carrier) (transferred to LOADHAUL Ltd):
910234/69, 910413/21/2/6/40/50/84/9.

910460 (coded BWA) and 910465/9 (coded BXA) were subsequently rebuilt with telescopic bodywork but this thought to have been later than 1995.

BDA Class (originals)

Most of the earlier BDA class wagons were either converted or transferred to the CCE department but 861 still remained to be transferred on 1st January 1994, 549 to LOADHAUL Ltd, 34 to MAINLINE FREIGHT Ltd and 278 to TRANSRAIL Ltd. As far as is known, none were painted in SECTOR livery but some of the early vehicles painted freight brown when delivered did receive repaints.

950211, taken at Grimsby Docks in May 1992. This BDA has been repainted in flame red/black livery but with a small double arrow symbol added on the centre line. (Author's Ref No 16923/DL)

950705, taken at Hoo Junction, Rochester in December 1988. It was more usual for flame red/black repaints to have the RAILFREIGHT symbol as well as the Double Arrow, as seen here. (Author's Ref No 14367/DL)

BDA Class (BEA, BFA conversions)

BEA (Bogie Steel Carrier; Tall stanchions)
This conversion was ongoing on 1st January 1994, only 6 vehicles being transferred to LOADHAUL Ltd. No photograph is available but they could be considered as the air-braked equivalent of the old BHV class (see previous volumes). Known numbers were as follows:

950017, 950392, 950475/6, 950513/5/27/49/53/5/6/9/64/6/8/9/76/80/5/9/, 950600/3/6/10/1/3/4/6/7
/20/6/7/36/45/7/51/3/7/8/60/3/71–3/5/9/80/5/92/5/7, 950703/4/7/15/23/7/9/35/7/9/49/51–3/5/7/61/3/5/6
/73/5/7–9/83/6/7/94/5/7–9, 950800–2/11–3/5/8/21/5/6/9/30/2/4–6/8/9/43/6/50/2/8–60/4/6/8
/70/2/5/7/8/81/2/4/7/8/95/6, 950903–5/7/10/2/4/6/7/9/21/3/7/33–6/41/2/4/5/7–50/2/4–6/9/60/2/3/5/6
/8/9/73–5/80–2/90/6/7/9, 951000–3/5–7/9/14/22/3/5–7/32/3/5/40/1/3–5/7–51/4/5/7/8/61/3/5–8
/72/5–7/80–3/5/6/90/2/5/7–9, 951101/2/5/8/9/11–3/6/8–20/2–4/6–31/4/5/7/8/40/3/7/50/1/5/7/9
/60/2–5/8/70–3/5–7/9/81–7/8/92/8, 951200/1/6/7/9–11/3/6/7/21–3/7/8/31/5/6/8/42–4/6/8/9.

BFA (Bogie Steel Carrier 52T)
This conversion had been initiated in the mid-1980s and the differences were slight. The capacity was reduced and one known traffic flow was BSC Scunthorpe to Rotherham. 89 vehicles were transferred to LOADHAUL Ltd on 1st January 1994. Known numbers were as follows:

950249, 950494, 950507/16/9/26/9/31/8/44/51/61/3/73/4/83/90/5–8, 950607/9/21/33/7/8/48/50/6/61/2/6/9/76/7/
82/8/94/6/9, 950700/2/18/9/34/6/45/70–2/85, 950806/28/37/45/62/91, 950930/1/84, 9510002/3/88, 951153/74.

950661, taken at Rotherham, South Yorkshire in October 1988. As well as the amended BFA code, this vehicle is also lettered BSC SCUNTHORPE. This example was in freight brown livery but others were recorded on the same occasion in flame red/black. (Author's Ref No 14110/DL)

There appears to be some conflict with the numbers of these conversions and others from the BDA class. If possible, numbers should be confirmed with photographs. Such are 950534/5/45/67/74/5/90/8, 950618/21/30/41/61/89/91, 950700, 950930.

BDA Class (BMA, BTA conversions)

BMA (Bogie Steel Carrier, Wide Body)
This conversion, which also included the BPA class (see page 71), had been initiated in the mid-1980s; new bodywork, with tall fixed ends, low bolsters and tall stanchions set at wide spacings, was fitted. One vehicle, 950131, was painted in yellow/executive grey SECTOR livery with Metals Sector symbols. The joint fleet was split between LOADHAUL Ltd (58 wagons) and TRANSRAIL Ltd (36 vehicles) on 1st January 1994. Known numbers were as follows:
950003/7/12/3/6/20/1/3/5/8/32/9/43/51/8/62/9/70/3/5/9/80/3/9/99, 950101/3/21/2/5/31/3/5/40–3/6/7/54/5/60/73/6/8/80/91/5/6, 950200/3, 950523/6/83, 950607/33, 950745/85, 950833, 950930/1/84, 9510002/3/88, 951153/74.

950160, taken at Tinsley Yard, Sheffield in May 1992. The changes from BDA to BMA can be well seen in this view. Livery is flame red/black, as are all such conversions except 950131 noted above. (Author's Ref No W16999/DL)

There appears to be some conflict with the numbers of these conversions and others from the BDA class. If possible, numbers should be confirmed with photographs. Such are 950012/21/5/69/73/9, 950125/31/60/78/95/6, 950203.

BTA (Bogie Timber or Pipe Wagon)
This conversion had been initiated in the mid-1980s; very tall stanchions, with bracing, were fitted to carry logs or large diameter pipes. No details are available of 1st January 1994 transfers. Known numbers were as follows:
950017/91, 950123/87/91, 950523/45/81, 950668, 950839.

950123, taken at Dumfries, Scotland in October 1988. The livery of this BTA conversion is rail grey sides with flame red ends. (Author's Ref No W14203/DL)

There appears to be some conflict with the numbers of these conversions and others from the BDA class. If possible, numbers should be confirmed with photographs. Such are 950091, 950123/91, 950523/45/81, 950668.

BGA, BHA, BJA Classes

These were a group of vehicles built in 1990 as experimental steel wagons. They were basically all to the same design but came in different lengths. They were changed numerous times over the years and the photographs show the condition in 1992. The BGA and BHA classes passed to LOADHAUL Ltd on 1st January 1994 and the BJA class passed to TRANSRAIL Ltd. Building details are below:

961000 to 961003	BGA BOGIE STEEL (Short)	1990	4065	RFS (DONCASTER)
962000 to 962003	BHA BOGIE STEEL (Medium)	1990	4066	RFS (DONCASTER)
963000 to 963003	BJA BOGIE STEEL (Long)	1990	4067	RFS (DONCASTER)

961001, taken at Tees Yard, Middlesborough in June 1992. This view shows the flexible hood in the partially opened position. The hood was flame red and the rest of the vehicle black. (Author's Ref No W17104/DL)

961002, taken at Tees Yard, Middlesborough in June 1992. This is the short design without the hood and also lettered for European working. (Author's Ref No W17106/DL)

962000, taken at Tees Yard, Middlesborough in June 1992. This is the medium version with hood fully closed. It is also lettered for European working. (Author's Ref No W17110/DL)

962002, taken at Tees Yard, Middlesborough in May 1992. This is the open version of the medium vehicle, again marked for European working. (Author's Ref No W17107/ DL)

963000, taken at Tees Yard, Middlesborough in May 1992. This is the covered long version. All these vehicles had v-section floors in the well for coil traffic. (Author's Ref No W17111/ DL)

963003, taken at Tees Yard, Middlesborough in May 1992. None of these wagons appeared to do much work and may have been an attempt before Privatisation to win back traffic from privately owned ferry wagons. (Author's Ref No W17105/DL)

BPA Class (originals and BMA)

Significant numbers of BPA class wagons had been transferred to the CCE department but the following remained in normal revenue traffic in 1990: 965026/31/3/6/42/4/52/6/62/70/2.

Some had also been converted to BMA class wagons in 1987 (see page 68) for details of conversion and totals transferred on 1st January 1994). Numbers of known wagons were as follows: 965029/32/4/5/8–41/3/5–51/4/5/8–61/3–9/73/5–9.

It should be noted that no vehicles remained as BPA in 1994 to transfer. However, some of those transferred to the CCE reverted to revenue-earning. The situation was further confused by a later conversion to BNA class wagons, which were very similar but appear to have had higher stanchions.

965046, taken at Tinsley Yard, Sheffield in May 1992. As with the BDA conversions noted earlier, new ends were fitted and replacement bodywork. The BPA conversions retained the flame red/ black livery that they carried from building. (Author's Ref No W17002/DL)

965076, taken at Grimsby Docks in May 1992. This appears to be a typical load and regular destination for the BMA class. (Author's Ref No W16920/DL)

BRA and XVA Classes (all conversions)

All the BRA class wagons (965700–967649) were transferred to the CCE department in the early 1980s and none were ever transferred back to revenue-earning traffic. One wagon is noted as a BRA Bogie Steel Re Bar as being transferred to TRANSRAIL Ltd on 1st January 1994; it does not appear to have one of the above vehicles and cannot be identified at the time of writing.

The history of the XVA class wagons (990000–990049) is somewhat confusing. They were coded BXA from 1983 but no photographs of them with code are available.

By 1988/89, at least two (990016 and 990024) were operating as RRA runner wagons with all upperworks removed.

990016, taken at Warrington Dallam in October 1988. This view shows the RRA conversion with the trestles completely removed. Livery was black. (Author's Ref No W14131/DL)

By 1991, the whole fleet (except 990025, which had been withdrawn) had received coil cradles and were recoded BOA. These all passed to LOADHAUL Ltd on 1st January 1994 but were in storage. In 1996, the survivors were reconverted to RRA again, 16 still in use at the time of writing.

990016, taken at Cardiff, Tidal Sidings in June 1992. This wagon is seen in its later BOA form, with four red coil cradles loaded laterally. It had been withdrawn by the time of writing. (Author's Ref No W17066/DL)

Air-piped Bogie Steel-carrying Wagons (all types, BCW, BDW conversions)

The conversion of vacuum-braked Bogie Bolster wagons of various classes was initiated in 1983, involving the BDV class of 42T Bogie Bolster D wagons and then the BCV class of 30T Bogie Bolster C wagons, as well as the derivatives of both. None survived in revenue earning traffic to be transferred on 1st January 1994. Some were repainted in flame red livery, with rail grey ends and black solebars and bogies. Known examples are listed alphabetically.

BCW (Bogie Bolster C 30.5t)
B923103/4/6/7/10/1/4–6/9/23/4/7/30–2/4/7/40/1/6/55/60/9/71/2/4/7/83/8/9/93/4/6–8, B923201/3 /11/7/22/4/5/30/4/5/40/7/50/1/5/66/8/9/71/3/5/8/80/2/4/6/90/2/9, B924400/6/8/11/2/6/8/24/32/6/7 /42/3/6/7/9/50/6/62/73/8/84/6/92/8, B924503/6/12–5/26/7/30/44/6/61/2/4/74/8/81/6, B924604/7–10 /2/8/23/7/30/2/7/47–9/56/7/63/9–72/4/5/80/7/93/5/9, B924704/10/2/22/4/33/6/41/7/9/50/2/3/7/63/7 /74/5/7/82/4/93/8.

B924612, taken at Hoo Junction, Rochester in July 1989. As well as receiving air through-pipes, the BCW class also received blue nylon straps to replace the original chains. Livery is rusty bauxite. (Author's Ref No W16331/DL)

BDW (Bogie Bolster D 45t)
B927800/3/5–10/2/4–6/8–21/4/5/7–33/5–41/4/5/7–9/53–64/6/7/70–2/4/6/7/9/80/2/4/6/7/9–94/6–9, B927900–3/7– 16/8–20/3/4/6–30/2–42/4–8/51/2/5/7/9–61/3–6/8/9/72/4–6/8/9/82/3/5–90/3/6/7/9, B928001/3/6/8–13/7–9/21– 3/6/8–31/3–7/40–4/6/7/50/4–9/61/3/6–8/70/3–8/82–7/90/1/3–8, B928100/2–9/11/2/5/7/9–22/4–30/2–4/7/9– 43/5/7/8/50/2/3/6–9/61/2/4/5/7/70–5/7/9/80–2/4–90/3/4/8.

B928054, taken at Hoo Junction, Rochester in December 1988. This BDW conversion has received the air through-pipes and blue nylon straps. It has been repainted in flame red livery with rail grey ends. (Author's Ref No W14370/ DL)

Air-piped Bogie Steel-carrying Wagons (all types, BHW, BSW conversions)

BHW (Bogie Bolster C 30.5t with tall stanchions, ex BHV)

B923192, B923212/21/3/85/8, B924413/23/6/40, B924510/1/28/39/48/52/5/82, B924633, B924701/14/29.

BSW (Bogie Bolster D 42.5t with tall stanchions, for timber traffic)

This appears to have been a fairly short-lived conversion, first recorded in 1988 and apparently being transferred to the departmental fleet in 1992. All known examples came from the BDW fleet listed on the previous page and had very tall, large section stanchions to stabilise a load of logs. Known examples were as follows:

B927809/47/87, B927908/16, B928031, B928132/75/7/88/93.

B927887, taken at Plumstead, South East London in December 1988. This BSW conversion has received flame red livery, with rail grey ends, black bogies and solebar. The load of timber was windfall from the North Downs to the south of London. (Author's Ref No W14355/DL)

B927908, taken at Perth Yard, Scotland in June 1992. By the 1990s, these conversions had been phased out and this example has chalked lettering suggesting transfer to the S and T department. The flame red/rail grey livery has an unusually large symbol. (Author's Ref No W17148/DL)

Air-piped Bogie Steel-carrying Wagons (all types, BTW conversions)

BTW (Bogie Bolster T 30.5t with tall stanchions, for pipe traffic)

B923100/5/20/2/5/6/33/6/8/9/43/4/8/9/52/4/7/8/62/4/5/7/8/73/5/8/8, B923204–6/9/14/6/8/9/26/31/7/42–4/6/
8/9/54/6/62/3/5/72/4/7/9/94/8, B924402/4/19/21/30/3/9/44/8/52/4/5/7/8/63/4/8–70/5–7/81–3/5/7/91/3/7,
B924502/5/8/17/9/20/2/33/5/7/41/5/50/1/3/6/7/63/5/8/70/3/80/5/9/90/8, B924600/1/5/6/15/6/20/2/34/
8–40/3/4//53/4/9/64/5/73/7/9/84/90/4/7, B924703/6/8/9/13/5/26/32/7/42/4/56//60/1/4/5/9/76/8/81/5/94/4.

Note: The following were coded BQW but this is probably an error for BTW: B923132, B924780

B924620, taken at Warrington Arpley in November 1983. The BTW conversion carried three large diameter pipes, as seen here, and the conversion replaced chains with blue nylon straps. The livery is rusty bauxite. (Author's Ref No W13495/DL)

B923105, taken at Warrington Arpley in November 1983. The BTW conversions normally operated in block trains of similarly loaded wagons without brake van. The livery is rusty bauxite and both BTV and BTW codes are carried. (Author's Ref No W13491/DL)

VIX Wagons (Leyland motor-car parts vans)

These vans were actually a little earlier than the review period, the conversion being carried out in 1977, but they were just going out of service in 1983 and will be recorded here. These were 1962-vintage Ferry Vans which had the sides replaced by curtain sides; they were intended to carry British Leyland lorry engines. Livery was blue with white symbols. Numbers were as follows:

21 70 219 6 000–0 (GB787246); 21 70 219 6 001–8 (GB787114); 21 70 219 6 002–6 (GB787231);
21 70 219 6 003–4 (GB787215); 21 70 219 6 004–2 (GB787272); 21 70 219 6 005–9 (GB787286);
21 70 219 6 006–7 (GB787185); 21 70 219 6 007–5 (GB787263); 21 70 219 6 008–3 (GB787228);
21 70 219 6 009–1 (GB787195); 21 70 219 6 010–9 (GB787143); 21 70 219 6 011–7 (GB787171);
21 70 219 6 012–5 (GB787317); 21 70 219 6 013–3 (GB787112); 21 70 219 6 014–1 (GB787104);
21 70 219 6 015–8 (GB787311); 21 70 219 6 016–6 (GB787330); 21 70 219 6 017–7 (GB787192);
21 70 219 6 018–2 (GB787249); 21 70 219 6 019–0 (GB787302); 21 70 219 6 020–8 (GB787337);
21 70 219 6 021–6 (GB787273); 21 70 219 6 022–4 (GB787248); 21 70 219 6 023–2 (GB787183);
21 70 219 6 024–0 (GB787250); 21 70 219 6 025–7 (GB787314); 21 70 219 6 026–5 (GB787208);
21 70 219 6 027–3 (GB786997).

By 1982, the painted number was 21 70 239 6 000 to 21 70 239 6 027; this would have changed the final digit also.

21 70 219 6 018–2, taken at Battersea, South West London in April 1979. When new, these vehicles were very eye-catching in the blue BL livery. Note that the data panel is on the end, as it could not be placed on the side. (Author's Ref No W7724/DL)

21 70 239 6 024–8, taken at Peterborough in October 1982. In very faded blue livery, two BL vans await their fate. (Author's Ref No W12299/DL)

CAR Class (air and vacuum-piped brake vans)

The brake vans which had been coded CAR under the TOPS scheme had been in service since the inception of the merry-go-round coal hoppers. 101 such vehicles were transferred on 1st January 1994, LOADHAUL Ltd receiving 12, MAINLINE FREIGHT Ltd receiving 7, TRANSRAIL Ltd receiving 66 and RAILFREIGHT DISTRIBUTION Ltd receiving 2. 14 were withdrawn and unallocated. Known numbers were as follows:

B954524/8/31/6/8–40/2/4/6/7/50/2/3/6/66/8/76/7/80/3/6/95/6, B954600/3/12/3/5/7–21/5/7/9/30/5/6/41/2/4/5/9/51/5/8/61/8/76/80/2–4/7/91–3/5/7–9, B954709/11/3/6–8/20/3–5/7/32/4/9/40/5/6/50/7–9/62/5/7–9/75/9/81/6/8/93/4, B954801/5/7/13/6/8/21/2/6/9/32/4/7/40/2/7/51/2/4/6/60/2–5/72/4/6/7/9/85–7/990/4/8/9, B954901/8/12–4/6/8/9/21/6/8/33/5/6/9/48/50/2 /62/4–6/71/8/82/8/9/91/5/9, B955002/6/7/9/14/8/9/24/5/7/38/9/41/7/8/60/3/6/7/71–4/6/7 /81/3/6/7/90/1/7/9, B955102/5/9/10/3/5/22/3/30–2/4/6/9/44/6/51–3/63/76/87/90, B955211/9.

B954821, taken at Bristol East Depot in March 1989. This view shows the plain side of the brakevan; the air-pipe operating valve connections were inserted through the opposite side. Livery is flame red sides above the ducket, rail grey lower sides and ends. (Author's Ref No W15608/DL)

955006, taken at Bristol, Avon in March 1989. This example retains the original bauxite livery with yellow panels. The sides are lettered TO BE USED ON AIR BRAKED TRAINS ONLY and the ends AIR PIPED. (Author's Ref No W15675/DL)

B954862, taken at Eastleigh, Hampshire in March 1992. This van has received sector livery with executive grey sides and yellow ends. The SECTOR symbol, unusually, is the yellow/red RAILFREIGHT DISTRIBUTION. The additional pipe work for the air-brake release valve is prominent. (Author's Ref No W16639/DL)

B954962, taken at Carlisle Currock Depot in June 1992. This van is also in yellow/executive grey sector livery but carries the more-common yellow/black COAL sector symbol. (Author's Ref No W17179/DL)

B955219, taken at Tees Yard, Middlesborough in June 1992. By no means all of the CAR brake vans had been repainted in SECTOR livery, and this example is in flame red/rail grey livery. Note the different angle of the additional pipe work, which was probably added by a different wagon works. (Author's Ref No W17112/DL)

Final analysis of BR wagon fleet from nationalisation to privatisation

The first years of the BR wagon fleet development were taken up by delivery of the final orders of the pre–Nationalisation companies and then repetition of the designs. Few of the vehicles lasted into the 1980s, especially if they were unfitted.

DB900108, taken at Reading, Berkshire in May 1992. Some former special wagons, such as this FLATROL, survived in the CCE department to transport mechanical diggers to track relaying sites. Already vacuum through-piped, it has now received an air through-pipe and is coded ZVR. (Author's Ref No W16881/DL)

From the mid-1950s onwards until the late 1960s, BR attempted to introduce new designs and innovations to try and stave off the encroachments of road haulage. Some designs, such as the COVHOP, remained in service well into the late 1980s. Others, like the PRESFLO, although remaining in service for a long time, were superseded by private owner designs.

BCC10845, taken at Inverness, Scotland in June 1992. Blue Circle Cement, the owner of this French-built wagon built in 1981, was a prolific user of PRESFLO wagons when the design was first introduced, owning a large batch. As the limitations of the design became apparent, they were replaced by non-BR designs. (Author's Ref No W17115/DL)

The two big steps forward of the 1960s, the merry-go-round hopper wagons and the Freightliner trains, really forced BR into the 20th Century. Both classes of vehicle were air-braked and this one factor really made a difference.

601996, taken at Elgin, Scotland in June 1992. One Freightliner flat was converted in 1979 to FJA configuration, with buffer beams and normal couplings at both ends, for whiskey tank traffic. It was still in use in 1991 and possibly in 1994. 601998 was presumably similar but had vacuum through-pipes and was coded FJB. (Author's Ref No W17119/DL)

The other important change came in the early 1970s with the introduction of the TOPS computer system. The outward manifestation of this was the visible wagon code but the hidden side was more important. For the first time, every wagon could be traced and numbers of wagons actually required to cater for fluctuating traffic levels could be determined. There could never again be the excessive numbers of wagons built as had happened in the 1950s and 1960s.

B902607, taken at Micheldever, Hampshire in March 1992. TOPS codes in the "R" series were used for wagons that were considered as part of the normal fleet but carried no load. This wagon is an RFQ Match wagon for LUL stock and was converted from a BR passenger chassis of the CCT class. New freight numbers were required for accountancy purposes and these conversions were numbered in a vacant block in the special wagon series. It is seen here in use as an oil train barrier wagon. (Author's Ref No W16647/DL)

A feature of the 1980s was the rapid livery changes, at least on paper, of the air-braked fleet. Starting with freight brown, then changing to maroon, then again to flame red/rail grey, and finally yellow/executive grey Sector livery, virtually all of these liveries could be seen together at one time.

200245, taken at Avonmouth Docks in March 1989. This VBA van had been delivered in freight brown livery. Having probably skipped the maroon livery stage, it passed onto flame red/rail grey and was probably withdrawn in this condition. (Author's Ref No W15714/DL)

The liveries of many of the wagons painted in Sector Livery were initial trials.
Had there been no change of government policy towards British Rail, no doubt many more would have been done. As it was, things became even more colourful under Privatisation. Three companies, LOADHAUL, MAINLINE FREIGHT and TRANSRAIL, were set up, with at the very least new logos and eventually new liveries as well. These were subsequently acquired by EWS Ltd, which added yet another livery variant. As was normal with wagons, repainting took a long time and trains could be a melange of any of the above-mentioned colour schemes.

360853, taken at Peak Forest, Derbyshire in February 1989. Only two HEA class wagons were given Sector livery and this was interpreted as executive grey bodywork with yellow framing. Note the red/ yellow RAILFREIGHT DISTRIBUTION symbol rather than the COAL symbol, reflecting their intended domestic rather than industrial traffic use. (Author's Ref No W15308/DL)

The rapid transfer of many air-braked revenue earning wagons to the departmental fleet seemed very surprising at the time but, upon reflection, it was necessary to transport the materials required by the various departments at higher speeds. The existing stock was of no use so newly built or converted stock had to be used.

DC965009, taken at Workington, Cumbria in June 1992. Unusually for a vehicle transferred to the Chief Civil Engineers department, this former BPA was recoded YNA but was not issued with a FISHKND name, as all the other air-braked transfers were. Livery remained flame red when this photograph was taken. (Author's Ref No W17156/DL)

Rather more understandable at the time was the conversion of numerous air-braked wagons to convey new types of load or to replace time-expired unfitted or vacuum-braked stock.

OTA wagons, taken at Hoo Junction, Rochester in May 1989. One of the more interesting developments was the conversion of wagons to convey timber. Although originally envisaged before the event, the large number of trees blown down in the so-called 1987 Hurricane saw many such wagons operating in Kent , Sussex and South East London in the vicinity of the North and South Downs. These particular wagons operated to Kronospan Ltd, Chirk, North Wales. (Author's Ref No W16197/DL)

In general, no air-braked wagon was wasted. If the conversion was useful for something else, such as the timber wagon conversion being used to carry sleepers for the CCE department, they continue in service at the time of writing.

DC201070, taken at Eastleigh, Hampshire in March 1992. This vehicle has an interesting history. One of the batch of VDA class vans with Taperlite suspension, it became a curtain-sided van VHA prototype (see page 30). It was then converted to an OTA, with modified ends from the VHA period. Finally it is seen here as a ZRA Sleeper wagon still in blue Kronospan livery. (Author's Ref No W16631/ DL)

The fleet that passed to the Privatised companies in 1994 in general remains the essence of the freight wagon fleet in use over ten years later. Certainly new types have been taken into service but many of the classes listed above are still to be seen. The following table quotes 2008 figures.

BAA Class: 141 wagons; BBA Class: 307 wagons; BCA Class (ex BAA): 52 wagons; BDA Class: 350 wagons; BEA Class (ex BDA): 306 wagons; BFA Class (ex BDA): 54 wagons; BGA Class: 4 wagons; BHA Class: 2 wagons; BIA Class (ex BBA): 12 wagons; BJA Class: 4 wagons; BKA Class (ex BAA): 1 wagon; BLA Class (ex BBA): 163 wagons; BMA Class (ex BDA): 16 wagons; BMA Class (ex BPA): 9 wagons; BNA Class (ex BPA): 25 wagons; BPA Class: 10 wagons; BSA Class (ex BBA): 29 vehicles; BTA Class (ex BDA): 31 wagons; BWA Class (ex BBA): 9 wagons; BXA Class (ex BBA): 19 wagons; BZA Class (ex BAA): 97 wagons; CDA Class: 131 wagons; CDA China Clay (ex HAA): 1 wagon; CEA Covered Hopper (ex HEA): 45 wagons; FNA Class: 50 wagons; FPA Conflat (ex SAA): 69 wagons; FPA Conflat (ex VCA): 8 wagons; HAA Class: 1222 wagons; HBA Class (HDA with canopy): 71 wagons; HCA Class (HAA with canopy): 23 wagons; HDA Class: 116 wagons; HEA Class: 113 wagons; HFA Class (HAA with aerodynamic canopy): 336 wagons; HMA Class (HAA with modified brake): 635 wagons; HNA Class (HAA rebodied with modified brake): 12 wagons; HSA Scrap Wagons (ex HEA): 3 wagons; MEA Class: 501 wagons (total includes later additions); MFA Class (reduced-height ex MEA): 35 wagons (total includes later additions); OAA Class: 50 wagons; OBA Class: 291 wagons; OCA Class: 207 wagons; ODA Class: 1 wagon. OTA Class (ex OBA): 15 wagons (may actually refer to PLASMOR conversion wagons); OTA Class (ex OCA): 86 wagons; OTA Class (ex VDA): 64 wagons; RBA Class (ex VAA/VBA): 3 vehicles; REA Match Class (ex VDA): 8 vehicles; RLA Match Class (ex VDA): 8 vehicles; RNA Runner Class (ex HEA): Total not established (part of HEA total); RRA Class (ex BOA): 15 wagons; RRA Class (ex OBA): 53 wagons; RRA/RRB Runner (ex SAA/SAB): 31 wagons; RRA Class (ex VCA): 2 wagons; RRA Class (ex VDA): 19 wagons; SDA Class (ex SPA): 20 wagons; SEA Class (ex SPA): 22 wagons; SHA Class (ex SPA): 1 wagon; SPA Class: 328 wagons; SSA Class: 130 wagons; VAA/VBA Classes: 19 vans; VGA Class: 149 vans; VKA Class (ex VGA): 100 vans. (Note: The above list includes pre-1995 conversions that were recoded but excludes totally post-1995 conversions. As indicated, some totals are speculative or enhanced).

Hoo Junction Yard – A personal appraisal

I started my railway career in 1963 at this small, remote yard on the banks of the Thames in North Kent. It primarily dealt with traffic from BP Isle of Grain refinery and the cement industry of North Kent and was also a repair yard.

My career fairly quickly took me away but, especially from 1968 onwards when I collected my wages there, I regularly visited the yard and recorded stock there. I also introduced many fellow wagon enthusiasts to the somewhat dubious delights of the bleak North Kent marshes that Hoo Junction occupies.

The yard had its up and downs. It seemed doomed when BP closed the refinery but the site became the construction point for the Channel Tunnel and Hoo Junction became busy again. Again, when this project was completed, and all the local cement works had closed, it again awaited its fate. The introduction of container services and aggregate traffic to and from Grain and the continued traffic from Cliffe and Sheerness all kept things ticking over. Finally, the decision to make Hoo Junction a "virtual quarry", served by trains from Grain, has meant it has long outlived many larger yards.

My own wanderings, both looking for wagons and career moves, took me away and, particularly in the mid-1980s, when I could no longer keep up with developments due to lack of access to BR records, I kept away. A chance visit in the run-up to Christmas 1988 revealed much change and inspired me to traverse the country from then until mid-1992 to record many of the photographs found in this volume. I will close with a selection of what I found in the December 1988 visit.

201005, taken at Hoo Junction on 1st December 1988. In flame red/rail grey livery, but with unusually placed symbols, this VDA with Taperlite suspension also has the Carlisle Currock fox symbol. (Author's Ref No W14489/DL)

400012, taken at Hoo Junction on 22nd December 1988. Despite being a failure in the original design, the SAA/SAB class have served well in other capacities. This one retains the vacuum through-pipe and is an RRB Runner wagon. (Author's Ref No W14387/DL)

460839, taken at Hoo Junction on 22nd December 1988. The SPA class, both in original form and when converted, has served well. Although there were rod coil conversions available, an SPA was just as frequently used for such traffic. (Author's Ref No W14376/DL)

950320, taken at Hoo Junction on 17th December 1988. The conversion of unfitted Bogie Bolster D wagons to the air-braked BDA class obviously made economic sense and this was another very successful class. (Author's Ref No W14366/DL)

200271, taken at Hoo Junction on 22nd December 1988. The early vans have had quite a long service. This particular example, which has received flame red/rail grey livery, is in use as an oil train barrier wagon. (Author's Ref No W14446/DL)

230116, taken at Hoo Junction on 22nd December 1988. One class that did not see long service was the VEA. Intended for military traffic, the short wheelbase probably indicated a lower speed and they were not as useful once no longer needed to serve cramped military depots. (Author's Ref No W14436/DL)

ADC210271, taken at Hoo Junction on 7th December 1988. The transfer of air-braked stock to the various departments was necessary. This former VDA, in flame red/rail grey livery, is delivering parts to Hoo Junction carriage and wagon depot. It was eventually rebuilt as a ballast wagon. (Author's Ref No W14487/DL)

DC110296, taken at Hoo Junction on 7th December 1988. Most of the OBA class transferred to the CCE as ZDA BASS wagons can still be seen on ballast trains carrying the small items. This one however, freshly repainted in yellow/ rail grey livery, has been withdrawn. (Author's Ref No W14491/DL)

DC112054, taken at Hoo Junction on 7th December 1988. The OCA class were also thinned out by transfers. This one retains flame red livery with crudely repainted code and number. It was later transferred back to traffic as an OCA. (Author's Ref No W14512/DL)

DC112142, taken at Hoo Junction on 7th December 1988. Some OCA wagons had the doors fixed and were reclassified ZCA SEAHORSE. This one has received the full yellow/ rail grey repaint but appears to have subsequently been withdrawn. (Author's Ref No W14495/DL)

DC950112, taken at Hoo Junction on 7th December 1988. This former BDA has received the full yellow/black repaint and carries the YAA BRILL code. It was another vehicle subsequently restored to revenue-earning use. (Author's Ref No W14493/ DL)

ADB733228, taken at Hoo Junction on 7th December 1988. Wagons from the traditional era were few and far between by the late 1980s, except for the BCW/BDW group. This was one survivor, in use carrying CM and EE stores to Hoo Junction. (Author's Ref No W14490/ DL)

ADS56296, taken at Hoo Junction on 7th December 1988. A more surprising survivor was this ex-SR bogie brake van. The fact that it was air-piped was the major factor. Both this, and the ZDX above, are in olive green livery. (Author's Ref No W14511/DL)

Conclusion and future plans

This brings the story of the revenue-earning wagons delivered between 1948 and 1994 to an end, but this was never the full story.

Inherited Stock

BR inherited far more revenue-earning wagons than it built and a future series will cover this fleet in as much detail as it can be. Lack of photographs and fleet details mean that the pre-Grouping stock, in use up until the late 1950s, will not receive full coverage. The Grouping period stock, including the Private Owner wagons that became part of the BR fleet in 1948, will be covered in more detail.

Privately-owned Stock

Although it was the intention of the political masters of BR to eliminate such stock after 1948, this did not happen. Although I do not have access to photographs and details of some designs, a pretty accurate picture can be presented in a separate series. This will also include coverage of stock owned by European railways or based there, which entered the country via the train ferries at Dover and Harwich and now via the Channel Tunnel.

Departmental Stock

There was already a large fleet of non-revenue-earning wagons available that BR inherited in 1948 for the use of the various companies, and these were grouped into a specially numbered fleet with codenames of a "watery" flavour (the FISHKND). This fleet will also be examined, probably in two books, a pre-TOPS and a post-TOPS volume.

In closing this book, may I say thank you to old colleagues, such as Paul Bartlett, Peter Fidczuk, Trevor Mann, and the many others who have kept the wagon flame alight. Also to be thanked are the newcomers, such as the Inter-City-Railway-Society, who produce books of wagon details. Without their help, I could not have written this volume. Photographs alone tell only part of the story. It was my realisation that wagons from specific Lot numbers differed greatly in appearance which led me to seek out the history from BR records. This was denied to me in later years, hence some of the problems in compiling conversion details after 1984, but it is nice to know that others have taken the trouble to seek out such details.

Other Books in this Series

Volume 1: Wagons of the Early British Railways Era – A Pictorial Study of the 1948 to 1954 Period

David Larkin is well-known for his study of British Railways goods wagons, and this book pays particular attention to those ordered by BR in the earliest years of its existence. The "Big Four" pre-nationalisation companies all had outstanding wagon orders under construction in 1948, and these continued to be delivered with their original numbers, albeit with new prefix letters.

In addition, the newly-created BR acquired a fleet of wagons from the erstwhile Ministry of War Transport. These are also considered in this book, together with the early BR orders for wagons based on the "Big Four" designs and on its own early standard designs in the period up to the eve of the "Modernisation Plan" of 1955.

Profusely illustrated, this book includes lot and diagram details, wagon number ranges, builders' and livery details of vehicles as diverse as Lowfit wagons, open wagons, containers and container wagons, mineral wagons, ventilated vans, railtanks, cattle wagons and brake vans. ISBN: 978-0-9544859-8-6

Volume 2: Wagons of the Middle British Railways Era – A Pictorial Study of the 1955 to 1961 Period

In this volume David Larkin continues to use his of knowledge of British Railways goods wagons to review the middle years of BR, and this book pays particular attention to the vast numbers of wagons inspired by the Ideal Stocks Committee and built under the 1955 Modernisation Scheme.

Profusely illustrated, this book includes all the usual lot and diagram details, wagon number ranges, builder's and livery details and lists at some length the route lettering carried by these vehicles. The final examples of such types as single bolsters, banana vans and ventilated fruit vans are covered, as is the emergence of new types like the Presflo and Covhop. ISBN: 978-1-905505-06-7

Volume 3: Wagons of the Final Years of British Railways – A Pictorial Study of the 1962 to 1968 Period

In this volume David Larkin looks at the final flowering of vacuum-braked stock, and the development of air-braked stock in the final years of British Railways, such as "merry-go-round" coal hoppers and Freightliner flat wagons. The batch of vacuum-fitted prototypes that eventually led to the general fleet of air-braked opens and vans is also covered. In addition, David also considers the effect of the change of corporate image for British Rail on wagon liveries, as a prelude to his continuation of the series into the British Rail era.

Profusely illustrated, this book includes lot and diagram details, wagon number ranges, builder's and livery details of a diverse set of vehicles. ISBN: 978-1-905505-08-1

Volume 4: Wagons of Early British Rail Era – A Pictorial Study of the 1966 to 1982 Period

In this volume David Larkin turns to the British Rail era. Although British Rail technically came into being a few years earlier, 1969 has been chosen as the starting point for this volume as it was the first full year of non-steam operation. 1969 was also the year that large numbers of mineral and hopper coal-carrying wagons began to be totally rebodied, rather than just being patched up.

At the same time, orders were placed for the first air-braked general purpose open and van designs, and a major step forward was the introduction of the TOPS computerised wagon record system in 1972. This greatly simplified wagon codes to three-letters, and enabled each wagon to be tracked.

Vacuum-braked wagons were only built in small numbers and involved conversions, but further air-braked designs appeared, including open wagons, vans, plate wagons, and domestic coal hoppers. The air-braked fleet was separated from other wagons, firstly by code (ABN), and then by name – Railfreight. Compatible privately-owned wagons operated with BR-owned stock on set routes, echoing the old Condor and Speedlink services and on a par with Freightliner services.

Profusely illustrated, this book includes lot and diagram details, wagon number ranges, builder's and livery details of a diverse set of vehicles. ISBN: 978-1-905505-10-4

THE (X) FILES™

CONSPIRACY THEORY –
THE TRUTH, SECRETS & LIES

TITAN

WWW.TITAN-COMICS.COM

THE X FILES

"YOU CAN KILL A MAN... BUT YOU CAN'T KILL WHAT HE STANDS FOR."

THE MOMENT HIS SISTER WAS ABDUCTED, FOX MULDER'S QUEST FOR THE TRUTH BEGAN. BUT AS THE FABRIC OF DECEIT AND LIES UNRAVELED TO REVEAL A GLOBAL CONSPIRACY OF A COLOSSAL SCALE, A PERSONAL QUEST FOR ANSWERS BECAME A CRUSADE TO UNCOVER THE UNIMAGINABLE TRUTH FOR AN ENTIRE GENERATION.

THWARTED AT EVERY TURN BY A SHADOW SYNDICATE WHOSE UNSCRUPULOUS BEHAVIOR KNEW NO BOUNDS, MULDER AND SCULLY BECAME UNWITTING PAWNS IN A FATAL GAME. WHILE THEIR INVESTIGATIONS LEAD THEM CLOSER TO THE TRUTH, THE INTRICATE WEB OF DECEIT BECAME INCREASINGLY ELABORATE UNTIL IT WAS IMPOSSIBLE FOR AGENTS AND VIEWERS ALIKE TO DETERMINE WHERE THE LIE ENDED AND THE TRUTH BEGAN.

FROM DOUBLE AGENTS AND ALIEN BOUNTY HUNTERS TO ALIEN ABDUCTIONS, THE BLACK OIL, SCULLY'S CANCER AND EVERYTHING INBETWEEN, OVER THE COURSE OF NINE THRILLING SEASONS THAT TURNED *THE X-FILES* INTO A GLOBAL PHENOMENON, VIEWERS HUNG ON EVERY TWIST AND TURN AS MULDER PURSUED THE TRUTH AND SOUGHT TO PROVE HIS BELIEF - THAT A SHADOW GOVERNMENT WAS ACTING IN COLLUSION WITH EXTRA-TERRESTRIALS TO COLONIZE THE PLANET INTO A SLAVE RACE.

THIS VOLUME COLLECTS TOGETHER SOME OF THE BEST FEATURES AND INTERVIEWS FROM *THE OFFICIAL X-FILES MAGAZINE* TO CELEBRATE ONE OF THE GREATEST CONSPIRACY THEORIES OF ALL TIME. NOW SEE FOR YOURSELF THAT THE TRUTH REALLY IS OUT THERE.

THE X-FILES
- CONSPRIRACY THEORY
ISBN: 9781782763734

PUBLISHED BY TITAN A DIVISION OF TITAN PUBLISHING GROUP LTD., 144 SOUTHWARK STREET, LONDON SE1 0UP.

THE X-FILES™ & © 2016 TWENTIETH CENTURY FOX FILM CORPORATION. ALL RIGHTS RESERVED. THE X-FILES™ AND ALL OTHER PROMINENTLY FEATURED CHARACTERS ARE TRADEMARKS OF TWENTIETH CENTURY FOX FILM CORPORATION. TITAN AUTHORISED USER.TCN 0828

COLLECTING MATERIAL PREVIOUSLY PUBLISHED IN

THE OFFICIAL X-FILES MAGAZINE 1993-2002.

NO PART OF THIS PUBLICATION MAY BE REPRODUCED, STORED IN A RETRIEVAL SYSTEM, OR TRANSMITTED, IN ANY FORM OR BY ANY MEANS, WITHOUT THE PRIOR WRITTEN PERMISSION OF THE PUBLISHER.

A CIP CATALOGUE RECORD FOR THIS TITLE IS AVAILABLE FROM THE BRITISH LIBRARY.

FIRST EDITION MAY 2016
10 9 8 7 6 5 4 3 2 1

PRINTED IN CHINA. TITAN.

Editor
Natalie Clubb

Senior Designers
Rob Farmer, Andrew Leung

Contributing Editor
Martin Eden

Senior Executive Editor
Divinia Fleary

Art Director
Oz Browne

Studio Manager
Emma Smith

Publishing Manager
Darryl Tothill

Publishing Director
Chris Teather

Operations Director
Leigh Baulch

Executive Director
Vivian Cheung

Publisher
Nick Landau

ACKNOWLEDGMENTS
Titan Would Like to Thank...
The cast and crew of *The X-Files* for giving up their time to be interviewed, and Josh Izzo and Nicole Spiegel at Fox for all their help in putting this volume together.

94

C O N T

64

80

84

58

E N T S

168

14

Here's **everything you need to know**
about Mulder, Scully and their long search for the truth

mytholo

by Deep Throat

All heads turn as a horrified Agent
Mulder steps inside his office and
surveys the extensive damage wrought
by some unknown arsonist (although the
list of suspects begins with a certain cigarette-smoking man). Water pools on the
floor and white smoke still hangs in the
air, the only signs of the blaze that deci-
mated his world.

The X-Files, his singular passion of
the last five years, the cause for which
he has risked proverbial life and limb

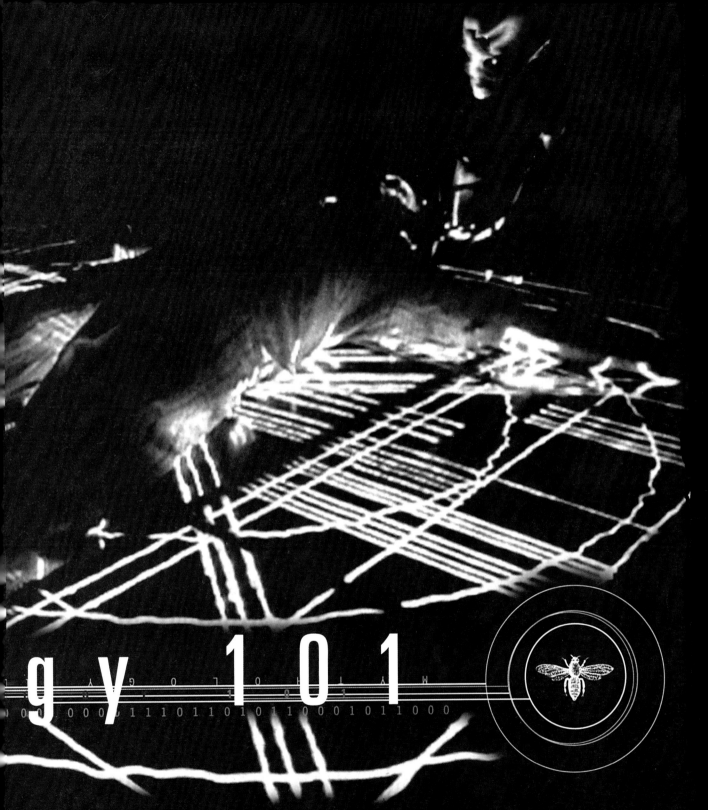

gy 101

untold times, are reduced to a smoldering pile of ashes. Only his eternally loyal partner Dana Scully dares advance, embracing him tightly enough to keep him from breaking apart under the weight of the tragedy. The agents are demoralized with hardly enough resolve to sustain them in light of these recent events. For all intents and purposes, it appears as though the nefarious Syndicate, with its deadly plan against humanity, has won.

Perhaps this really is "The End." But the aptly named Season Five cliffhanger only signals the close of *The X-Files*' first chapter. The persevering Mulder and Scully have not yet begun to fight the future, which promises exploding office buildings, deadly swarms of insects, conniving conspirators, arctic climates and assorted treachery as the duo takes to the big screen for more adventures in *The X-Files* feature film.

Just how did two dedicated government agents on a mission to find the always elusive "truth" get themselves into this fine mess? Through a series of labyrinthine twists and turns complicated enough to leave even the most die hard *X-Files* fan somewhat befuddled. In this season-by-season overview of the series' mythology, we highlight the groundbreaking, can't-miss episodes that have led Agents Mulder and Scully to their shared destiny.

The Quest Begins

PILOT: Agent Dana Scully, a doctor who's spent two years in the FBI, is partnered with Fox Mulder, an expert profiler who's been given the nickname "Spooky" because of his obsession with paranormal phenomena. Scully's charge: to evaluate the validity of Mulder's work on the X-Files, which are unsolved and unexplained cases that the FBI would prefer to ignore altogether.

On their first case together, the two agents investigate a series of youth murders in Oregon, South Dakota and Texas that Mulder believes involve alien abduction and experimentation.

Despite her skepticism, Scully finds evidence that might support Mulder's theories. When she returns to her superiors to report on the case, she brings with her the metal implant found in the nose of one of the dead teens. Asked about her partner's views on the case, she simply states that Agent Mulder believes "we are not alone."

As the episode ends, Mulder calls to tell Scully that all records of the case had been erased. Meanwhile, the mysterious Cigarette-Smoking Man—one of the men who has teamed Scully with Mulder—is shown depositing the implant in a bin, next to similar evidence, in a huge Pentagon storage room.

DEEP THROAT: Mulder and Scully

MYTHOLOGY 101—FIRST SEASON: The conspiracy builds in "The Erlenmeyer Flask" [above] and the pilot for the TV series [below]

investigate an Air Force base where Mulder suspects pilots are testing aircraft that have technology not entirely of this earth.

When a test pilot at the base has what appears to be a nervous breakdown and then disappears—the sixth pilot from the base to do so in recent weeks—Mulder is intrigued. That interest is intensified when he is approached by an enigmatic stranger who happens to know a great deal about Mulder and his work. This man, known to Mulder only as "Deep Throat" (the *nom de guerre* of Watergate's famous mole), warns Mulder to stay away from this particular case.

Mulder and Scully nonetheless continue to investigate, travelling to the air base. When the latest "lost" pilot is suddenly and mysteriously returned with no memory, Mulder suspects he's been brainwashed. Sneaking onto the base, Mulder witnesses an incredible craft just before he is apprehended, drugged and incarcerated. Scully is able to get Mulder released, but he has no memory of what he saw. Deep Throat contacts Mulder again and urges

him to continue his work, saying that he can help him in his quest for the truth.

THE ERLENMEYER FLASK: Deep Throat tells Mulder that a truck is transporting an actual E.B.E. (Extraterrestrial Biological Entity) across country, sending Mulder and Scully after the one piece of evidence that may confirm all of Mulder's beliefs.

When a researcher is killed by a mysterious man with a crew cut, Scully takes samples of the researcher's viral work to a colleague, Dr. Carpenter, where they discover that the sample tissue's DNA possesses a fifth and sixth nucleotide that exist "nowhere in nature."

Meanwhile, Scully discovers that Mulder, tracking the supposed E.B.E., is caught by Crew Cut Man and that Dr. Carpenter and her family have been killed in a "car accident." Desperate, Deep Throat gets Scully access to what he calls the original alien tissue to trade for her partner's life.

Unfortunately, there is treachery afoot: As the exchange (which again leaves the agents without any concrete evidence of alien existence) is completed on the side of a road, Deep Throat is shot dead. "Trust no one," Deep Throat tells Scully with his last breath. Soon thereafter, Mulder and Scully learn that the X-Files have been shut down and that they are being reassigned.

The Plot Thickens... 2:

LITTLE GREEN MEN: With the X-Files officially shut down and Mulder and Scully working apart, Mulder begins to doubt his own beliefs. But when an ally urges him to investigate an abandoned satellite tracking station, he heads for Puerto Rico. Mulder searches the station and finds a lone man there, hysterical with fear. The man speaks only Spanish, and Mulder is unsure of what he is saying, until the man draws a picture of the head of an alien being. The man runs away into the jungle, and by the time Mulder finds him, he is dead. Mulder returns to the station, and the equipment comes to life. A bright light blasts through the door. Mulder shields his eyes as he waits for whatever is outside to come in.

DUANE BARRY: Mulder is called in to negotiate a hostage situation with Duane Barry, a former FBI agent who claims to have been abducted by aliens. The hostage situation is resolved, and Barry is taken to the hospital. Yet when metal implants are found throughout Barry's body, Mulder believes this to be proof that Barry was abducted. He gives an implant to Scully, who remains unconvinced until she impulsively runs the implant over a grocery store price scanner. The check-out register is overloaded with binary information. Scully returns home and phones Mulder. Yet as she leaves Mulder a message on his machine, she is startled by a noise at her window. Someone is out there...

ASCENSION: Mulder rushes to Scully's apartment, but she's gone: Duane Barry somehow escaped and kidnapped her. Desperate to save her, Mulder takes his new partner, Alex Krycek, and tracks Barry to a Virginia mountaintop. He finds Barry, but Scully is gone. Barry later mysteriously dies. Mulder suspects Krycek, but the agent disappears without a trace. Though Mulder's superior, Assistant Director Walter Skinner, can't protect Mulder from the dark forces within the government, he can do the one thing they fear most—re-open the X-Files.

ONE BREATH: Scully appears in a Washington, D.C., hospital, close to death. Enraged, Mulder tries to find out who brought her to the hospital, but no one seems to know. A woman gives Mulder a pack of cigarettes—and the Cigarette-Smoking Man's address. Mulder breaks into CSM's apartment and holds a gun to his

MYTHOLOGY 101—SECOND SEASON: "Anasazi" [top] and "Little Green Men" [below]

head, but Mulder leaves without any answers. Scully's family decides to remove her from life support. Mulder sits in his darkened apartment, resigned to the imminent death of his partner—and the phone rings. Scully has awakened.

COLONY: Mulder and Scully are approached by a man claiming to be a CIA agent who says that a group of recently murdered doctors—all of them identical—were part of a Soviet cloning project. But when Mulder, Scully and the CIA agent find the next doctor, the agent morphs into the murderer, using a strange stiletto to kill the doctor. Mulder is called home to Martha's Vineyard, where he meets a woman claiming to be his sister, Samantha. She tells Mulder the cloned doctors are actually the aliens who raised her, and the Bounty Hunter is an

alien as well—and can transform himself to appear as anyone. That night, Scully answers her motel room door, finding Mulder. But then, her cell phone rings. It's Mulder....

END GAME: The "Mulder" in Scully's room morphs into the Alien Bounty Hunter. He captures Scully and tells Mulder he wants to trade her for Mulder's sister. Mulder arranges to have a sharpshooter at the meeting spot. But the shooter misses and both Samantha and the Bounty Hunter topple into a river. Samantha's body is found the next morning—yet the body inexplicably dissolves into a bizarre green liquid. Mulder is shocked to find several other women all looking like Samantha. The Bounty Hunter arrives, and Mulder is knocked unconscious, awakening to find the Samantha clones gone. Mulder follows the Bounty Hunter to the Arctic Circle. There, the Bounty Hunter beats him and leaves him—but not before telling Mulder his sister is alive.

ANASAZI: A man known as "The Thinker" gives Mulder a tape containing proof that the government knows about aliens. But the files, which contain Scully's name, are encoded in Navajo. Mulder's father is visited by the Cigarette-Smoking Man—then is shot and killed by Alex Krycek. After confronting Krycek, Mulder awakens in New Mexico. Mulder finds a boxcar packed with bodies that appear to be alien. The CSM arrives and firebombs the boxcar... and maybe Mulder.

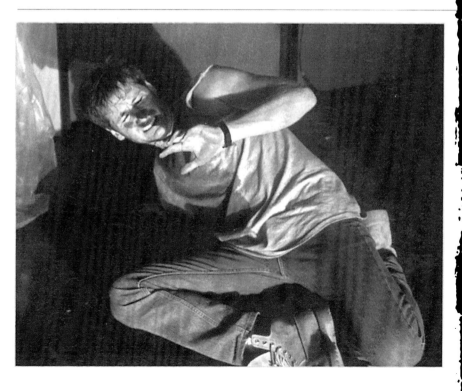

Black Oil, Dark Deeds

THE BLESSING WAY: Mulder is saved by Navajos. Scully discovers a small computer chip implanted in her neck. At Mulder's father's funeral, Scully is visited by a Well-Manicured Man who warns her that someone she trusts will attempt to take her life. A paranoid Scully believes that Skinner is the man sent to kill her, and the two end up in an armed standoff inside Mulder's apartment.

PAPER CLIP: Mulder finds Skinner and Scully pointing guns at each other. Skinner tells the agents that he has the digital tape. He convinces the agents that he should guard it. Scully learns that her sister has been shot. The agents track down a doctor who may have been developing an alien-human hybrid. He directs them to a mine where they find thousands of medical files—including one on Mulder's sister. Meanwhile, Krycek steals the tape from Skinner. But Skinner has an ace up his sleeve: a Navajo man who has memorized the tape's contents and passed them on to others of his tribe.

NISEI: Mulder thinks a video of an alien autopsy is real—and is even more convinced when he finds the man who sold him the tape dead. The agents capture a Japanese man near the murder scene, but they are ordered to let him go—he is a Japanese diplomat. Mulder takes satellite photos and a list of names—all members of the Mutual UFO Network—from the man. Scully investigates the group and is shocked when several of its members—all women—recognize her as a fellow abductee. Mulder discovers that the spy photos were tracking a secret train traveling across the country. Mulder finds the train... and leaps onto it.

731: Mulder's informant X tells Scully that the key to everything is the implant from her neck. Taking the implant to an FBI analyst, Scully discovers that it is a microchip that replicates human memory. She later finds a modern-day leper colony filled with horribly disfigured humans. A squadron of soldiers capture Scully. On the train, Mulder discovers what appears to be an alien-human hybrid. But before he can get a good look, he is jumped by a man claiming to be with the National Security Administration. What's more, the man says there's a bomb on the train. Mulder eventually escapes... thanks to some help from X.

PIPER MARU: A French salvage ship arrives in San Diego, its crew suffering from massive radiation burns. The only member of the crew not suffering from the burns returns home and an oily substance jumps from him into his wife's body. Mulder tracks a salvage broker to Hong Kong, where he is shocked to find Alex Krycek trading the

secrets from the tape he stole from Skinner. The diver's wife is also in Hong Kong, still carrying the black oil. Back in D.C., Skinner, who had been warned not to pursue the investigation of Melissa Scully's death, is shot. While Scully rushes to the hospital, Mulder surprises Krycek in a Hong Kong airport and forces him to confess the location of the tape: It is in a locker in Washington, D.C. Yet just before the two enemies board the plane back to the States, Krycek encounters the diver's wife in the airport bathroom. The oil jumps again—into Krycek.

APOCRYPHA: Krycek escapes and hands the tape over to the Cigarette-Smoking Man. Scully searches for Skinner's assailant and is suspicious when Skinner is inexplicably transferred to another hospital. She rides along, and the ambulance is soon ambushed by a gunman. Scully runs him down and discovers him to be the man who shot Skinner and killed her sister. He tells Scully that the man she wants is Krycek—and Krycek has gone to an abandoned missile silo. The agents race to the silo, but the Cigarette-Smoking Man and his squadron arrive and drag Mulder and Scully away. Inside the silo, Krycek lays on top of a strange-looking craft, convulsing. Finally, the black oil oozes out of his eyes, nose and mouth and seeps inside the craft.

TALITHA CUMI: When a gunman goes berserk inside a fast food restaurant, a gentle man heals the wounded. Mulder and Scully search for this healer, known as Jeremiah Smith. Yet Mulder is sidetracked when he learns from X that his mother has suffered a stroke shortly after she had a confrontation with the Cigarette-Smoking Man. Scully discovers that there are several "Jeremiah Smiths" all over the country, all identical. Yet just as Jeremiah begins to explain this mystery to Mulder and Scully, the alien Bounty Hunter arrives to kill Jeremiah.

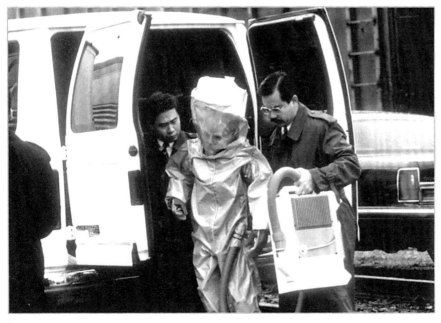

MYTHOLOGY 101—THIRD SEASON: Mulder's mother in "Talitha Cumi" [top] and an alien/human hybrid from "Nisei" [bottom]

Send in the Bees

HERRENVOLK: Pursued by the Bounty Hunter, Mulder attempts to bring the mysterious healer, Jeremiah Smith, to his dying mother. But Jeremiah first shows Mulder a farm worked by children—sets of boys and girls who are exactly identical. Also swarming around the farm—thousands of deadly bees. Eventually, the Bounty Hunter catches up with Mulder and Jeremiah, and Jeremiah disappears.

Mulder is also dealt a blow when his informant, X, is murdered. But before he dies, X scrawls out "SRSG" in his own blood. This leads Mulder to the office of the United Nations' Special Representative to the Secretary General. There, he encounters his new informant—Marita Covarrubias. Meanwhile, the Cigarette-Smoking Man brings the Bounty Hunter to Mulder s mother's bedside—where the Bounty Hunter heals the ailing woman.

TUNGUSKA: When a deadly substance believed to be an alien organism—the black oil—is discovered inside a rock that may have come from Mars, Mulder and Scully try to determine the rock's origin. This leads Mulder to Russia, where he comes upon his old enemy Krycek. Both are captured and imprisoned in a gulag. Back in Washington D.C., a Russian assassin named Peskow is killing everyone associated with the Mars rock. Meanwhile, Mulder is subjected to a sinister experiment in the gulag: He is exposed to the black oil.

TERMA: Mulder eventually escapes the gulag, hijacking a truck and taking Krycek with him. The two are separated when the truck crashes. Mulder is saved by a peasant family, Krycek by a group of one-armed men. Mulder learns that all the villagers cut off their left arms to save themselves from the mysterious "black cancer" tests. Krycek learns about this first-hand—the one-armed men hold him down and chop off his arm.

MEMENTO MORI: Scully's worst fears about her abduction are confirmed when she is diagnosed with inoperable brain cancer. As Scully begins treatment at a medical facility doing experimental cancer research, Mulder learns that the facility contains clones—and that Scully

MYTHOLOGY 101—FOURTH SEASON: Mulder fenced in in "Tunguska" [above] and Scully looking for answers in "Herrenvolk" [below]

was one of the unwitting "mothers" for the clones' creation.

ZERO SUM: An express mail worker is killed by a swarm of bees, and an unlikely operative for the Syndicate—Skinner—is sent to destroy the body and all evidence. It's part of a deal the assistant director has cut with the Cigarette-Smoking Man to save Scully's life. After the bees attack and kill an entomologist Skinner consulted, Mulder discovers the bees are carrying a mutated version of smallpox. Fearing he's been set up for a murder charge, Skinner ambushes CSM in his apartment, but doesn't kill him because CSM may be able to save Scully. After Skinner leaves, the Cigarette-Smoking Man receives a phone call from a woman who vows to continue to mislead Mulder—Marita Covarrubias.

DEMONS: Mulder wakes up in a motel room covered in blood with no idea how he got there. Possibly being framed for two recent murders, Mulder is incapacitated by a powerful vision in which he sees his mother and the young Cigarette-Smoking Man in an embrace. Incensed, believing his own mother may have had something to do with Samantha's abduction, Mulder goes to his mother's home, where he argues with her, to no avail. Though plagued by amnesia, Mulder is able to clear his name. But disturbing questions remain unanswered.

GETHSEMANE: Mulder goes into the Canadian mountains to witness a fantastic discovery that could prove the existence of alien life, only to find all but one of the scientists who made the discovery murdered. Scully, meanwhile, pursues a man who reveals that the alien conspiracy was a hoax created to discredit Mulder. Scully relays all this to Mulder, providing seemingly irrefutable evidence, and Mulder is shattered by the news that he has been misled for years. Scully reports back to Section Chief Blevins—the man who originally assigned her to the X-Files—that everything Mulder believed is false, and that she was contacted that morning to identify a body inside Mulder's apartment—Mulder is dead of an apparently self-inflicted gunshot wound to the head.

Twists and Turns

REDUX: Despondent over his inability to uncover the truth and his apparent victimization by an elaborate government hoax, Mulder is about to shoot himself when he discovers an operative lurking in an upstairs apartment. He kills the agent, who, it turns out, had him under surveillance at the behest of someone at the FBI. Mulder infiltrates a secret facility where he encounters a tipster who claims that the hoax Mulder has been drawn into dates back to the days after World War II, when the military was desperate to continue the wartime arms build-up. Mulder discovers a room containing dozens of "alien" bodies and a warehouse containing a massive index system, which contains a card reading "Dana Katherine Scully." Scully, meanwhile, learns that cells contained within a possible alien specimen she's obtained are the beginnings of a new life form. Scully performs a test, concluding that her cancer resulted from being deliberately exposed to the organism.

REDUX II: Mulder is confronted by the Cigarette-Smoking Man, who provides him with a metallic vial that contains a tiny microchip that he says will cure Scully's illness. The chip is implanted in her body and the cancer goes into remission. The Cigarette-Smoking Man next arranges a meeting between Mulder and his sister, Samantha, who reveals that some time after her abduction, she was taken to a hotel room and told that CSM was her father. Samantha then disappears, leaving Mulder no means of locating her. Later, the Cigarette-Smoking Man asks Mulder to work for him. At an FBI hearing, Mulder identifies Section Chief Scott Blevins as the mole who had ordered him put under surveillance. Blevins is shot and killed, the murder made to look like a suicide. Simultaneously, CSM is shot. As he lays dying, he glances at a photograph of a teenaged Mulder and Samantha.

CHRISTMAS CAROL: While visiting her brother during Christmas, Scully becomes embroiled in a case involving Emily, a 3-year-old child. After looking into the girl's adoption records and ordering genetic tests, Scully learns that she is the girl's biological mother (the child was born during Scully's alien abduction three years earlier). She petitions to adopt the girl, but her application is rejected.

EMILY: A thick, fibrous cyst is discovered on Emily's neck. When a doctor removes a biopsy sample, it oozes green bubbling fluid. Emily slips into a coma and dies. At the funeral, Scully, referring to what she believes were genetic experiments conducted on the little girl, tells Mulder there is still evidence of what the men did to Emily, but when she lifts the casket lid, she discovers only small sandbags inside.

PATIENT X: In the former Soviet Union, two boys see a UFO, then an area filled with burning automobiles and a screaming man, his body ablaze. Krycek, in the company of a unit of Russian soldiers, captures one of the boys. Krycek phones the "Syndicate," offering to trade the boy for all research pertaining to a vaccine for the black oil, but Marita Covarrubias steals away with the boy, only to be infected herself.

THE RED AND THE BLACK: Rescue workers sift through a secured area, which is filled with blackened corpses. An abductee named Cassandra Spender—the mother of FBI Agent Jeffrey Spender—has disappeared, perhaps taken again by aliens. Scully, who was with Mrs. Spender the night she vanished, doesn't have a clear recollection of what transpired. Mulder tells Scully that X-rays have revealed the presence of implants inside the people who were killed and recounts his belief that the U.S. government manufactured and implanted the chips as part of a bio-chemical weapons project. Meanwhile, a spacecraft crashes at an Air Force base. A faceless "alien" drags one of his comrades from the wreckage. Members of the Syndicate study photographs of the alien and realize he is a resistance fighter, part of a battle against alien colonists.

THE END: A woman from Mulder's past, Agent Diana Fowley, returns. Another figure from the past—the Cigarette-Smoking Man—also turns up and is reunited with the Syndicate, which orders him to track down a young boy with tremendous psychic ability. CSM tracks down his own son—Agent Jeffrey Spender—and reveals his identity. Meanwhile, Mulder's office is destroyed in a mysterious blaze. It appears as though all of the agent's work has gone up in smoke. ●

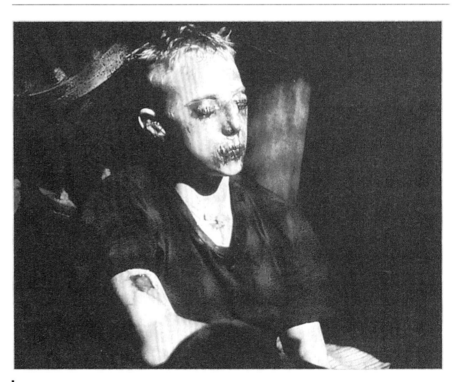

MYTHOLOGY 101—SEASON FIVE: The conspiracy took unexpected turns in "The End" [top] and "Patient X" [bottom]

THE Ⓧ FILES

DARKNESS FALLS

HOW DID AN EASYGOING SURFER END UP SCARING TV-PHILES THE WORLD OVER? AN EXCLUSIVE INTERVIEW WITH THE CREATOR OF *THE X-FILES*

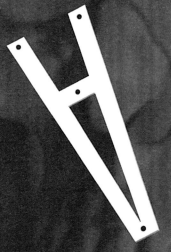

Profiles of Chris Carter all begin on the same note: He's a blond, good-looking, affable Southern Californian, partial to casual dress and first names... for cryin' out loud, he's even a dedicated surfer who got his start as a writer working for *Surfer* magazine. Point being: He's not the guy you'd expect to be the driving force behind the hectoring murderers and corrupt conspiracies that are seen weekly on *The X-Files* and *Millennium*.

So saith the outsiders, at least. But for anyone who works with Carter, the beach-bum bearing is a mirage of sorts—it soothes only temporarily before reality hits like a tidal wave. Yes, to all outward appearances, Carter could have been the real-life model for *Baywatch*'s Mitch Buchannon, but he's also much more than that. The dark shadows that often slash under his eyes aren't sunburn, and the streaks of white in his hair aren't from too much salt water. Television's golden boy works hard, and he works *all* the

BY DOUGLAS PERRY

time. In his own way, he's as obsessive as his most famous creation, *The X-Files'* Fox Mulder, a character driven by a deep suspicion of exactly the kind of self-absorbed, back-slapping, cliquish suburban subculture that the 40-year-old writer-producer supposedly embodies.

The result isn't just challenging stories that are well presented, it's an entirely new kind of television—dark, cinematic, one in which subtext is so carefully and powerfully woven into the mood of the shows that fear and anticipation and pain and melancholy

seem to swoop and dive in the night, threatening at any moment to take form out of the very air the characters breathe. The critics have responded to all this smashing of convention with awards and praise aplenty (though naysayers still can be found here and there, like wannabe Cassandras). And Carter has become not simply a behind-the-camera power broker but a celebrity—a rare accomplishment for a creator of episodic television (quick, name two others you would recognize on the street!). Beyond all that, Carter's work ethic and personal appeal

also have brought about a unique atmosphere at Ten-Thirteen, Carter's bustling production company, where astonishing success somehow seems to have made everyone actually *redouble* their efforts.

"Not only is there Chris' vision and commitment," offers Kim Manners, one of *The X-Files'* director-producers, "but he shares the opportunity to actually be a filmmaker. 'Hey, you're a filmmaker,' he says. 'Do your best work. Make this your best.' He inspires that in everybody."

We decided to see for ourselves.

Q: *At the Golden Globes,* The X-Files *won, one right after the other, best actor and best actress in a dramatic series, and—for the second time in three years—best dramatic series. It was quite a night.*

A. Yes, yes. It was truly unanticipated. We've been nominated a number of times and often we go and don't win anything. We're always just happy to be nominated, and so when all of a sudden it happens 1-2-3, it's, well, a paranormal phenomenon.

Have you had time to savor it?
The euphoria lasted about 12 to 15 hours, then it was, 'Uh oh, we've got deadlines.'

Your public persona is that of the quintessential surfer: easygoing, at peace with yourself. But your work on The X-Files *and* Millennium *suggests a man on the edge. Is either of these a true portrait?*
I don't know. I live a pretty simple life. I'm a fair person and not a paranoiac in the psycho sense. But I have an acute sense of what makes us afraid and what we're fearful of, and that fear interests me. And I happen to be a hard worker and a person who would prefer to succeed than fail. So all that is what you see [in my shows].

Is evil an aberration in human nature, or is it something we all must fight within ourselves?
Evil exists; we cannot deny that it is out there and that it affects us. I'm not sure what its nature is, but I'm certainly very interested in exploring the subject.

Why do you think that is?
I think it's a fundamental interest of everyone. We all deal with evil, with unconscionable acts—it's unavoidable. We deal with temptation, with resistance to temptation and with everything that goes along with that struggle. In this modern world, everything is explained away now by psychology, every behavior has its set of psychological terms. But I think that pure evil, true evil, exists out there and it defies the efforts of [psychologists or social scientists] to understand or define it.

What does sin mean to you?
In the Judeo-Christian sense, there's sin against God or nature or others, but I don't think my moral guide catalogues things [only] that way. [Sin] can be very personal.

Guilt certainly plays a role for Mulder. James Wolcott recently wrote in The New Yorker *that, "Mulder, once a worthy successor to Sherlock Holmes, has been remodeled this season into an action hero with a mean streak... and the coarsening of his character is part of the general downgrading of the show." Do you feel the tone of* The X-Files *has significantly changed this season?*
No, it hasn't changed. I think there have been some other voices in the mix this season, new voices. And they've done some new things on the show, but the show is very elastic. Some of the criticisms he makes are valid, but I think he singled out

Do you feel that this season's "Tunguska" and "Terma" episodes were as logistically difficult as, say, the "Duane Barry" two-parter or the "Anasazi" trilogy?
The "Anasazi" trilogy was logistically very difficult. We had to re-create the Southwest of the United States in Vancouver. We had to take, for example, something like 15,000 gallons of paint to paint the rock quarry we used red. There were all types of difficulties. Certainly, it offered the most difficult production problems we've ever faced. Of course, we write this stuff in anticipation of production problems that we'll have to solve along the way. But when you have an explosion like you have at the end of "Terma," and you have helicopter shots and big gulag shots—all that work is executed by the show's directors, in this case Kim Manners and Rob Bowman, as well as the producers, and they all did an unbelievable job.

the perpetrators of the violence that we are all so appalled by; it's not a desensitization of it. [*Crash*] is about characters who have to find new and greater thrills in order to get excited; *Millennium* is about a man who wants to make the world as safe as he can for his wife and his daughter. That's why he goes out, in spite of great pain to himself, to try to catch these people.

Yet sometimes it seems as if Frank Black is numb from it all, numb from the pain and sickness and violence he's seen.
He's not. In fact, he's much too raw; he remains very calm and placid because he must keep a perfect center. If he doesn't, he'll go into some terrible tailspin. So he is not numb to it at all; he is just calm about it in that he must be very thoughtful in order to get these violent criminals. It's quite the opposite [from *Crash*]; he's really quite heroic.

"I'M NOT A <u>PARANOIAC</u> IN THE PSYCHO SENSE. BUT I HAVE AN ACUTE SENSE OF WHAT MAKES US <u>AFRAID</u> AND WHAT WE'RE FEARFUL OF, AND THAT <u>FEAR</u> INTERESTS ME."

a couple episodes and makes a blanket comment that is very inaccurate.

You've said your original objective for The X-Files *was simply to scare the heck out of people. Has that objective evolved over the course of the show's run?*
No, it's the same.

The fourth season has shown us that the conspiracy to hide the truth about alien contact has a wider reach than even Mulder may have imagined. Where did the idea of a Russian "alien" connection come from?
From the very beginning we've all imagined that if we had X-Files [here in the U.S.], so did the other superpower. And the "Tunguska" story is a real one; the turn-of-the-century event there that knocked down a clutch of trees still has not been explained.

Did you do a lot of research on that supposed meteorite crash in Russia?
As much as I could do, given the limited time I had.

Have you ever had a story idea that you thought was fantastic, but it was so horrifying you just couldn't bring yourself to put it on film?
You can always go that far. The secret is finding the way to do it and be restrained; to do it in a tasteful manner, if you will. That's what makes it an X-File—what you don't see, how you pull back, how you make it believable, how you create the scare. The idea of something very, very dark without actually showing it. There are only so many ways to show death or violent death. The scariest thing is not the death itself but the anticipation of it.

In your new show, Millennium, *Frank Black doesn't really have the luxury of anticipating. Death is all around him. His reaction to it makes me think of David Cronenberg's film,* Crash, *which, it has been argued, is about how desensitized we've all become.*
I don't think you can compare the two. Here [in *Millennium*] we have a man in Frank Black, a heroic character, who is selflessly going out and trying to bring to heel

The flashes he has; do they represent visions or the education and experience that he brings to bear?
Yes, that is what it is; because he's been doing it for so long he is able to imagine what the killer saw, what inspired the killer, what is going through his mind.

Are you interested in showing more of the methodology of what he does, how he is able to figure out what a killer is seeing or thinking? Is there a way to show the actual nuts-and-bolts criminal-analysis process in a dramatic way?
Well, I think we are doing that by showing it visually. [Frank Black] has talked about it on the show. What has to happen as the series progresses is that we have to start showing the way *other* people see the world; it might not make sense to us, but he makes sense of it for us.

Do you have the same emotional commitment to Millennium *that you do to* The X-Files?
Yes, but it's different because my work load has doubled. There are certain things that I

THE (X) FILES   17

cannot do on *Millennium* that I *always* did the first three years on *The X-Files*, such as going on every technical survey and being involved in every part of the process. But there are only so many hours in the day. I have to put some of those things aside [on *Millennium*] and let other people do them. I walked down to the set the other night and looked at all the faces and was a little taken aback: I almost didn't recognize some of the people because I hadn't seen them in so long.

Stephen King has recently expressed interest in writing an episode of The X-Files. Will that happen?
I don't know. I haven't spoken with him recently. If it's going to happen, I think it'll happen kind of magically and mysteriously, like Stephen himself.

When you're dealing with writers who are "outside the fold," so to speak, how concerned are you that they might not understand the characters and the show as well as you do?
There's always that concern, even with writers inside the fold. But you take someone like Stephen King, who is a wonder—you cannot offer anything other than support for his desire to do it. After all, he's bigger than we are.

A few critics have said that Scully is kidnapped or assaulted or menaced too often, far more so than Mulder. Do you think that's a fair criticism?
It is fair in that, mathematically, it's probably true. But it really isn't a fair criticism, because whenever Scully gets into these predicaments there's a good chance she can get herself out of them.

It's not always Mulder going to save her.
Right. And she's saved Mulder a number of times in ways that people don't add up. When she shot Mulder in "Anasazi," she was saving him, which is a strange way of saving someone.

It was rather unconventional.
[Laughs] Yes.

Do you think that means she understands Mulder better than Mulder understands her?
Well... I think it's fair to say they both

understand each other very well.

As you well know, many fans have become so attached to Mulder and Scully that they'd like to see more about their personal lives. Do you feel the characters could be successful if removed from specific paranormal or conspiracy stories?
Well, I'm just not interested in doing that.

> **"EVERYTHING IS EXPLAINED AWAY NOW BY PSYCHOLOGY, EVERY BEHAVIOR HAS ITS SET OF PSYCHOLOGICAL TERMS. BUT I THINK THAT PURE EVIL, TRUE EVIL, EXISTS OUT THERE AND IT DEFIES ALL EFFORTS TO CATALOGUE OR DEFINE IT."**

Do you worry that it would negatively affect either the chemistry between Mulder and Scully, or the structure of the show, if one of them had an ongoing personal relationship with another character?
If it worked for the kind of stories we want to tell, it would be fine. But if it didn't, it would be a needless part of the show, a distraction, since you would have to stop and deal with that part of somebody's life.

So your approach, dramatically, is more like, say, Law & Order than NYPD Blue: the characters fit into the specific episod-

ic plots rather than the plots growing out of the characters' personal lives.
There are shows that are about the characters and their lives, and this is one of them. It just so happens that we learn about the characters and their lives through the telling of X-Files.

Much has been made of David Duchovny offering story ideas. How does his input affect the direction of his character?
It doesn't really. When someone like Mulder's father dies it obviously affects Mulder; it affects the way he looks at the world, the way he approaches his life and his job. So we make those decisions [about the character], and David and I both made that decision together in that story. But the characters were set from the very beginning [of the series], so what changes is their focus, their attitudes and their motivations, but they are still essentially who they were as originally written.

Both David and Gillian won Golden Globes for their performances. How do you think they've grown as actors since the beginning of the show?
Both of them were very good actors to begin with. And when you are talented and you work 13 hours a day, 10 months a year, you are bound to develop something that goes beyond technique, which is true artistry. I see that in their work; I see it in how they approach moments, the way they approach a scene. I think the fact that they both won a Golden Globe in the fourth year is not just because of the popularity of the show but because they're both worthy of being called the best.

Mulder and Scully's chief nemesis, the Cigarette-Smoking Man, has had a higher profile lately. Do you think the almost whimsical "Musings of a Cigarette-Smoking Man" episode, which shows him as a frustrated and untalented adventure writer, has made him less threatening and less mysterious to the audience?
Some people think so, but it certainly humanized him. But of course you must remember those were just *musings*. We don't know if the story is the man's own fictionalized creation, the mythologizing of his own life, or if it is real.

Will there be a return to the "government experiments on humans" theme?
Yes, we've got some interesting episodes

coming up through the middle of the season that will play on that. They aren't two-parters but are kind of loosely connected mythology arc [episodes].

Have the hoopla and attention that the show has generated over the past couple of years made it more difficult to sustain your original vision for The X-Files? Do you feel a lot of pressure–from the ratings or Internet chat groups or the press–to continuously top yourself?

I have to say because of directors like Kim Manners and Rob Bowman and David Nutter and Bob Goodwin, the answer is that far more often than not, it comes pretty damn close to what we originally imagined. And certain parts end up even better.

Has the script for the upcoming X-Files movie been finished?

The script is being written. I'm writing it, and Frank Spotnitz helped me work on the story.

Did you have to do some convincing in order to get Gillian and David to give up their summer vacation?

No, they are perfectly willing and ready to do it. It's going to be done sometime, so why not do it now?

Will Season Five be the last one for The X-Files?

No.

A lot of people will be happy to hear that.

The pressure has been there from the very beginning; it heightened around the time the show really took off, which was in year two. So now, here in year four, the pressure is about the same and we're used to it. We approach every episode the same way every day, which is: Is it good enough? Can it be better? Will this work? Can we fix it? Can we refine it? That's the way we approach it every day, so we're still doing the same stuff, the pressure doesn't mount from all the attention. It just makes you know that what you're doing is appreciated.

How often does the final product on screen match the picture you originally had in your head; how often do you feel you've completely nailed it?

Can you give us any hints as to what the story is about?

No. Sorry.

Is it true that next year's season-ender will be a cliff-hanger, and the movie will provide the resolution?

Yes, that's what I would like to do.

Is that fair to audiences?

Why not? I've done [cliffhangers] every year. It's the same thing I do every year with The X-Files.

What about the poor soul who happens to miss the season-five cliffhanger; will he have a hard time following the movie?

No, it will work for him, too.

Do you have a set plan for how long you'd like the series to run, or if you'd like a film franchise to grow out of it?

I'd love to do, just as we've done with the TV show, a whole series of movies.

What does the future hold for you professionally?

I'd love to write something that isn't a screenplay. I'd love to direct and I look forward to directing television or feature films. I'll keep busy.

Any specific plans yet?

I've got ideas that hopefully I can bring to fruition, but right now I have a very full plate, and I have to keep my eye on the two balls that are being pitched to me. ●

X marks the spot

Dave Hughes takes a look at the pilot episode, the genesis of *The X-Files*

There's something quite extraordinary about the pilot episode of *The X-Files*, and it has little to do with the story. What is truly remarkable about *The X-Files*' first ever episode is that, unlike almost every other pilot show, it does more than simply set up the characters and situations which will become the staples of the series. It hints at far more complex matters – subplots, character nuances, inter-personal relationships, background details and more – the importance of which will only become clear as the series progresses.

Re-watching the pilot show after four subsequent seasons and almost 100 episodes is therefore an immensely rewarding experience, and a surprising one. One comes away from it less with a sense of how far we've come, than how much *The X-Files*' creator (and pilot scriptwriter) Chris Carter had pre-planned for the series which he hoped would follow.

At first glance, several things are unique to the pilot episode: most obviously, it has no opening titles and no theme music. Instead, the programme is preceded, for the first and only time, by a tabloid-style caption which reads:

THE FOLLOWING STORY IS INSPIRED BY ACTUAL DOCU-MENTED ACCOUNTS

This is a little like saying, 'The following story isn't true, but others might be.' The absence of a title sequence and Mark Snow's music means that the episode uniquely moves directly from the atmospheric,

chillingly underscored opening teaser – in which a girl in a nightdress is pursued through an Oregon forest, *Evil Dead* style, by an approaching figure surrounded by swirling leaves and an eerie light – to the meat of the story itself.

The FBI's Dr Dana Scully is assigned to the errant agent Fox 'Spooky' Mulder to report back upon (and hopefully debunk) his work on the bureau's unofficial 'X' Files. Scully already knows of Mulder's reputation (and even his nickname) from her time at the FBI academy, and therefore the first example of her soon-to-be-omnipresent skepticism comes when she first learns that she is to be his new partner.

Mulder's character, too, is established early: his opening line, "Nobody down here but the FBI's most unwanted," illustrates both his standing within the bureau and his sense of humor. This is possibly the first example

of a 'Mulderism' – The X-philes' term for Mulder's witticisms.

"It was important to me that he have a sense of humor," explains Duchovny, "and to have a certain strength from the fact that he really didn't care what other people thought. Those were the two major decisions I made. This was not a person that cared whether he was liked or even cared whether he was believed – and that lent him a kind of irreverence and a kind of power. I think the greatest power you can have is when you don't care what people think."

The Cigarette Smoking Man, first glimpsed in Blevin's office as Scully is briefed, clearly agrees; his own status is quickly established – he is powerful enough to smoke unchallenged in a government building, despite the fact that it's illegal in the US. His importance is reinforced by the closing scene; a scene echoed 23 episodes later in "The Erlenmeyer Flask."

Chris Carter says that it was always his intention to make the

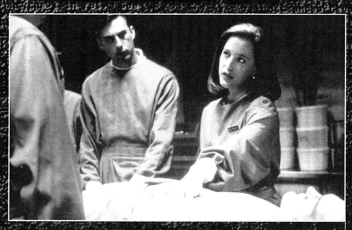

'higher-ups' the true villains, rather than the bureau itself. "I always saw the characters at the FBI as being not the ultimate bad guys, but the middlemen, [so that] the people above them, represented by the Cigarette Smoking Man, were the people who were pulling the strings – the puppeteers, if you will."

The depiction of Mulder and Scully and the implied significance of the Cigarette-Smoking Man are not the only X-Files elements established in the pilot. The facts about the abduction of Mulder's sister are relayed, not merely to give his investigations into the paranormal a personal angle, but to give his character an element of sympathy, which Scully might otherwise find lacking.

Surprisingly, the sexual tension between the two agents – later to become an implied staple of the series – is also far more obvious in the pilot episode than any other to date. The scene in which Mulder examines a scantily-clad Scully, by candlelight, for marks left by aliens remains one of the series' most overt acknowledgements of the unrequited sexuality between the partners.

"I love that scene," says Carter, perhaps offering a clue as to why he decided to cut scenes between Scully and her boyfriend, Ethan (check the boxout). (Another scene, in which Mulder and Scully literally howl at the moon, was also cut.) Finally, the destruction of the agents' evidence by someone who feels they may be getting too close to the truth would become another recurring element of the show. "This thing exists," Mulder tells his new partner in frustration. "The government knows about it. And this is the closest I've ever gotten to it."

Carter's original inspiration for the series is well-documented. "First and foremost, what I wanted to do was scare

SCULLY IN BOYFRIEND SHOCKER!

Anyone who has read Brian Lowry's The Truth is Out There: The Official Guide to The X-Files may recall a throwaway comment about a throwaway character. In the background information for the pilot episode, it is said that "Carter's original script also has Scully in bed at the end with a boyfriend, named 'Ethan Minette', who was excised before the final cut." There is, however, a little more to it than that...

In Carter's script for the episode, Ethan (a television journalist) makes a very clear impression as someone quite important to Scully – though not quite as important as her job. After she learns that her new assignment will take her to Oregon, on the other side of the United States, she has to break the news to Ethan that their holiday is off...

people's pants off," he is fond of saying.

"I said I wanted to do something as scary as a show that was on when I was a kid – *Kolchak: The Night Stalker*. I came up with *The X-Files*... as a new way to explore paranormal phenomena." Other inspirations are more obvious. The scenes in which the agents' car loses power and shuts off is straight out of *Close Encounters of the Third Kind* (a homage which Carter acknowledges when Mulder knocks at Scully's motel room claiming to be Steven Spielberg).

In addition, Agent Scully seems at least partly inspired by Jodie Foster's portrayal of FBI Agent Clarice Starling in *The Silence of the Lambs*, which may explain why Carter had a clearer idea about Gillian Anderson's character than Duchovny's. "When I first went in for the pilot audition," the actress says, "it was very obvious that Chris Carter had a strong, solid and concrete formula for who Scully was, and he guided me through whenever he felt I was getting off track. I was still trying to formulate who she was for myself in the pilot episode."

Although the pilot show's visual effects were a walk in the park compared to some of the things achieved in the series which followed, there were a number of shots which proved problematic. "We had to get a girl's nose to bleed on cue," Carter says of one particularly troublesome scene. "We had to run a tube up through the girl's hair, down her forehead, along one side of her nostril, and shoot her in profile. That tube was covered by thick, flesh-colored make-up. And it worked. I can't believe it worked! Toby Lindala, who did the special effects, is one of our biggest assets on the show. He came through heroically."

Another special effects artist whose first of many tasks on the show came with the pilot was visual effects supervisor Mat Beck, who would remain with the show until the end of the third season (even writing one episode – season three's "Wetwired"). "They were trying to figure out how to make a vortex of leaves swirl around this character," he says. "I said I'd do it, and after the pilot I got a message from Chris Carter saying he was delighted with how it went, and he wanted to work with me again. And the rest is... whatever the rest is!"

With the pilot show finally completed under the direction of Robert Mandel, whose feature film credits include the hit thriller *F/X: Murder by Illusion*, Carter's next obstacle was convincing the executives at Twentieth Century Fox that the intriguing premise offered by the pilot could be converted into a series. The reaction to the pilot could hardly have been better. "It was a riveting plot," remembers Bob Greenblatt, head of Fox's drama development. "We were all really excited about it.

"When we screened it for a group at the company, it was one of the most well-received screenings we've ever had. Then we did some test market focus groups here in Los Angeles [where they show a programme to a cross-section of the viewing public], which was equally positive... I was always concerned that, first of all, the story be very clear, and secondly, that people buy it, because we were asking them to make this big leap of faith and suspend their disbelief. And people were eager to do it!

"It was the right time for this kind of show," he adds, "because people are so curious and interested in what's possibly going on out there."

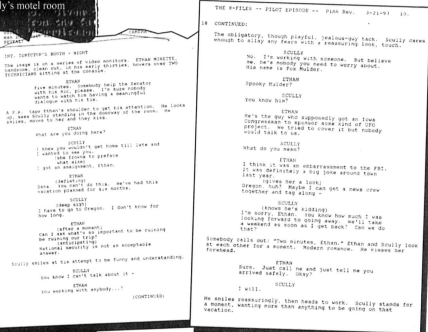

His only other appearance in the episode is in the mentioned scene near the end, where Scully receives a call from Mulder as she is trying to get to sleep.

The editing of his scenes takes a soap opera aspect out of the episode that, had it remained, would have perhaps built up more of the perceived sexual tension between Mulder and Scully. With a potentially jealous boyfriend in the mix, this would have only highlighted the fact that Mulder and Scully *could* become involved. Who can say what twists and turns the series may have taken if Ethan had stayed?

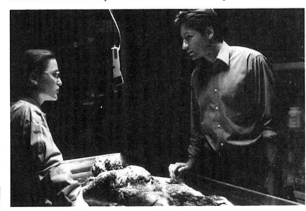

THE (X) FILES

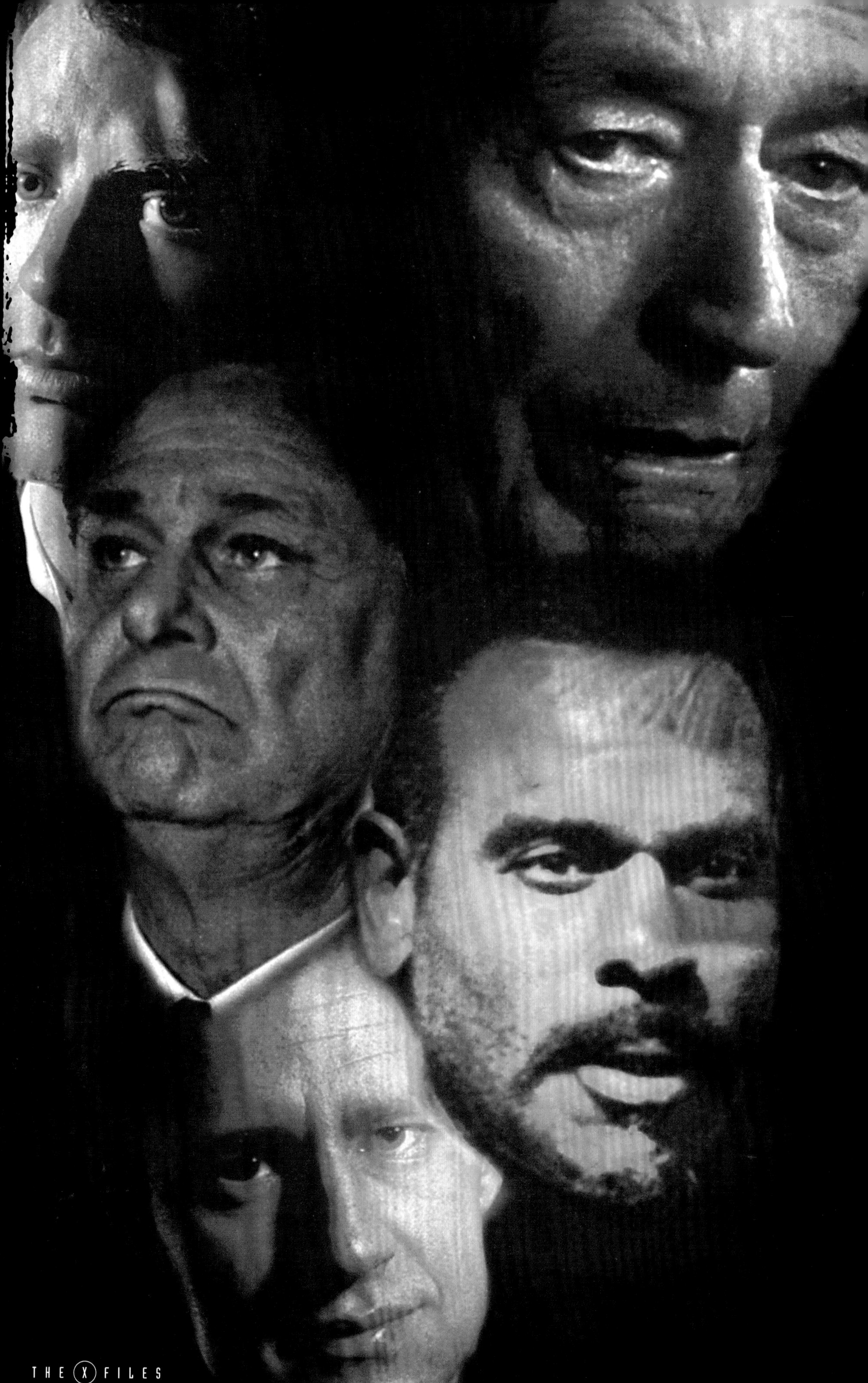

The cast of characters sacrificed to The X-Files' *mythology arc speak from beyond the grave*

RETURN OF THE LIVING DEAD

By Chandra Palermo & Gina McIntyre

War is hell.

No question about it. Particularly when the conflict in question involves two feuding alien races whose battleground is about to become Earth and a conspiracy to conceal the truth about the future from the inhabitants of the planet. Logically, events of such magnitude are bound to catch innocent (and not so innocent) bystanders in the crossfire. While *The X-Files'* roster of characters lost in action is substantial when compared to other series, in Chris Carter's dark world of espionage and deceit, it's par for the course. Here's a recap of some of the key figures who have given their lives for the cause.

[A.K.A. JERRY HARDIN]

"There are all kinds of ways to assume this character could come back, not the least of which is he's an alien."
—Jerry Hardin

ULTIMATE DEMISE: In Season One's finale "The Erlenmeyer Flask," the informant was shot and killed during a fateful hostage exchange, during which Scully bartered an alien foetus in return for Mulder's freedom from kidnappers.

CORONER'S REPORT: It's been more than five years since Deep Throat gave Mulder a clue to solving the mystery behind *The X-Files'* ongoing global conspiracy. But his parting words to Scully, "Trust no one," have achieved a life of their own as one of the series' most popular catch phrases. The character, too, has achieved his own kind of immortality, living

on as one of the most beloved figures in the show's mythology. And no one is more surprised about the turn of events than the actor who portrayed the Syndicate mole, Jerry Hardin.

"To this day, I am recognized almost all over the world as a result of having played Deep Throat," Hardin says. "It's an extraordinary phenomenon."

Hardin has dozens of stories about encounters with avid fans, ranging from hearing cries across a busy Paris airport of, "Hey, Deep Throat! Yeah, baby!" to being grabbed so forcefully by an Australian autograph seeker that he feared he was being mugged. "It's been a long time since that first season, so I'm assuming it will fade soon," he says. "But it hasn't faded yet."

As astonishing as the continued recognition might be, Hardin was even more impressed with the ability of *The X-Files'* writing team to turn the character into such a strong, intriguing presence. "My take on what they were doing with Deep Throat, and subsequently with other characters similar to mine, is it was a writers' device to dump a lot of exposition in a big hurry. So

the question was, how do you do it in an interesting and entertaining way?" he explains. "I think the mystery of the character was a very determining factor in the audience's fascination with him. So often, people who are charged with exposition like that are boring or the audience is not taken with them."

Hardin has kept busy with theatre, film and television roles, such as those in *The Associate*, *Ghosts of Mississippi* and *From the Earth to the Moon*, but he is still disappointed that he never had the opportunity to more deeply explore Deep Throat's identity.

"David [Duchovny] and I came up with all kinds of explanations that [Deep Throat] actually was an alien or he was David's father because the backstory was never discussed," Hardin says. Adding that he would love to return, he jokingly points out, "There are all kinds of ways to assume this character could come back, not the least of which is he's an alien."

2. SUBJECT:

ULTIMATE DEMISE: An assassin's bullet fells the informant in the hallway of Mulder's apartment building in the Season Four première "Herrenvolk."

CORONER'S REPORT: Death hasn't slowed down Steven Williams. With his buddy-cop show *L.A.*

Heat airing regularly in syndication and the second season of his cable series *Linc's* on Showtime (both in the US), the man who portrayed the mysterious X is enjoying an abundance of screen time in his *X-Files* afterlife. Even with his hectic schedule, though, Williams says he would love to return to the series for one final fling.

"I'd like to see him kill the whole cast," Williams says, laughing. "X just shows up one day and he's very angry, and he takes out everybody."

If anyone could do it, it would be X. Appearing in only 12 episodes, the menacing character earned the distinction of being perhaps the most slippery and inexplicable ever to appear on the series. When the end came, however, actor Steven Williams says he accepted his fate graciously. He'd always known his days were numbered and rather than bearing a grudge, he decided to make the most of his final exit.

"I looked at it as [my tribute to] James Cagney and Edward G. Robinson," Williams says. "They would take forever to die! They'd be riddled with bullets, and they'd run nine or 10 blocks and stumble up a set of stairs. [X's death scene] had a little bit of that element with that whole dragging his body down the hallway back to Mulder's doorway and then writing this thing in his own blood. It was a noble ending. Even in his death throes he was still trying to help Mulder, sending him on to his next contact."

Almost one year after his murder, X resurfaced in flashback in Season Five's "Unusual Suspects" to skulk about top-secret warehouses and intimidate the Lone Gunmen. As the series embarks on its seventh season, Williams says he has even bigger plans for another appearance of the man with no name. "My ideal scenario is he saves Mulder's butt one last time," he explains. "Mulder's about to go down the tubes and this mysterious shot rings out from someplace and saves Mulder's butt yet again. You pan to a set of feet with a long trenchcoat leaving the room. Maybe we only see him from the back, but you know that it's X. He'd only have to show up briefly, but I think that would just

" X "

[A.K.A. STEVEN WILLIAMS]

knock the fans' socks off. Or we find out that Scully is an alien, and he takes out Scully. He saves Mulder from Scully just as they're finally getting ready to get together romantically. That would about kill him for good."

3. SUBJECT: AGENT PENDRELL
[A.K.A. BRENDAN BEISER]

ULTIMATE DEMISE: The lovelorn lab tech jumped in front of a bullet meant for Scully in Season Four's "Tempus Fugit"/"Max" two-parter.

CORONER'S REPORT: Until the past two somewhat 'shipper-friendly seasons, proponents of a more-than-platonic relationship between Mulder and Scully counted on Agent Pendrell to prove romance could blossom at the FBI. So when the forensic expert, who backed up Scully's scientific analyses while secretly pining for her, sacrificed himself for his lady love, he could have easily won a nomination for sainthood. But Brendan Beiser, the actor behind the fan-dubbed "Lab boy," wasn't impressed by being shot in the heart in the local watering hole.

"I thought, 'What a jerk. What's he doing drinking anyway at four in the afternoon?'

PHOTO BY KHAREN HILL

CASUALTIES OF WAR: [clockwise from above] Brendan Beiser, Steven Williams, X's final bow, Deep Throat and Mulder in "Deep Throat"; Jerry Hardin

BETTER OFF DEAD: [clockwise from above] Brendan Beiser, John Neville, Chris Owens, the Well-Manicured Man in *The X-Files* feature film

"He took a bullet for Scully, that was nice. But she could have leaned over and kissed him at the very least."

-Brendan Beiser

That's usually what Mulder does, not me," insists Beiser, a consummate jokester. But he reluctantly concedes, "I suppose it was somewhat heroic. He took a bullet for Scully, that was nice. But she could have leaned over and kissed him at the very least."

While the actor's heartstrings were being tugged on-screen, his future on *The X-Files* dangled just as torturously off-screen. Rumors about his end ran rampant in the weeks leading up to the filming of what became his final episode.

"It went something like this, if I recall: He wasn't going to be [killed] and then he was going to be and then he wasn't going to be, and it was like a tennis match basically," Beiser explains. "They weren't sure. So one day I finally just got the script. I had heard all sorts of rumors, but then the script was just given to me and there it was."

Not surprisingly, Beiser didn't take the news well. "That's when the drug abuse started, I suppose," he jokes.

In a rare serious moment, the Vancouver resident admits that he does miss his character. He's kept busy with stints in independent films and Canadian television roles, not to mention gardening and visits from his mum. But the actor still dreams of the day when Pendrell will return "with a flowing red cape and a blue shirt with red underwear pulled over his pants and a large 'P' on his chest," he enthuses. He even has his own idea for the name of the episode marking the character's resurrection: "The P-Files."

4. SUBJECT:

WELL-MANICURED MAN

ULTIMATE DEMISE:
One of The Syndicate's top ranking officers, the Well-Manicured Man perished inside an exploding car in *The X-Files* feature film.

CORONER'S REPORT:
The Well-Manicured Man had been dead for months when actor John Neville filmed his final episode as the dignified Syndicate member. The accomplished British stage and film veteran had suffered his fate during the summer feature shoot, only to appear in the mythology episodes that were filmed during the regular Season Five schedule. So when it came time for the season finale "The End," a sense of impending doom confronted Neville.

"I said to Chris Carter, 'Well, that's it then,'" he explains. "'This episode leads into the movie. I get killed. It's been great. Thank you, bye bye.' He whispered in my ear, 'No, no, no, John. Nobody ever dies on this series.' So I said to

[A.K.A. JOHN NEVILLE]

PHOTO BY KHAREN HILL

him, 'Well then, you do realise that I got out the other side of that car.' And he laughed. He said, 'Well done, John.'"

Carter's prophecy nearly came true in Season Six when Neville received a summons to *The X-Files'* set for the flashback sequences in the revealing "Two Fathers"/"One Son." "I was phoned and asked to do two episodes, which in fact I couldn't do because I was directing the three plays of the Greek tragedy, The Orestia, for the graduating class of Ryerson [Polytechnic University in Toronto]," he explains. "And they said, 'Oh well, we'll call you later.' Well, that hasn't happened yet, but it leads me to suppose that somehow I will be magically resurrected."

In the meantime, he's kept busy, appearing in films like *Urban Legend* and *Goodbye Lover*, working on an upcoming new TV series called *Amazon*, directing plays and receiving a doctorate from the University of Toronto. The highlight of his post-*X-Files* work, however, has been to work with director István Szabó on the upcoming film *The Taste of Sunshine*.

Nevertheless, he still misses the intriguing nature of the Well-Manicured Man. "I always think that the great thing about my character was that the audience never knew whether I was good or evil," Neville explains. "That makes it something very interesting to play, of course, but it also intrigues the audience and makes them want to watch."

5.SUBJECT: JEFFREY SPENDER
[A.K.A. CHRIS OWENS]

ULTIMATE DEMISE:
Murdered by his own father, the nefarious Cigarette-Smoking Man, Spender presumably died inside his basement office at the FBI. His body was never recovered...

CORONER'S REPORT: Given
his penchant for sabotaging Mulder's work on the *X-Files*, Jeffrey Spender might not have won too many popularity contests with fans of the series. But his unexpected demise at the conclusion of Season Six's "One Son" still proved shocking, particularly to the character's alter-ego, Chris Owens.

"I had just finished doing an interview for *People*," Owens explains. "There had been a phone call [from] Mr. Carter's office. I called back and spoke to Chris. He said, 'You're going to get some news in the next episode. It's rather drastic. I rarely do this but I think it's important for the story.' I said, 'What are you going to do, fire me?' He said, 'Well, no, but I am going to kill you.' I was really surprised. He said, 'You've got to trust me.' I said, 'Well, I do. I trust you implicitly.' He said, 'Well, trust

no one.' After I hung up the phone, I was sitting there. It was one of those rare days in L.A. where it was rainy outside and dark. I was sitting at my table, and a few seconds later a script arrived under the door. I thought, 'Oh my god, I'm living *The X-Files*.'"

His surprise is understandable. Owens thought that his *X-Files* training had prepared him for anything – in the past two years, he had already portrayed three characters on the show: Spender, the Great Mutato in "The Post-Modern Prometheus" and the young Cigarette-Smoking Man in "Musings of a Cigarette-Smoking Man." The dramatic turn of events in two-parter "Two Fathers"/"One Son," however, was simply unprecedented. Spender evolved from a hard-shelled cynic bent on sabotaging Mulder's lifelong work to an earnest believer in his colleague's quest for the truth. Few *X-Files* characters have traveled such an emotionally taxing path in such a short time.

There is some hope that Owens will again appear on the series. According to the

always vague Chris Carter, the actor could resurface in a number of ways. "How about alive?" Owens suggests, laughing. "Chris mentioned flashbacks as a possibility. I'm not sure how Spender would fit into that because of his brief association with the FBI, unless it's something to do with his mother, perhaps. It's funny. Spender hasn't even been mentioned since that gunshot. It's surprising that an FBI agent can be shot at the by FBI and there's no mention. It's bizarre. But I'm sure Chris has his plan, whatever it may be."

"I said, 'What are you going to do, fire me?' [Carter] said, 'Well, no, but I am going to kill you.'" -Chris Owens

6.SUBJECTS:
THE SYNDICATE

THE DEAD NEXT DOOR: [clockwise from top] Scully and Spender in "The Red and the Black"; Don S. Williams as the First Elder; The Syndicate circa 1972 in "One Son"

ULTIMATE DEMISE: After years of orchestrating perhaps the most wide-reaching conspiracy ever perpetrated, the powerbrokers of The Syndicate were wiped out by flame-wielding alien rebels.

CORONER'S REPORT: You don't rise to the rank of First Elder by losing your cool in a crisis situation. So it's not too surprising that when actor Don S. Williams, who portrayed the mysterious fellow, read the

scripts for mythology blow-out "Two Fathers"/"One Son," he accepted his apparent demise with quiet resignation.

"My immediate reaction was that time has come, I guess," Williams remembers. "I figured it was going to happen sooner or later. Chris Carter obviously has a grand plan, and it was time for those developments in the grand plan. That was the reaction, so I started thinking about what a good time I'd been having."

Williams cites working with longtime peers William B. Davis and John Neville as highlights of his three-season stint on the series. Since the character

first surfaced in Season Three's "The Blessing Way," the Elder has overseen the actions of his dastardly colleagues and had a hand in some of the greatest hoaxes ever perpetrated. It was only fitting, then, that he and his Syndicate cohorts met such an elaborate end.

"It was filmed in a hangar," Williams says of his final scene. "It was quite a powerful building to be in. It made one feel about as large as an ant. It was a wonderful location. It was an all-night shoot. It's very tiring because you're doing something other than what you normally do at that time, but the adrenaline gets up because of the work at hand. It just comes with the job. I'm used to night shoots from my directing experience."

In the meantime, Williams can be seen in the upcoming thriller *Reindeer Games*. "I play Ben Affleck's Uncle Ray," Williams says. "He's a little different [from the First Elder]. I'm not in a shadowy room, let's put it that way. It was wonderful. It was especially nice because John Frankenheimer has always been one of my favorite film directors and to work with him was really interesting."

Just because the actor is pursuing other roles does not mean that he would be too busy to return to *The X-Files*. "It's good work and I'd love to see him return," Williams says. "I think I would like to return as a kind of Trojan horse for the rebel aliens. That would be the twist that I would be working for them." ◆

"NISEI"

Scully discovers a bizarre connection between her abduction and the female members of a UFO group...

THE BUILD-UP:

An investigation into an alien autopsy video puts Mulder and Scully on the trail of a conspiracy involving a group of Japanese scientists, which, in turn, may hold some answers to Scully's mysterious abduction. The man behind the autopsy video is found dead, but at his home the agents find evidence linking him to a group called the Mutual UFO Network. While Mulder pursues another line of enquiry, Scully visits the home of one of the 'MUFON' group's members, Betsy Hagopian...

THE SCENE:

BETSY HAGOPIAN'S HOUSE; ALLENTOWN, PENNSYLVANIA

(Scully listens to the MUFON members.)

LOTTIE HOLLOWAY: I don't know, when I opened that door and saw you standing there? It was like a revelation. The image of your face was so clear to me.

SCULLY: But why is it that I don't remember you?

PENNY NORTHERN: All you remember in the beginning is the light, and then sometimes the faces of the men who perform the tests.

(Scully stares at her until her memory begins to return. She sees some kind of tube attached to her belly button. Her stomach grows large as two figures, presumably aliens, watch in the background. Scully looks away from Penny and Lottie.)

SCULLY: How do you know that you're not mistaking me for somebody else?

(Lottie looks over to Diane.)

DIANE: You have the mark, don't you?

(Scully looks over at her.)

SCULLY: What mark?

DIANE: Here.

(Diane sits down backwards in front of Scully and pulls down the back of her shirt, revealing a small scar on the back of her neck.)

DIANE: On the back of your neck.

(Scully looks at it, then closes her eyes.)

LOTTIE HOLLOWAY: We all have them. It's where they put the implants.

(Lottie nods to the other women in the room, who all, one by one, take out various capsules, medicine bottles and containers, each holding an implant inside. Scully looks at them, her feelings building inside her.)

THE SIGNIFICANCE:

An important revelation about what may actually have happened to Scully during her abduction in Season Two. This powerful scene, particularly the haunting image of the women producing their implants, leaves the viewer reeling. In true X-Files style, answers only lead to more questions.

THE FACTS:

● Gillian Barber (Penny Northern) also appeared in Season Two's "Red Museum". In that episode, the catchphrase was "He is one." Here it is "She is one." Spooky!

● Blimey – Scully's hair! The sleek, shorter bob she wears nowadays is so much sexier.

EPISODE CREDITS

Episode #3x09
First US airdate: 24/11/95
Written by: Chris Carter & Howard Gordon & Frank Spotnitz
Directed by: Rob Bowman
Main actors this scene:
Dana Scully: Gillian Anderson
Penny Northern: Gillian Barber
Lottie Holloway: Corrine Koslo
Diane: Lori Triolo

Compiled by Kate Anderson

SECRETS AND LIES

by Gina McIntyre

PARANOIA ISN'T A
RECENT PHENOMENON—
CONSPIRACY THEORIES
HAVE BEEN AROUND
SINCE THE DAWN OF
CIVILIZATION

These days, it's hip to be scared. Just ask most people on the street if they trust the media, big business or politicians—the resounding answer will be no. And given the number of uncovered scandals over the years, be it Watergate, Iran-Contra, the S&L failures or Bill Clinton's woes, a paranoid worldview where conspiracies abound and meetings conducted in secret determine the fate of the planet almost makes sense. In fact, believing that the powers that be often work against the best interests of the people whom they supposedly serve might rightly be considered more the trademark of the astute political observer rather than the fringe eccentric printing leaflets from his basement.

But the notion that the conspiracy theory has only recently emerged from the dark cellar of peripheral politics into the bright light of mainstream consciousness is wrong. Sure, technology has created almost unlimited venues to disseminate conspiracy theories, but off-the-wall ideas about nefarious, power-hungry cabals are not a product of the Information Age. Neither the nature of conspiracy theories nor the number of people who subscribe to them has changed over the last two centuries, experts say. Throughout history, there have always been suspicious minds seeing sinister patterns and plots in the world around them.

"Most people throughout history and today don't like chance [and] want to impose order on the chaos that lies around us," explains Lacey Smith, a Northwestern University history professor and author of *Treason in Tudor England: Politics and Paranoia*. It's a question of human nature, he says. "There is a marvelous scene between Eeyore and Winnie the Pooh. Eeyore has just discovered that he is missing his tail. He is a paranoid type, and he says somebody stole it. And he said, 'It's so like people to do this.' And Pooh says, 'What are you talking about Eeyore? You just lost it.' There are two kinds of people in this world—the Eeyores and the Poohs."

Even in the cradle of civilization, conspiracy theories enjoyed their own cultural cachet. Way back in ancient Mesopotamia, people who fell ill or were vexed by some other kind of problem were quick to assume that they were the victims of a vendetta, postulating that their misfortune

was the result of an evil spell cast by a malevolent deity or a group of conniving foes. Sometimes, the persecuted said, these conspirators had a greater purpose, but mostly they tormented their victims for sheer amusement.

The same attitude prevailed among the toga-sporting citizens of ancient Rome. Many espoused theories that secret agents conspired against them or their government, and, in some cases, they weren't necessarily too far off the mark: A healthy dose of paranoia might have kept Julius Caesar from suffering that famous knife in the back.

"The conspiracy theory is as old as man, if only because it makes so much sense," Smith says. "Let's say you walk out of your house and on the doorstep, there's a banana peel. You step on it, and you slip and break your leg. There are two basic questions that immediately rise to your mind. One is, 'Why is this happening to me?' The other question is, 'How did that banana peel get there in the first place? Somebody put it there.' That is the enemy theory, a form of conspiracy."

As the "they're out to get me" concept grew in popularity, it became a tool of bigotry. All it took was a little misinformation about some ethnic or religious group other than one's own, and bam, those people became the enemy. Take early Christians, for example. Some considered them cannibals whose ritual of Communion involved the consumption of the flesh and blood of their saviour and feared the sect's attempts to convert the world to their way of thinking. In reality, of course, the celebrants were simply imbibing wine and wafers, but the paranoid believed otherwise.

Ironically, early Christians themselves were quick to point the finger of conspiracy. They held Jews responsible for the death of their messiah, a grudge that developed over the centuries with lasting and lethal ramifications. Citing a "conspiracy against Jesus" for nearly 1,000 years after the crucifixion, some early Christian writers, seeing themselves in competition with Judaism, called Jews everything from murderers to agents of the devil to authors of a plot to control the world.

In 1096, with the beginning of the Crusades, an all-out assault on Jews got underway, with conversion the preferred course of action and annihilation a close second. In 1306, King Philip IV of France expelled Jews from his country on the grounds that they "dishonor Christian customs and behavior in innumerable ways." Almost 200 years later, Protestant Reformer Martin Luther made a number of similar statements, concluding that Jews are "enemies."

Unfounded as it was, the belief in an alleged Jewish conspiracy to dominate the world became one of the most widely adopted theories, says Northwestern University assistant professor of religion Benjamin Sommer. Sometimes, it's easier for people to believe that an omnipotent "*They*" control the fate of the universe: A simple, if delusional, explanation for the evils in society can assuage the individual's need for a rational answer.

"When bad things are happening that you have no control over, it's nice to be able to put a name and a face on them because then you can begin to imagine that maybe somebody somewhere will handle the problem. Once you can put a face on the bad things that might be happening to you—your town has been overrun by bubonic plague or the stock market crashes and there's a depression—then, at least, you can imagine that there's something that can be done about it," Sommer says. "[In this case], if you say the problem is the Jews, then you know where the Jews are and even if you yourself don't necessarily go out and get all of them, you can imagine that somebody somewhere in the world could do that."

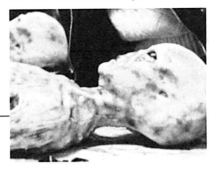

NO TRUST ONE

During the Middle Ages, the conspiracy theory began to take on its contemporary form with the evolution of the universal dominion theory, which encapsulated fears about secret bids for world hegemony. The reigning fear wasn't that the forces of evil were up to no good in the neighborhood: now the bad guys were out to take over the world.

"[The theory] claims that it's inevitable for religious reasons, as well as an analysis of human nature, that various regimes will try to dominate the entire world, not only through explicit political means but through various subversive, subtle means," says University of Chicago historian Steven Pincus.

With the development of a more sophisticated kind of conspiracy theory, the focus shifted from Jews to Catholics. In 16th century England, Pincus explains, fear was rampant that "Papists" (i.e., agents of the Pope) would subvert the government in their attempt to turn the world to Catholicism, torturing innocent Anglicans until they were forced to recant their faith. And the prime emissary of the Catholic plot? For the English, that was plain to see: it had to be their old enemies, the French.

"Conspiracy theories have to do with imperfect knowledge about information. You have to have some sort of basis of truth to believe this is going to happen," Pincus says. "The English were obsessed with the notion that there was a French conspiracy to take over the world. They located this conspiracy in attempts to make French the language of high culture,

to disseminate French fashion.

"And the French had exactly a mirror opposite image of the British," he continues. "They'd claim attempts to make tea a marker of civilization was part of a British attempt to take over the world since the Brits controlled most of the world's tea resources. During the Napoleonic regime in France, the Brits claimed the French were trying to get control of the whole world again, [only] Napoleon just wasn't as subtle as his predecessors. Similarly, the Napoleonic rhetoric was that the Brits opposed France because they wanted control of the world."

While Catholics were believed to have evil motives, they weren't the only perceived agents of the devil skulking about Britain. It was widely believed that witches and other worshippers of evil were engaged in a grand conspiracy to overthrow the Christian world so iniquity could run amok. "There's this belief that the devil has lots of different people working for him. There were theories in Europe that there were enormous numbers of witches out there. You didn't know who they were, but

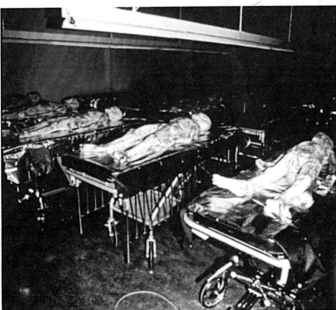

E.T. CONSPIRACY:
"GETHSEMANE" [FAR LEFT],
"REDUX" AND "REDUX II"
SUGGESTED THAT THE
"ALIENS" SEEN BY
ABDUCTEES MIGHT BE
FAKES CREATED BY THE
GOVERNMENT

they were trying to take over the world. They were trying to undermine Christendom," Sommer says.

That theory proved so infectious even the

ruling class adopted it, Smith adds. For example, in 1511, when riots against foreign merchants erupted in the streets of London and King Henry VIII asked Sir Thomas Moore to ascertain the reasons behind them, his investigation focused on ferreting out a corrupt agitator, not on resolving perceived economic tension. "He immediately started looking for the evil person who put these evil ideas into the heads of the apprentices who organized this riot. In other words, conspiracy theory at work," he explains.

The anonymous Evil Doer also emerged in high profile pieces of entertainment. Instead of *The X-Files*, the masses looked to Shakespeare for their doses of conspiracy lore. "In the 16th century the notion of the enemy out there–the evil guy who is after you, was universal," Smith says. "Remember honest, honest Iago from *Othello*? In a way, [that play] is advising you never to trust your friend because your friend may conceal behind the façade of friendship an evil person. In the 16th century, you get an eruption of fear of the devil, of fear of evil in society and of plays similar to *Othello* that say, 'Be on the lookout. Never trust anybody.'"

Sage wisdom indeed for New England settlers living in a certain Massachusetts town. The Salem witch trials of 1692 parlayed fear of the devil into a bitter neighbor-versus-neighbor battle in which your closest friend might accuse you of frolicking naked in the woods with Lucifer.

BELIEVE THE LIE

Another kind of conspiracy theory began to evolve in the early 1700s coinciding with the founding of the Freemasons. Due in part to the secrecy surrounding membership in the society, rumors sprang up accusing the Masons of heresy and treason, according to Jonathan Vankin, author of *Conspiracies, Cover-Ups and Crimes* and co-author of *The 60 Greatest Conspiracies of All Time.*

"[Freemasonry] was seen as a very subversive force, and there was an element of truth to that. In the 18th century, the masonic order was a refuge for intellectuals, scholars and radicals—people who today would be called Communists or Socialists—to get together and express themselves and to try to act on their ideals, ideals that in a monarchy like France were not thought of very highly by the establishment," Vankin says.

The wagging tongues assailing the bricklayers' order described them as a new incarnation of the Knights Templar, a mysterious group who protected Christians traveling to and from Jerusalem during the Crusades, but were suspected of having their own, selfish motives.

Founded in 1119, the Templars resembled a monastic order—members took vows of poverty, chastity and obedience—with one major exception: They waged wars. To finance their battles, the Knights inadvertently founded deposit banking, securing large sums from their partons based on their reputation for great nobility. It was their wealth, and the mystery that surrounded their order, that put them right behind the Jews on King Philip's hit list. The monarch dissolved the order in 1307, burned its members at the stake and confiscated their holdings. But numerous conspiracy theorists alleged that the order had gone underground and was simply resurfacing as Masons, quenching their need to wage war by promoting the advancement of the French Revolution.

Cashing in on the secret society buzz, a

IS THE TRUTH OUT THERE?: EPISODES LIKE "REDUX" [LEFT] AND "GETHSEMANE" [ABOVE RIGHT] TURNED REAL-LIFE PARANOIA ABOUT ALIEN COVER-UPS INTO TENSE DRAMA

law professor named Adam Weishaupt founded his own Order of the Perfectibilists, better known as the Bavarian Illuminati, with the lofty goal of ultimately controlling the world. *Really.* After passing the secret rites of initiation, the more than 3,000 members of Weishaupt's order were expected to follow their leader's mandates with the strictness of a cult. Specifically, members, most of whom already belonged to the Freemasons, were directed to

infiltrate as many secret societies as possible to spread their doctrine. By the mid 1780s, though, a few of the order's loose-lipped acolytes let slip just enough details to get the organization outlawed.

Not that legal banishment made the order any less notorious. Rumors continued to assert that the Illuminati were alive and well and up to all sorts of mischief. Some even said Weishaupt

had fled to the United States, assassinated George Washington, then successfully impersonated him. Mostly, though, the Illuminati were thought to be biding their time until all of the necessary elements fell into place to achieve the "New World Order" they dreamed of. Yes, the same phrase that President George Bush so proudly hailed as the slogan of the decade originated 200 years ago in Bavaria. (And if you think that

didn't send a big red flag to conspiracy mongers, think again.)

DENY EVERYTHING

Conspiracy theories about secret societies and their relationships to the legions of Hell are still plentiful in the 20th century—for evidence, just look to all the present-day paranoia about baby-murdering Satan worshippers. But the black-robed devotees of evil faded into the background with the resurgence of political and racially motivated paranoia. Specifically, anti-Semitism resurfaced in the late 1800s with the publication of *The Protocols of the Meetings of the Learned Elders of Zion*. The book purported to describe secret meetings of the leaders of a worldwide Jewish conspiracy, even though it was actually based on an 18th century French pamphlet blasting Freemasons.

"[It said] Jews pretended to be in

BEHIND THE $CHEMES

Cooking up a good conspiracy theory is relatively easy, but trying to unearth theories that have been right on the proverbial money is not. In fact, despite the pervasive nature of conspiracy theories in history, only a handful have later been proven to be true.

Among the real-life conspiracy elite is the CIA's MKULTRA programs, mentioned by author Jose Chung in the classic "Jose Chung's 'From Outer Space.'" From 1953 to 1973, the government conducted mind-control experiments on often-unwitting participants who were hypnotized, administered doses of LSD and other chemicals and subjected to all sorts of bizarre tests. The programme awarded one scientist a grant to work on "depatterning," in which ongoing

patterns of the patient's behavior were broken down by means of particularly intensive electric shocks in addition to hallucinogens. Some subjects suffered brain damage and other debilitations, including one person who sued the government and won an out-of-court settlement in 1988. The goal of the programme? The creation of mind-controlled assassins, a la *The Manchurian Candidate*.

The CIA was also behind multiple assassination attempts on Fidel Castro. Aside from the disastrous Bay of Pigs invasion, the agency concocted all sorts of plans to eliminate the Cuban dictator, including dousing him with LSD, presenting him with poisoned cigars and staging the second coming of Christ in order to incite a rebel-

lion among Cubans. Finally, the government enlisted professional help from the mob, but, for some mysterious reason, every attempt on the dictator's life failed.

But perhaps the most frightening conspiracy theory-come-true is the United States government's biological weapons campaign. Following World War II, the U.S. granted amnesty to Japanese scientists from a research outfit called Unit 731. The government wanted access to the results of their experiments, most of which involved testing lab-manufactured diseases on humans. During the war, the researchers engineered everything from the bubonic plague to meningitis, then administered it to prisoners of war

(including American G.I.s), sometimes additionally forcing the *homo sapien* guinea pigs to stand naked in sub-zero weather until their limbs froze, ostensibly to determine the effects of disease in cold temperatures.

In 1950, the U.S. government began running tests of its own. A lawsuit against the feds filed by the family of a San Francisco resident who died after a rare strain of bacteria was sprayed over the city revealed details about 300 open-air germ tests conducted between 1950 and 1969. In 1972, an official ban on the development and use of biological weapons went into effect. The experiments supposedly stopped, but their legacy lived on in *X-Files* episodes like "Nisei" and "731."—*G.M.*

poverty and pretended to be powerless as a way of masking the fact that they were, in fact, in positions of great power and through setting up democracies, which was beginning to happen in parts of Europe by the late 19th century, they were able to determine the destiny of the world," explains Sommer.

Originally penned in Russian, *The Protocols* were translated into a number of other languages during the 1920s and distributed across the globe. Despite its obviously ludicrous content, the Nazis quickly adopted the book as gospel. "[The Protocols] were widely distributed in Germany. Serious people, serious newspapers that talked about them dismissed them as fraudulent, but millions and millions of people believed them," Sommer says. "They were really put very effectively to use. They

were certainly quite influential."

By the end of World War II, the tragic consequences of that influence had been made clear to the world. Open anti-Semitism faded. But a powerful new kind of paranoia quickly rose to take its place. Rabid anti-Communism, already widespread before the war, breathed new life—and respectability—into the conspiracy theory. Republican Sen. Joseph McCarthy announced that the Red Menace had infiltrated the United Nations, the State Department and even the Pentagon as part

of a conspiracy "so black that, when it is finally exposed, its principles shall be forever deserving of the malediction for all honest men."

Red-baiting demagoguery would fade with the end of the Cold War, but a mish-mash of other paranoid worldviews remain. The treatment these get from the general public and the mass media is somewhat schizophrenic: certain theories are embraced, while others are tossed on the loony-bin heap. Theories accusing certain government officials of impropriety are readily accepted, but those targeting every government agency from the CIA to the Food and Drug Administration, not to mention the perennially popular World Financial Syndicate, are instantly discredited as bunk, perhaps rightly so. "Somehow you've got Jewish Catholic Communist Capitalists who are all the same person, or the same group," Sommer quips of overzealous believers who try to wrap all the different conspiracy theories into one not-so-neat package.

For Vankin, the distinction between the believable and the dubious is more or less arbitrary. Although some theories are obviously fatally flawed, some of the more plausible, such as those

SUSPICIOUS MINDS

Author Jonathan Vankin spent years trying on the mindset of a conspiracy theorist, extensively researching the topic and interviewing its biggest proponents. After publishing two books on the subject and maintaining conspire.com, a frequently updated Web site, he knows the loopy world of paranoia pretty well. We asked him to pick his three favourite conspiracy theories, all of which are mentioned in his book *The 60 Greatest Conspiracies of All Time*:

"Apolloscam": Basically, man never went to the moon. The government faked the whole thing, creating sets of the lunar landscape in a Nevada warehouse. Before the astronauts

stepped in front of the camera, they were living it up in Vegas, gambling and gals paid for by Uncle Sam.

"The Candy-Coated Conspiracy": The decision to add fluoride to drinking water was not, as those wily Feds claimed, an effort to promote dental health. It was instead,

according to urban legend, an ingenious way to diminish the sex drives of Americans and placate the candy lobby: Parents would count on fluoride to protect their children's teeth, leading to an all-out sugar-fest for the country's youngsters.

"Anglophobia": Hegemony resurfaces with the fear that the Brits are plotting to regain control of the world. And by what means? Why, by running a covert drug operation to ensure that unsuspecting countries are lulled into apathy until the British Empire can again reign supreme. Libertarian supreme and former presidential candidate Lyndon LaRouche is perhaps the premiere Anglophobe.

And, Vankin adds, wild and

wacky theories keep rolling in all the time via e-mail, which has surpassed typewritten pamphlets, street-corner preaching and word of mouth as the most-popular method for spreading unconventional worldviews.

"When something happens like the death of Princess Diana—our Web site was getting e-mailed minutes after the news reports appeared [with messages saying], 'British intelligence did this. The Royal Family did this. It's all a cover-up!'" he says. "After the John Denver tragedy, we got [an e-mail message] from someone about *Bob* Denver [of *Gilligan's Island* fame] and how he was stockpiling food in a cabin in Montana. And I kept thinking, 'Gilligan? Gilligan's a survivalist?'"—*G.M.*

concerning the assassination of John F. Kennedy, are not thoroughly, or impartially, investigated.

"It's interesting that 34 years [after JFK's assassination], there are still extreme reactions on the part of the major media against anyone who comes up with any kind of conspiracy theory about it. It's fascinating to me that that provokes such a reaction when it seems so clear that there was some sort of conspiracy involved," Vankin says. "You hear things like, 'It's been 34 years. Someone would have come forward.' The fallacy is that a lot of people have come forward, and they're either not believed or they're discredited or they're not taken seriously.

"A lot of people have talked," he continues. "No one person with the whole story, but I doubt any one person ever knew the whole story. When you have something like that, I would think it would be like any big corporate operation. If Microsoft is working on new software, there's usually not any one person who knows absolutely everything, except maybe one person at the top. I would imagine that's the way a major political assassination would work, too."

THE TRUTH IS OUT THERE

Years ago, Vankin predicted that the 1990s would become the conspiracy theory decade. In a way, his prophecy has come to pass: increasingly, people are beginning to realize that, when it comes to "the facts," what you see is not necessarily what you get. The media might not be part of a vast conspiracy, but reporters, producers and networks often do have their own agendas. In the Information Age, it might be easier to get information, but it's easier to manipulate it, too.

"It's so hard to come up with explanations for why things are the way they are, why political situations go wrong, why our social climate is so screwed up," says Vankin, a professed

X-Files fan. "Conspiracy theories and paranoia are the natural result of wanting to affect a larger world but not having the tools to do it.

"Conspiracy theorizing is a very individualistic way of forming explanations for things," he continues. "It's your individual understanding of the world, not the understanding you get from the nightly news. I think it's good that people are becoming more skeptical and more questioning of authority and of the government and the information received through the media."

For some, that might mean assuming that AIDS was a deliberate attempt to eradicate certain elements of the American population or swearing that the Department of Defense planted a bomb inside an Oklahoma City office building to destroy top-secret documents. But for others, that admonition to be aware, to really examine things from all sides, can be enlightening, mind-opening and, ultimately, positive.

"The Internet has made it more acceptable to express non-mainstream points of view," Vankin points out. "People are aware that there is a multiplicity of viewpoints

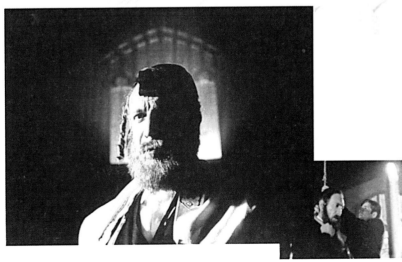

and ideas and thoughts out there, and that we're not just limited to what the networks and the big newspapers tell us." ●

Here Among Us

John Ainsworth takes a look
at the production of
The X-Files' first major
conspiracy two-parter:

"Colony" and
"End Game"

D o aliens exist or is there some other more
'rational,' but elusive, explanation for close encounters
of various kinds? This was the question originally planted in the minds of the audience by *The X-Files* and per-
sonified by the strikingly different approaches of the two
lead characters. For a season and a half the series trod its
ambiguous line well but with the two-part story "Colony"
and "End Game," the aliens came out of the closet.

A shape-shifting alien bounty hunter crash-lands in the
Arctic Sea. Following his rescue he escapes and begins to
hunt down and kill a group of alien clones that are
attempting to combine human and alien DNA. At the same
time, Mulder receives an urgent call from his father and trav-
els home to discover that his sister Samantha, who was apparently abducted by aliens when she and Mulder were still children, has returned.

"Colony" and "End Game" were a big step forward for
the series, both in terms of the ongoing conspiracy story arc
and how the television-viewing public was receiving the show.

"It was around this time that *The X-Files* finally exploded
into bigger than life," explains Rob Bowman, *X-Files* producer
and director of "End Game." "These were the sweeps
episodes, [the ratings for which are used to set the advertising
rates for the year], and the scripts became enormous, requiring
several units to shoot them."

"'Colony' is a crystallization of the mythology of the series,"
adds *X-Files* creator and executive producer Chris Carter. "It
came about kind of inadvertently. David Duchovny had wanted to
do an alien bounty hunter story."

Although Chris Carter and David Duchovny are credited with the
story for "Colony," it was actually writer Frank Spotnitz who first proposed the exploration of what happened to Mulder's sister.

"It's been so many years since Mulder has seen his sister – what if someone
shows up and says she's his sister? What would he make of this?" wondered
Spotnitz. "Chris saw how that could immediately fit in to what he and David had
already been talking about for the two-parter and I was brought on to do the second part."

"Colony" opens with a scene that actually takes place towards the conclusion
of the story, as Chris Carter explains: "Mulder comes in, frost-bitten, to a hospital
on the verge of death and [there is] what I think is a very poignant voice-over
about his search for extraterrestrial life and his knowledge that they have
begun to colonise – that they're here. It was a different way to tell a
story. I've always wanted to tell a story backwards like that, an
inspiration I took from the original *Frankenstein*, which is
told the same way."

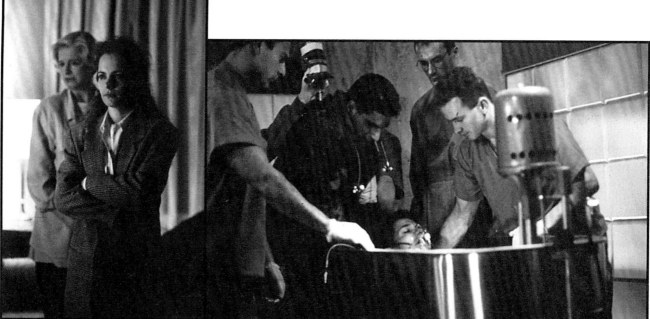

Above left: An emotional time for the Mulders, as Samantha comes home; Above right: Mulder only barely survives his encounter with the bounty hunter in the Arctic

"The perfect dilemma" – Mulder must choose between Samantha and Scully

The alien bounty hunter ruthlessly pursues his goal of eliminating the group of renegade alien clones by masquerading as a CIA agent and even advertising in newspapers for information on the whereabouts of his targets. The clones, like the bounty hunter, are near-indestructible; they can only be killed by a puncture wound at the base of the neck.

While Mulder joins his parents and is amazed to discover that his sister has returned home, Scully is left to continue the investigation alone and attempts to locate the renegade clones before the bounty hunter can bump them off. Apparently successful, Scully is able to take the identical doctors into protective custody. However, the alien murderer uses his shape-shifting abilities to out-manoever her and, masquerading as an official, he is able to gain access to the imprisoned clones and carry out his deadly mission.

Scully, realizing that she may now also be on the alien's hit list, takes precautions by checking into a motel and waits for the elusive Mulder to contact her. Scully is relieved when Mulder finally arrives; but her relief turns to horror when her mobile phone rings and she discovers that the caller is the real Mulder!

"I'd always wanted to do a scene where Scully is on the phone talking to Mulder and he arrives at the door [at the same time]," confesses Carter. "You'll see at the end of 'Colony' that it's truly one of the great transitional two-part connections in the series and ends up being a great way to come back in the subsequent episode, 'End Game.'"

While Scully is taken hostage by the shapeshifter, a submarine discovers the alien's craft in the icy waters of the Arctic. Some kind of sonic attack from the craft renders the submarine powerless and they are left to drift below the solid ice.

Samantha, meanwhile, has been explaining the details of her absence to Mudler. Following

her abduction, she was placed with one of the renegade clones as a kind of foster parent – and she too is now being pursued by the bounty hunter. A call from Scully confirms Samantha's belief that Scully's abductor wishes to make an exchange – Samantha for Scully. Convincing Assistant Director Skinner to help them stop the bounty hunter, Mulder agrees to go ahead with the exchange. However, it goes horribly wrong when the alien is shot and plunges into an ice-cold river with Samantha.

"The dramatic set-up of Mulder having to choose between his sister and Scully is the perfect dilemma," proclaims Carter who is rightly, proud of the moment. "How do you choose between two people who are so important to you...? It's really one of those nervous moments for the audience, and for Mulder..."

Pursuing a lead left by Samantha, Mulder's investigation leads him to a clinic where he discovers a group of young women identical to Samantha. They are all clones, and they explain that the girl who claimed to be his sister was also a clone; the deception was merely a way to enlist his protection from the bounty hunter. His real sister is still alive, they say, and they know where she is.

Mulder, angry that he has been used, makes to leave but is stopped and knocked unconscious by the bounty hunter, who has come to conclude his dark business. When Mulder finally awakes the women and the bounty hunter are long gone.

Intent on finding his sister, Mulder seeks out his informant, X, and demands to know the location of the bounty hunter's vessel so that he might pursue him. With the information from X, Mulder heads north. Later, learning of his disappearance, Scully attempts to discover where Mulder has gone. When Skinner refuses to help her, she resorts to contriving a meeting with X at Mulder's apartment. X also refuses to assist her, and immediately leaves. But on his

way out of the apartment building, X encounters Skinner who attempts to learn Mulder's whereabouts by more physical methods.

Steven Williams relished his character's encounter with Mitch Pileggi's Skinner. "Up to this point the only one I was really interacting with was Mulder, so the whole elevator fight with Skinner was exciting for me and one of my favorite scenes as an actor.

"Mitch and I loved that! What Mitch and I were wondering was, do these guys know each other? They must, because they both seem to know a little bit about everything, but when they met in that hallway there is the moment of, 'Do we know each other?' We never resolved that ambiguity...

"Now, what intrigued me about it is that they have this fight, and the last scene you see is X with a gun in Skinner's face, saying 'I've killed men for less'. Then, in the next scene, you see Skinner showing up looking kind of beat up and he's got the information about Mulder, so the audience assumes he beat up X. How can that be? The last scene we saw was X with a gun to this man's temple. No way he got the drop on X and beat him up – he would have just blown Skinner away! I think what happened is that Skinner talked and convinced X that they are both on the same team, that they both need to save Mulder. I think that the audience were glad somebody kicked X's butt and made him give out some information!"

In the frozen Arctic, Mulder finds the submarine that was attacked by the UFO: it was obviously forced to surface hurriedly, its conning tower thrust through the ice.

From a visual standpoint alone, the submarine is the highlight of the whole two-part story and has certainly ingrained itself in the minds

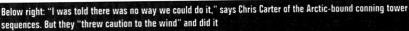

of the production crew.

"We rented a submarine that was being decommissioned from the Canadian Navy," explains producer Joseph Patrick Finn. "We used it on three different episodes: as an ice-breaker in 'Colony,' the submarine in 'End Game,' and as a ship in 'Død Kalm.' It was just an incredible set piece that we were able to use."

"I was told there was no way to do it," says Carter. "But we sort of threw caution to the wind and said let's give it a try. To do that, we had to truck in 140 tons of snow onto a sound stage and refrigerate the stage for five days. We built a conning tower that rose and fell only five feet. It never actually sunk into the ice as it appears. So we had all kinds of restrictions. We had to shoot it as Arctic night. We had to shoot it against black backdrops. There were restrictions galore."

Once inside the submarine Mulder discovers that the crew are all dead, save for one frightened lieutenant. Mulder rightly suspects the lieutenant of being the shape shifter and, after handcuffing himself to the man, demands to know where his sister is. Mulder's suspicions prove to be correct and, despite his precautions, the alien gets the better of him. At the mercy of the alien, Mulder begs to know the whereabouts of Samantha. However, all his assailant will tell him is that she is alive. Dragging him by his cuffed wrist, the alien throws Mulder out of the sub and severs the chain of the handcuffs.

Rob Bowman reflects on the high production standards achieved in the closing scenes of "End Game": "In the last act, Mulder and this alien hit man are having a vicious fight and Mulder is dangling off the top of this conning tower when the thing starts to submerge. He drops to the ice and is nearly crushed to death. I swear to God, it was like something out of *Die Hard* and we did it on a stage.

"'End Game' really is an example of what

The X-Files can do best, because it was a huge production. We had built a full-scale mock up of the conning tower with articulated wings!"

Executive Producer Bob Goodwin felt that the dramatic advancement in what *The X-Files* was able to achieve in production was in direct relation to the acclaim that the series had begun to receive. "We won the Golden Globe for best television drama, and the ratings kept growing, and growing. *The X-Files* started popping up on magazines everywhere you looked, so naturally we felt like we had to keep [bettering] ourselves. That's how you get to something like the refrigerated submarine-coming-through-the-ice set that we built for 'End Game.' That would have done a film crew proud."

After a long recovery from his ordeal, Mulder wakes to discover that the submarine and the assassin have disappeared. Scully asks him if he found what he·was looking for. He tells her no, but he has found something that he though he'd lost – the faith to keep on looking for the truth.

"I think the two-parter of 'Colony' and 'End Game' was extremely ambitious," admits Carter. "It encompassed a couple of desires from the first year that I couldn't fulfil. In [season one's] "Ice," I wanted to be at the North Pole, which is something we couldn't do. I also thought it was an interesting exploration of Scully and Mulder's different perspectives as well. I wanted to re-establish what their points of view were; to reaffirm her belief in science and his belief in the paranormal.

"I think that 'End Game,' for me, along with 'Colony,' is the backbone of the show. An important part of story-telling is to keep testing the character's faith. I think this has to take something away from Mulder, yet [it also] rejuvenated his energy to keep going to find his sister, to know that she was out there. There was something afoot and he was going to find out what it was." ◆

Below right: "I was told there was no way we could do it," says Chris Carter of the Arctic-bound conning tower sequences. But they "threw caution to the wind" and did it

AS NIGHTMARE SCENARIOS OF
ROGUE CLONES CAPTURE
THE PUBLIC CONSCIOUSNESS,
SCIENTISTS PONDER THE
DILEMMAS OF
DOLLY'S CREATION

Romancing the Clone

BY KRISTIN KLOBERDANZ

Illustration by Mike Smith

T he arrival of Dolly, the cloned sheep, wasn't just a scientific breakthrough — the Scottish lamb's birth gave rise to a range of wild scenarios that would be right at home on *The X-Files*, where cloning has been a feature of the show's mythology for more than two years. With the announcement that scientists had created a genetically identical lamb from a cell of an adult ewe, the most bizarre of science fiction plots moved from the realm of imagination to the real world, sparking

spirited debates among politicians, theologians, philosophers and bioethicists. The realization that the main barrier to human cloning is no longer technology, but society's often shaky ethics, has set the public buzzing with ideas about what can and should be done to legislate human cloning, genetic engineering and the Brave New World scenarios that may emerge from Dolly's birth. Could cloning solve infertility problems? Will clones be created solely for organ harvesting, or, worse yet, for purely narcissistic reasons? Will women be able to reproduce without the aid of men? Suddenly, the chilling plot of the '70s film *The Boys from Brazil*, in which several young clones of Hitler are discovered living in different parts of the world, seems all too frighteningly real.

somebody that you could harvest for spare parts—are evil things and shouldn't be done," says Thomas Murray, the director for the Center for Biomedical Ethics at Case Western University and a member of the Presidential National Bioethics Advisory Commission. "The tough question

view [that] human beings are purely defined by their genetics. In fact, you could have a clone of Hitler who ends up being a pacifist artist. Only the most hard-nosed genetic determinists fail to understand that so much of what we are is due to environment."

THE CLONE ZONE: In "Memento Mori" (above), Mulder stumbled across a lab in which alien-human clones were being created, and in Season Three's "Colony" (right), he encountered a clone of his missing sister, Samantha

While there may not be much clamoring for clones of past dictators, Dolly's arrival has given hope to many people whose desire to have children has been frustrated by the limits of current medical technology. One can argue that cloning would be a great solution for couples dealing with infertility problems: the child would look exactly like its mother or its father, but, due to its different environment, wouldn't be an identical replica. While most bioethicists have serious objections to human cloning, some are willing to concede that cloning *might* be a viable solution to infertility if human clones could be created without undue time and effort.

"Some people say, 'Well, what if we wanted to use this [technique] as a way of having a child that we couldn't [normally] have—a biologically related child?'" Murray says. "We really don't know how technically effective cloning might be, but what we do know is that it took 277 tries to make one Dolly. It took 29 implanted sheep embryos to get one viable clone—and that meant a lot of pregnant sheep. One of the features of this technique is that you've got to find women willing to carry this embryo in their womb, and would women be willing to do that if they knew the chance of success was one in 30? That seems pretty remote. The other infertility treatments are far from perfect, but they have a much higher success rate than that. It's clearly not going to be a preferred method of dealing with infertility. [I don't know if it will] ever be a permissible method of dealing with infertility."

The truth is, despite public fears and the likely passage of anti-cloning laws, someday, somewhere, human cloning will take place. Though many are outraged by such a possibility, after pondering the problem in the months since the announcement from Scotland, even medical ethicists are second-guessing the idea of an outright ban on cloning. It seems there just may be some situations in which the practice would be permissible, even prudent.

The Presidential National Bioethics Advisory Commission recently advised legislators that any endeavor to create a cloned human baby "would at this time be an irresponsible, unethical and unprofessional act." However, the committee also recommended that the cloning of humans cells for research purposes should not be restricted, which indicates scientists' ambivalence regarding this new technology.

"The nightmare scenarios—the cloning of dozens of Hitlers and the cloning of human beings so that you can have

is going to be: should you ever, under any circumstances, permit the cloning of a human being when the purpose is not evil? My initial response is, I think, like a lot of other people's initial response; the idea of cloning evokes memories of science-fiction movies and books, and in every case, the uses [depicted] were grossly immoral."

"This idea that we're going to end up with clones all over the place and, as one person said, with armies of Hitlers is absurd," counters Paul Root Wolpe, a senior faculty member at the Center for Bioethics at the University of Pennsylvania. "First of all, it is never going to be as easy or as much fun to clone as it is the old-fashioned way to create a baby. Second of all, the idea that a clone of Hitler is going to be a Hitler is a kind of genetic determinism that, ironically, Hitler used to kill millions of people. It's so ironic that everyone is talking about armies of Hitlers and don't even realize that what they do when they say that is validate that maniac's whole

But some ethicists don't think bearing a child is an inalienable right for everyone. "I still haven't heard a good reason [for human cloning]," says Arthur Caplan, director of the Center for Bioethics at the University of Pennsylvania. "If someone says, 'Well, I could use cloning to replace a dying child,' well, that's a reason, but it doesn't have any basis in what cloning is. You're not going to replace [the soul of a] dying child by cloning. I've heard people say, 'Maybe I could be immortal.' But you wouldn't be immortal—somebody who *looks* like you will be immortal. I've heard people say, 'Maybe we could use this technique to breed armies of supermodels or Dennis Rodmans or something.' Well, perhaps you could, but you'd have to control their environment, control their experience so that you'd get what you wanted. People don't understand that there's a big gap between having the same genes and having the same organism."

I f human cloning does eventually become a viable method of reproduction, other troubling questions arise. One that frightens many people is the notion that some individuals will want to have themselves cloned in order to "correct" their own childhoods.

"I was on 'Talk of the Nation,' a public radio show," Murray says, "and the first person who called said, 'I think cloning is great. I'd like to clone myself—then my wife and I could raise him the way I should have been raised.' That makes me very uneasy. That implies that somehow there's a right way to raise children and that, 'I know what [the right way] is and I can raise myself avoiding all those mistakes.' That's a hell of a burden to impose upon a child before its creation. Parents have children for all sorts of reasons, including no reason

at all, but that doesn't mean that we should provide the support of our science and our medicine to create children under circumstances that strike us as really worrisome."

Like many ethical issues, however, questions about cloning don't have cut-and-dried answers, and what may be deemed "worrisome" to some may be perfectly acceptable to others.

"One can imagine a number of situations in which cloning might be considered ethically acceptable to some people or even ethically demanded in some people's opinion," says Wolpe. "Let me give you an

Double Take

B elieve it or not, some people weren't shocked by the "Hello, Dolly!" headlines last winter. "Do you want a succinct description of my reaction?" asks Stanley Schmidt, editor of *Analog Science Fiction and Fact*. "'Ha! We told them so!'"

"I think it's safe to say that anyone who's acquainted with science or science fiction wasn't surprised," says Algis Budrys, novelist and editor of *tomorrowsf*, an on-line science fiction magazine.

Why the blasé responses?

Because cloning is old hat in the forward-thinking world of science fiction. Sci-fi writers have been exploring the scientific concept for years. According to Schmidt, one of the best clone stories ever was A. E. Van Vogt's *The World of Null-A*, which was first published way back in 1945. In the pulp classic, a scientist creates genetic duplicates of himself to help in the fight against a sinister conspiracy.

Budrys cites Jerry Sohl's 1952 novel *The Haploids* as his personal favorite. In it, women render men obsolete by using cloning to reproduce.

So after more than five decades of clone stories, is the idea tapped out? "Oh, heavens no!" cries celebrated novelist Gene Wolfe, who used cloning in his classic novel *The Fifth Head of Cerberus* (1972). "It's hardly started! We have just awakened the mass of people to the fact that it can be done."

Schmidt agrees that the news about the Scottish ewe won't put the kibosh on the clone sub-genre. "One of the funniest comments I've heard

is, 'A collective sob was heard from science fiction writers robbed of one of their favorite story ideas,'" he says. "That's ridiculous! There's going to be a new flood of clone stories. A lot of the inspiration is going to come from watching people react to the news."

Budrys sees a torrent of clone tales headed his way, too. He's just afraid that the stories won't just be *about* clones—they'll be clones themselves. "I'll probably bounce every one of them," he says. "They'll just be [redoing] what other people have already done."

Wolfe is more hopeful. "You can do story after story after story [on one subject], taking different angles because our world view changes. And when our world view changes, our view of clones or robots or what have you changes with it," he says.

Schmidt even thinks the legislators, ethicists, scientists and religious leaders who have been thrown for a loop by Dolly's big entrance ought to check out what science fiction has to say about cloning—but he doesn't think they will.

"Science fiction writers were anticipating all these things and thinking about the implications for decades while everyone else was either ignoring it or saying, 'That's just science fiction! It could never happen,'" he says. "And now they're [ignoring sci-fi] again. They never learn."

—Steve Hockensmith

example: Let's say you have a set of parents who both carry [the gene for] cystic fibrosis, and they had two children, both of whom had cystic fibrosis and both of whom died in their teens, as many CF kids do. And then, finally, they had a child who not only did not have CF but wasn't a carrier [of the gene]. Then something terrible happens to the child, let's say she gets hit by a car and she's lying in the hospital and she's brain dead, and the doctors say, 'That's it, she's gone.' Then the family says, 'Why don't we clone her, knowing that she's healthy, that she doesn't carry [the gene for the disease]. Otherwise, if we try again, we have a three in four chance of either getting a cystic fibrosis child or a carrier.' Well, under circumstances like that, we can imagine some people saying that's ethically acceptable.

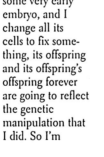

"Let me give you another example," he continues. "Let's say you have a lesbian couple. They're committed to each other, they love each other, they want to live together for the rest of their lives. They want to have a child. Up until now, they had to get donor sperm [in order to have a child]. But with cloning, what you can do is take the somatic cell, the body cell, from one of the women and the ovum from [the other] woman, inject the nucleus of the somatic cell into the ovum, which is what they did to create Dolly, and you could actually have a child that is the genetic product of the two women without a man. So in sense, they have an opportunity to reproduce themselves biologically, like any other couple.

"But if people are against cloning, they think cloning is wrong, then just wanting your own biological child will not be strong enough argument to allow it," Wolpe cautions. "Wanting a child that doesn't die from cystic fibrosis may be [enough of a reason]. But wanting your own biological child may not be."

Even if cloning never catches on as a human means of reproduction, many people are worried that gene therapy is just as dangerous. If you can genetically program a cow to produce richer meat and healthier milk, then the possibilities for genetic fine-tuning in

humans seem endless.

"I don't think we're going to find too many reasons to clone people, but genetically engineering them, trying to change them, trying to improve them, enhance them or eliminate undesirable traits—that's where we're going," ethicist Caplan says. "[Worries about whether] it's unnatural or whether people will abuse it and misuse it—those are legitimate concerns. I think we can handle it, I think we can create and implement controls and restrictions, regulations and guidelines, that'll allow us to proceed in ways that really are not risky or dangerous. But we haven't done that yet."

Of course, it's one thing to want to genetically program your child to have blond hair and blue eyes, but what if you want to make sure your child votes Republican and likes to wear plaid? After all, if scientists admit that you'll soon be able to design the family dog, are customized humans right around the corner?

"It's not going to be too long before you go to the pet store and say, 'I would like a half-German shepherd and half-schnauzer mix and I want it to be pink,'" says Wolpe. "With that you get the same kinds of ethical questions regarding the over-reaching of human beings. When I mess with a zygote or a blastocyst or some very early embryo, and I change all its cells to fix something, its offspring and its offspring's offspring forever are going to reflect the genetic manipulation that I did. So I'm

not only changing the life of that infant, I am changing the human genum forever and that is an extraordinarily ethically dangerous act as far as I'm concerned."

Genetic manipulation is already commonly used on farm animals, and scientists predict that soon we'll be able to drink fortified milk from vaccine-producing cows and get organs for transplants from our furry brethren. Some find those scenarios frightening, not to mention overly ambitious, but scientists in this field strongly resent the implication that they are "playing God."

"People get off on this idea that genetic engineering is a bad, evil deal and that we [should] get back to more natural ways to control disease," says Dr. Mark Westhusin, assistant professor of animal sciences at Texas A&M University. "This concept or idea of playing God kind of bugs me once in a while—Clinton even referred to it in some of [his speeches]—that scientists are playing God. We can't play God, that's ridiculous. I think about this in terms of, I'm not playing God, I'm serving God and I can't think of any better way in my life to serve God than to be working in a scientific area that is going to solve world hunger and is going to cure cancer and cure AIDS and make the quality of life better for people. To think that we're playing God because there's a few nuts out there who can dream up these evil applications is just ridiculous." ●

SEEING DOUBLE: The children Mulder met in "Herrenvolk" were clone drones

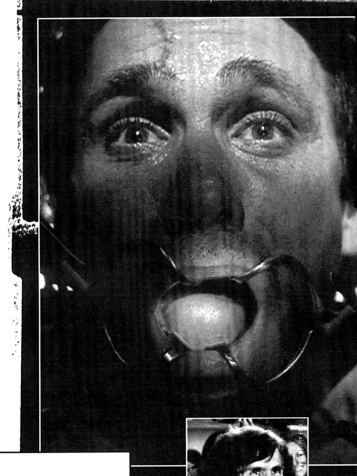

EPISODES: 2X05/2X06

DUANE BARRY

"Duane Barry" / "Ascension"

Before *X-Files* creator Chris Carter even started writing the legendary Season Two mythology episodes "Duane Barry" and "Ascension," his imagination locked onto one actor credible enough to play the pivotal guest role: Steve Railsback. After all, who better to portray dangerously overwrought alien abductee Duane Barry than the man who delivered a jaw-dropping performance as Charles Manson in the 1976 TV docudrama *Helter Skelter*?

"Chris told me he wrote the part for me and that if I didn't take it, he didn't know who he would ask," Railsback says. "At the time [in 1994], I didn't prefer to do episodic television, and I was going to say no. I hadn't even watched the show before. But when I read the script, I said, 'God,

STEVE RAILSBACK

this is good.' It renewed my faith in television."

Carter's hunch about the Hollywood veteran proved right on the mark. Railsback, whose résumé boasts a Golden Globe nomination for his performance in 1980's *The Stunt Man* in addition to producing, directing and writing credits, brought a mesmerizing intensity to the role of the disturbed former FBI agent who kidnaps Agent Scully and offers her as a guinea pig to his extraterrestrial tormentors. Even now, the actor, who most recently appeared in the film *Disturbing Behavior*, counts the role among his favorites.

"He's a sympathetic character who was sick of being laughed at and called a liar," Railsback says. "I prepared for the part by using my imagination and thinking back to what might have happened the first time Barry was abducted."—*Erik J. Martin*

ALSO KNOWN AS:

1997: "Col. James Vice" in *The Visitor*
1979: "Pvt. Robert E. Lee Prewitt" in *From Here to Eternity* (mini-series)
1976: "Charles Manson" in *Helter Skelter* (above)

1998: "Officer Cox" in *Disturbing Behavior*
1996: "Col. Pryzer" in *Barb Wire*
1993: "David Coppinger" in *In the Line of Fire*
1985: "Carlsen" in *Lifeforce*
1980: "Cameron" in *The Stunt Man*

GUEST X GALLERY

EVERYTHING'S Coming Up ''' ROSWELL

THE E.T. CAPITAL OF AMERICA IS BEING INVADED... AGAIN!

By Steve Hockensmith

photo illustration by Geoff Graham

In July of 1947, *something* crashed to Earth in the countryside outside of Roswell, N.M. Some say it was a flying saucer. Some say it was an experimental jet. The government says it was a surveillance balloon. The debate continues today.

But one fact about the infamous "Roswell incident" can't be disputed: All the brouhaha has been great for business. Every year, tens of thousands of curious tourists descend on the once-obscure community of 50,000. And unlike some visitors to Roswell, these out-of-towners leave behind plenty of physical evidence—about $2 million in cold, hard cash every year, the local Chamber of Commerce estimates.

GREATEST SHOW ON EARTH.

$3.25

$2.25

ENORMOUS UFO SHOWS

Benefitting the most from all of these close encounters of the tourist kind is Roswell's International UFO Museum and Research Center.

"As of today, we've had 166,056 people here in the last three-and-a-half years. That's a lot of people," says museum president Glenn Dennis. According to surveys of museum visitors, "68 percent of these people have come to Roswell on account of the UFO museum. It's unreal, isn't it?"

Dennis is familiar to Roswell aficionados as the undertaker who was supposedly asked for tiny alien-sized coffins by the military in 1947. He founded the museum in 1991 with Walter Haut, the Roswell press officer who wrote the famous

"Army Captures Flying Disc" press release, and Max Littell, a local businessman.

"The three of us who started this figured if we got 10 people a day we'd be lucky," Dennis says.

By that standard, Dennis and his museum have been very, very lucky indeed: Attendance figures topped 10,000 per month this spring. And it's not just the sheer volume of visitors that's impressive: Tourists from as far away as Japan, England, Greenland and Australia have made the long, hot journey across the dry Southwestern terrain to drop in on Roswell's museum.

"One Sunday alone we had eight foreign countries represented in two hours," says the museum's director, Deon Crosby, whose previous experience as a P.R.

maven included stints promoting the Senior Olympics and the Texas Beekeepers Association. "These people are coming in throngs."

Originally, visitors to the museum wouldn't have found much to justify the trip—just Dennis and Haut hanging out in a local bank's unused office space.

"They were there off and on," says Crosby, who joined the museum staff last year. "They would drink coffee and visit, and if anybody actually showed up [they would discuss the Roswell incident]. They didn't have a sign or anything."

But as more and more tourists started making the pilgrimage to the town—spurred by attention from *Unsolved Mysteries, Sightings,* a Roswell-inspired TV movie and hundreds of newspaper and magazine articles—the museum was able to trade up to better digs, eventually settling into a swanky, 12,000-square-foot renovated theater.

Today the museum features two video theaters, an alien autopsy display with props from the *Roswell* TV movie, exhibits exploring crop circles, cattle mutilations and other UFO-related topics, a snack bar offering "Andromeda lattes" and "Milky Way cappuccinos," and, of course, a gift shop (see sidebar).

According to the Tourism Association of New Mexico, the museum surpassed Carlsbad Caverns as the state's top tourist destination last year. That's quite an accomplishment for Roswell, a town that even Dennis admits is, "a long damn drive" from anywhere.

The museum has become the centerpiece of Roswell's booming tourist trade for a simple reason: There's not much else to see. There's a planetarium and an art museum. And cheese enthusiasts can visit the world's largest mozzarella factory, which isn't too far away. That's about it for local attractions.

As far as UFO-themed hot spots go, there's the International UFO Museum in downtown Roswell and the UFO Enigma Museum (a smaller competitor located in a former video store) outside of town. But there's no monument to the unknown alien, no splashy "Welcome to UFO City USA!" billboard, no park or roadside marker to commemorate the alleged crash site (the actual location of which is still a topic of fierce debate).

In fact, the good people of Roswell had pretty much forgotten the incident until a flurry of media attention put the controversy over the crash in the national spotlight in the late '80s.

"It wasn't a big deal," says Jack Swickard, general manager of the town's newspaper, the Roswell Daily Record. Until a few years ago, the only people who spoke to him about the crash were English tabloid journalists who would call up from time to time looking for information.

According to the burg's laconic mayor, Tom Jennings—a man so laid back he has to ask his twin brother how old they are—Roswellians have been satisfied to shrug off the crash as none of their business. "Who are we to say [what happened]?" he asks. "My father, who is 83 and still comes to work every day—we've laughed about it and stuff but never really sat down and seriously talked about it. The older people—I don't know if they don't care or what, but [their attitude is] it's just one of those things that happened."

"I was unaware of any of that back in the '50s when I came here. Nobody spoke about it," says William Brainerd, who moved to Roswell just six years after the incident and eventually served two terms as the town's mayor. "There was no street talk at all [about UFOs]."

More than 40 years later, things haven't changed much. "Most of the people in Roswell still don't [know much about the incident]. And they don't care. It's the people outside of Roswell who care and are interested in finding the answers," says Crosby. "I was the same way. It didn't really matter four years ago. Now that I'm in the business, I see the benefits and so yes, it does matter."

Even Roswell's younger residents aren't exactly intrigued by the incident that has made their town world famous.

"It doesn't come up that much except around the [annual summer] alien festival," says eighth grader Ian Allison.

According to Allison, tedium, not curiosity, is the biggest motivator behind debates on the subject. "Sometimes we argue about it because there's nothing else to do," he says.

"I never really hear about it," agrees his classmate, Audrey Collar. "I guess most [kids] think it was aliens. Well, they say they do. I don't know what they really think. They might just say that because they've heard it so many times" on TV.

Roswell's E.T. ennui is so acute that the town didn't even have a chapter of the Mutual UFO Network (MUFON) or any other UFO organization until last fall.

"My jaw dropped open in shock. My goodness, in Roswell? I thought that was terrible. That's why I got it started," says Beverly Fox, who founded Roswell's first MUFON chapter.

Fox moved to Roswell from Truth or Consequences, N.M., to be near the International UFO Museum. A dedicated

CRASH WORSHIP

Fifty years ago, Roswell, N.M., helped launch the era of flying saucers, alien abductions, *My Favorite Martian* and *The X-Files* by playing host to the first bona fide media event of the UFO Age. Now the city is welcoming back cameras, microphones and curious onlookers to commemorate the 50th anniversary of the incident that started it all.

Organizers of the city's annual "UFO Encounter" festival have pulled out all the stops for this year's celebration, to be held July 1-6 in venues all over town. UFO superstars like *Communion* author Whitley Strieber, psychiatrist John E. Mack and researcher Budd Hopkins will appear at a three-day conference; a "UFO Film Festival" will spotlight genre favorites like (of course) *Roswell*; the Roswell Community Little Theater will present the world premiere of "Ezekiel's Wheels," a new play linking alien abductions to the Old Testament; and a UFO Expo will give merchants a chance to abduct visitors' cash via books, videos, artwork, T-shirts and other knickknacks. Organizers have also scheduled an "Alien Chase" fun run, a "UFO Cycling Classic" bike race, and are hoping to line up artists like Sheryl Crow and the Foo Fighters for the Roswell Music Festival.

According to Deon Crosby, director of Roswell's UFO Museum and Research Center, every motel room in town was spoken for way back in April. Even faraway Artesia and Carlsbad, N.M., were booked solid by mid-spring.

Roswell mayor Tom Jennings has an interesting proposal for dealing with the hordes of curious visitors. "We're trying to get an ordinance passed that allows people to camp out in the city," he says. "They've got this stupid ordinance that

you can't camp out. We want to open up our parks and facilities so that people can crash in Roswell."

Not surprisingly, having UFO enthusiasts "crash" on the town's benches and curbs doesn't seem like such a great idea to everyone. "It's supposed to bring in 30,000 people. Hell, we can't take care of 'em," says Glenn Dennis, the museum's president and co-founder. "And I don't like rock bands and the kind of people they bring into town. We do not need a bunch of hype and crap and hullabaloo. I don't like it."

And Dennis says he is not alone. "I get phone calls day and night from the people that live here. They're driving me crazy," claims the plain-spoken 73-year-old. "Rock bands don't have a very good reputation with the dope and the drugs. [People] don't want that kind of atmosphere in our little community."

"I believe it's a generational problem," says Deon Crosby. "Do you know many 60-, 70- or 80-year-olds who enjoy listening to Sheryl Crow or Bush? If [Guy Lombardo was booked] they would probably love it. But the Guy Lombardo band doesn't bring in $10 million in major sponsors."

According to Mayor Jennings, the motivation for putting on the alien-themed extravaganza springs from a mixture of civic pride... and boredom. "Life is only as good as we make it. I guess that's something I learned growing up out here," he says. "If you wanted to have a party, you had to have your own. We've always made our own entertainment. Maybe this is [making] our own entertainment again—except on a bigger scale." —S.H.

UFO researcher, she has produced a self-published book on the subject (in which she theorizes that aliens are misguided meddlers trying to steal credit for God's accomplishments) and is hoping to finish another soon.

"I want to get it ready for the UFO festival that starts in July," she says. "Another girl and I have got a space rented in the convention center. I'm

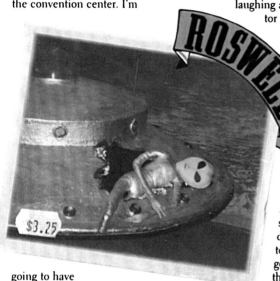

going to have my book on sale, and she's going to have a cookbook [with recipes] that will have names like 'Hot Spicy Meatballs from Mercury'—things like that with a UFO theme."

Fox says the locals are blasé about UFOs because "you don't care as much about what's in your backyard. It's just like people in Carlsbad aren't as enthusiastic about Carlsbad Caverns. It's right there. It's just a ho-hum, take-it-for-granted attitude."

U nfortunately, a few Roswell residents aren't just ho-hum about UFOs—they're downright hostile. UFO believer John Price has felt the sting of his neighbors' scorn more than once over the years.

"I've had [UFO non-believers] call me up and say, 'Take me to your leader,' or ask some serious questions then start laughing and hang up," says the director of the UFO Enigma Museum. "Or we'd have people call and make weird sci-fi noises."

A Roswell native who was always curious about the mysterious incident that the other folks in town didn't want to discuss, Price doesn't let the ridicule bother him. Most of the cranks are, "just people who haven't read any good research on this," he says. "If they come through the door and I can catch them face to face, usually we have a pretty good conversation and most of them leave with a little different attitude," he says.

But despite Price's faith, it would probably take more than "good research" to convince some of the other people in town. When local businessman Stan Crosby (Deon's husband) first proposed promoting Roswell's UFO connection a few years ago, he met stiff opposition. As a member of Main Street, an organization formed to help get downtown Roswell back on its feet

after a mega-mall sucked away business, Crosby came up with the idea of a UFO festival back in 1992.

"The then-president of Main Street didn't want to do it because she thought it was too controversial and she objected to it on religious grounds," he recalls. "So we did a chili cheese festival. We have a lot of dairies here and we grow chilies."

Though Crosby describes the chili cheese festival as a success, it didn't exactly capture the world's imagination or do much to help build a tourist industry in Roswell. So Crosby moved ahead with the festival idea on his own, a decision that didn't sit well with Tom Jennings' mayoral predecessor, William Brainerd.

"The mayor said, 'Absolutely not. I don't want to be looked at as a kook town. You will not do anything to promote the city of Roswell connected to UFOs—period,'" says Deon Crosby. "He did not want Roswell to be looked at as a community with what he called 'a trailer-park mentality.'"

N ow, five years and millions of dollars later, Brainerd is reluctant to discuss any opposition he might have had to what became the Roswell UFO Encounter, the annual festival that brought about 6,000 people to the town last summer. (This year's Encounter, a five-day celebration of the incident's 50th anniversary, is expected to draw 20,000 people or more—see sidebar.)

"There are two schools of thought," the former mayor says, choosing his words carefully. "One is that anything that has P.R. value [is good]. It's like the politician who says, 'I don't care what you write about me as long as you spell my name right.' There are the others who think Roswell is being held up to ridicule."

Originally, religious groups were vocal in their opposition to the International UFO Museum and the

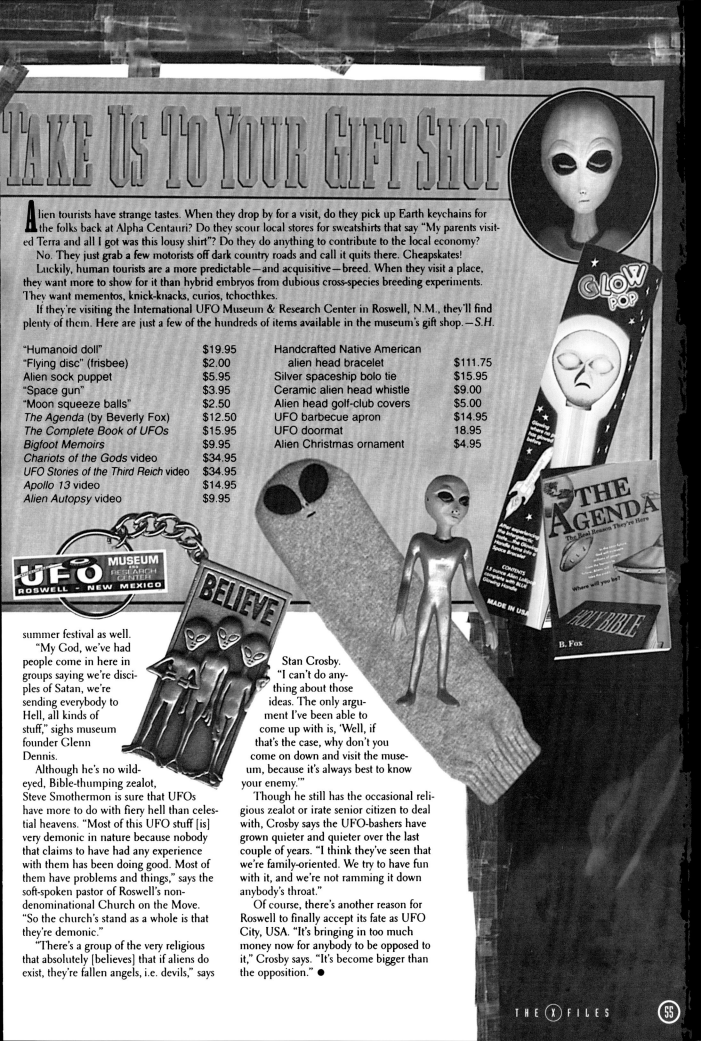

Take Us To Your Gift Shop

Alien tourists have strange tastes. When they drop by for a visit, do they pick up Earth keychains for the folks back at Alpha Centauri? Do they scour local stores for sweatshirts that say "My parents visited Terra and all I got was this lousy shirt"? Do they do anything to contribute to the local economy? No. They just grab a few motorists off dark country roads and call it quits there. Cheapskates!

Luckily, human tourists are a more predictable—and acquisitive—breed. When they visit a place, they want more to show for it than hybrid embryos from dubious cross-species breeding experiments. They want mementos, knick-knacks, curios, tchocthkes.

If they're visiting the International UFO Museum & Research Center in Roswell, N.M., they'll find plenty of them. Here are just a few of the hundreds of items available in the museum's gift shop. —S.H.

"Humanoid doll"	$19.95	Handcrafted Native American	
"Flying disc" (frisbee)	$2.00	alien head bracelet	$111.75
Alien sock puppet	$5.95	Silver spaceship bolo tie	$15.95
"Space gun"	$3.95	Ceramic alien head whistle	$9.00
"Moon squeeze balls"	$2.50	Alien head golf-club covers	$5.00
The Agenda (by Beverly Fox)	$12.50	UFO barbecue apron	$14.95
The Complete Book of UFOs	$15.95	UFO doormat	18.95
Bigfoot Memoirs	$9.95	Alien Christmas ornament	$4.95
Chariots of the Gods video	$34.95		
UFO Stories of the Third Reich video	$34.95		
Apollo 13 video	$14.95		
Alien Autopsy video	$9.95		

summer festival as well.

"My God, we've had people come in here in groups saying we're disciples of Satan, we're sending everybody to Hell, all kinds of stuff," sighs museum founder Glenn Dennis.

Although he's no wild-eyed, Bible-thumping zealot, Steve Smothermon is sure that UFOs have more to do with fiery hell than celestial heavens. "Most of this UFO stuff [is] very demonic in nature because nobody that claims to have had any experience with them has been doing good. Most of them have problems and things," says the soft-spoken pastor of Roswell's non-denominational Church on the Move. "So the church's stand as a whole is that they're demonic."

"There's a group of the very religious that absolutely [believes] that if aliens do exist, they're fallen angels, i.e. devils," says Stan Crosby. "I can't do anything about those ideas. The only argument I've been able to come up with is, 'Well, if that's the case, why don't you come on down and visit the museum, because it's always best to know your enemy.'"

Though he still has the occasional religious zealot or irate senior citizen to deal with, Crosby says the UFO-bashers have grown quieter and quieter over the last couple of years. "I think they've seen that we're family-oriented. We try to have fun with it, and we're not ramming it down anybody's throat."

Of course, there's another reason for Roswell to finally accept its fate as UFO City, USA. "It's bringing in too much money now for anybody to be opposed to it," Crosby says. "It's become bigger than the opposition." ●

"ANASAZI" "I strongly encourage you... to deny everything."

THE BUILD-UP:

Mulder has never been closer to the truth when he gets his hands on secret government files that provide evidence of UFOs. But the files – containing everything the Defence Department has compiled about UFOs since the 1940s - may contain one truth too many; a truth that Mulder may not be ready to hear: one involving his father... and the Cigarette-Smoking Man.

THE SCENE:

BILL MULDER'S HOME, WEST TISBURY, MARTHA'S VINEYARD, MASSACHUSETTS.

(The doorbell rings. Bill Mulder opens it. Standing on his porch is a smiling Cigarette-Smoking Man.)

CIGARETTE-SMOKING MAN: Hello, Bill.

BILL MULDER: *(The look on his face is a mixture of shock – and fear)* What are you doing here?

CSM: I've come on some pressing business.

BILL MULDER: We agreed that you would never...

CSM: That was a long time ago, Bill. There have been some unforeseen events.

(Cut to the two men sitting around a table, drinking.)

BILL MULDER: No one was supposed to know.

CSM: Who could have predicted the future, Bill? That the computers you and I only dreamed of would someday be home appliances capable of the most technical espionage.

BILL MULDER: The files should have been destroyed.

CSM: They should have, but they weren't. Regret is an inevitable consequence of life.

BILL MULDER: How do you know my son has them?

CSM: The man who stole them has come forward.

BILL MULDER: Oh God.

CSM: As always we maintain plausible denial. The files are only as real as their possible authentication.

BILL MULDER: My name is in those files.

CSM: The files have been encrypted of course. We have a certain luxury of time. We endeavored to prevent that fact from ever coming to light.

BILL MULDER: You wouldn't... harm him?

CSM: I've protected him this long, haven't I? Your son has been provident in the alliances that he's created. The last thing we need is a martyr in a crusade.

BILL MULDER: But if he should... learn of my involvement...

CSM: You're your own man, Bill. You always have been. But I strongly encourage you, in that event, to deny everything. *(Standing, he places a hand on Bill Mulder's shoulder.)* It's good to see you again, Bill. You look well.

THE SIGNIFICANCE:

Significant isn't the word. This is a monumental moment because it's the first time we see the Cigarette-Smoking Man and Bill Mulder together. And the revelation that Mulder's dad and Mulder's arch nemesis have a history; that he's part of the whole conspiracy is as shocking as discovering that Darth Vader was Luke Skywalker's father!

TRIVIA:

William B. Davis quit smoking in the late 1970s but smoked herbal cigarettes onscreen. A spokesman for the Canadian Cancer Society, and a national champion water-skier, he set up The William Davis Centre for Actors' Study in Vancouver. His movies include *Anthrax*, *Mindstorm* and *Out of Line*.

EPISODE CREDITS:

Season 2, Episode 25
First aired 19/05/95 (US) & 9/08/95 (UK)

Written by:
Chris Carter

Directed by:
R.W. Goodwin

Main actors this scene:
The Cigarette-Smoking Man: William B Davis
Bill Mulder: Peter Donat

Compiled by Kate Anderson

EPISODE GUIDE

THE (X) FILES™

3.2: "PAPER CLIP" Episode #3X02

Original US tx 29 Sep 95   Original UK tx scheduled for 12 March 96

RURAL WEST VIRGINIA and WASHINGTON, DC

The Scully/Skinner stand-off is interrupted by the arrival of another gunman, Mulder, who explains to Skinner the contents of the digital tape in his possession. Meanwhile, Scully's mother goes to the hospital looking for Dana and finds, instead, her other daughter - shot and in critical condition - just as Byers and Langly inform Mulder that the photograph he has of his father with The Cigarette-Smoking Man, circa 1973, pictures them with an evil Nazi war criminal, Victor Klemper, suggesting that America's 'Operation Paper Clip' - a dubious pseudo-scientific project utilizing the knowledge of several notorious Nazis - continued, unofficially, beyond the 1950s. Later, Frohike arrives with news of Scully's sister, but Mulder advises against a hospital visit: if Melissa was shot by mistake, her assailant must be still out there, looking for Dana... Instead, Albert Hosteen goes unbidden to Melissa's bedside, while Mulder and Scully visit Klemper, who leads them to a disused mineshaft in West Virginia before informing his former collaborator, The Well-Manicured Man, that Mulder is very much alive. The Well-Manicured Man, in turn, decides to take matters out of The Cigarette-Smoking Man's nicotine-stained hands and pay a visit to Klemper himself. An increasingly desparate Cigarette-Smoking Man reacts to the news of Krycek's two failed assassination attempts by car-bombing his own puppet - an attempt which, ironically, Krycek survives.

In West Virginia, Mulder and Scully are shocked to find huge banks of files containing birth details and tissue samples for thousands of people - including Scully herself *and* Mulder's missing sister, Samantha! Suddenly, Scully is surprised by a group of small grey creatures who rush past her just as, outside, Mulder sees a huge, brightly-lit ship take off. Interrupted again - this time by the gunfire of whoever has tracked them to the old mine - they escape and meet up with Skinner, who informs them of a deal he has made with The Cigarette-Smoking Man: the delivery of the only copy of the digital tape in exchange for his agents' lives...

Principal Credits

Produced by	Ten-Thirteen Productions for 20th Century Fox TV
Creator and Executive Producer	Chris Carter
Co-Executive Producers	Howard Gordon, R W Goodwin
Producers	Kim Manners, Joseph Patrick Finn, Rob Bowman
Supervising Producer	Charles Grant Craig
Co-Producer	Paul Rabwin
Music	Mark Snow
Visual Effects Producer	Mat Beck

Episode Credits

Written by	Chris Carter
Directed by	Rob Bowman

Special Agent Fox Mulder	David Duchovny
Special Agent Dana Scully	Gillian Anderson
Assistant Director Walter S Skinner	Mitch Pileggi
Victor Klemper	Walter Gotell
Melissa Scully	Melinda McGraw
Margaret Scully	Sheila Larken
Special Agent Alex Krycek	Nicholas Lea
The Cigarette Smoking Man	William B Davis
The Well-Manicured Man	John Neville
Frohike	Tom Braidwood
Langly	Dean Haglund
Byers	Bruce Harwood
William Mulder	Peter Donat
Albert Hosteen	Floyd "Red Crow" Westerman
Mrs Mulder	Rebecca Toolan
ER Doctor	Robert Lewis

F.Y.I.

The third part of Chris Carter's trilogy cannily asks as many questions as it answers - and provides a plethora of each.

Among its many other revelations, "Paper Clip" gives us the middle names of Fox (William, after his father) and Samantha (Ann) Mulder, and their birthdates as 13 October (Chris Carter's own birthday) and 21 November (his wife's) 1961 respectively.

For the second time (after "Duane Barry"), children were used to portray 'little gray men,' fitted into suits provided by special effects maestro Toby Lindala.

The episode is dedicated to Mario Mark Kennedy (1966-1995), an Internet-based X-Phile killed in an automobile accident.

Noteworthy Dialogue Transcript

SCULLY: "You said you didn't come here to kill me, Skinner - now prove it!"
SKINNER: "I didn't come here to have a gun shoved in my face, either!"

Unexplained Plot Discrepancies

The digital tape The Cigarette-Smoking Man is so intent on getting his hands on is apparently uncopiable - even by the finest hackers the US government has at its disposal. And does anyone know of a part of West Virginia that *isn't* rural!?

Right: Mulder Sr.'s murky past revealed

THE X-FACTOR

Steven Williams, the actor who intrigued us as 'X', chats

with Ian Spelling about X-Files fame, "The Truth" and beyond

The man made a mark. Steven Williams arrived on *The X-Files* scene back in Season Two, first portraying the mysterious and austere 'X,' Mulder's informant, in "Sleepless." He returned again and again – in such episodes as "One Breath," "Soft Light," "Nisei," "Wetwired" and "Talitha Cumi" – and even when a bullet finally took him down in "Herrenvolk," one could still feel his presence looming about the proceedings. X turned up briefly in the fifth season opener, "Unusual Suspects," but wasn't heard from again until "The Truth."

The X-Files Magazine caught up with Williams in the midst of filming the series finale.

THE X-FILES MAGAZINE: Before "The Truth" beckoned you back to *The X-Files*, it had been a while since you'd appeared on the show. How often were you still being recognized by X_philes as X?
STEVEN WILLIAMS: It was strange, man. Maybe it's that people that watch *The X-Files* didn't start watching until after I was gone, but I don't get recognized a whole bunch for *The X-Files*. What I get recognized most for is still [the police

drama] *21 Jump Street*. That's weird. But I think I know why. *21 Jump Street* is on all over, all the time. You'd be surprised. Here in Los Angeles, a lot of kids are seeing it for the first time. If *X-Files* fans recognize me, it's the avid ones, not the casual viewers. I think I ended up doing 12 or 13 shows as a recurring character over three seasons on *The X-Files*, whereas I was a regular on *Jump Street*. So there's not a lot of recognition from *The X-Files*, but what is there is awesome.

Ok, once and for all, who was X?
You know what? People ask me that, and I

"You just knew X was a cold-hearted son of a bitch and you didn't know who, why, what, where."

never thought about who X was. For me as an actor, the less I knew about X, the better it was for me. I didn't play the character or deliver his lines in any certain way. I tried to play him with as much ambiguity as possible, so that each individual who watched the show could make up his or her own mind about who X was. We just don't know. He remains a mystery to me. He remains a mystery to the audience. He remains a mystery to everybody. I wanted him to be this big enigma.

The interesting thing with the fans is that they wanted to see more of him, because the more they saw of him the more

they could try to figure out who he was, if he was a good guy or a bad guy. He's just a mystery.

This isn't just from an actor's point of view of "I want a job," but there was so much more to be said about X. There was so much more to be explored about him. They have excellent writers on *The X-Files* and I don't know why they didn't explore more of him. One of my favorite scenes with X was the one in which he had an encounter with the Cigarette-Smoking Man. They were sitting in a car and CSM says, "Somebody has been passing information onto Mulder," and X turns to him and says,

"That individual has not been revealed yet." And there was this look that said, "Who are these two guys? What are they to each other? Is CSM X's boss? Is X CSM's boss? Are they equals? What's the deal? Why is X keeping secrets from these guys?" It was one of those mysterious things. I have to say I was disappointed that they didn't explore this guy more, and I think a lot of the audience was disappointed.

Of the episodes you did, which moments are you most fond of?
I loved the episode with that scene between CSM and X. At one point I really wasn't

interacting with anyone but Mulder, so interacting with the other actors and the other characters was fun. I loved the scene with X and Skinner fighting on the elevator. Not only do I like Mitch as a person, but also you had these two guys, X and Skinner, and you're thinking, "Who are they? How will Skinner react to X? Would X kill Skinner on the spot?" He pulls a gun and says, "I've killed men for a lot less, but I'm going to let you go." I liked the quick encounter I had with Scully. But my favorite moment of all was in my first episode, where they were trying to get Scully's blood and I rescue Mulder. I think it was "Sleepless." I blow the guy away and I thought, "I like this character." And the scene looked great. You had the shadow on the wall and you saw the gun and "Blam!" You just knew X was a cold-hearted son of a bitch and you didn't know who, why, what or where.

ENCOUNTERING SCULLY IN "HERRENVOLK"

"I wanted X to be this big enigma. He remains a mystery to me. He remains a mystery to everybody."

Where do you think X is now?

I will never, ever really think he is dead. Absolutely not. As an actor I held out hope he wasn't dead, so that I could possibly come back on the show. But as part of the show itself, who knows? Maybe he is an alien. You have to remember that in the episode in which X was killed, Jeremiah Smith was around, and he was a guy who could bring people back. He had healing powers that could bring you back from the dead. So I've always had it in the back of my mind that Jeremiah found X in the hallway after he'd been shot and brought him back to life somehow.

Let's talk about the finale.

They didn't give me a script, so again it was a mystery to me. They called me and said, "We want you to appear in this episode." I'm happy to be back. I was frustrated by not being back for so long, but I said yes to this because I wanted to do it for those fans who really dug X, who dig me. I didn't worry about the number of lines or the money. I just did it for the fans. If they did an *X-Files* finale without X it would probably make a lot of fans sad, especially X fans. So I'm there. And if they ask me to be in the next *X-Files* movie, I'll be there, too.

So what else have you been up to lately?

I'm keeping busy, but it's been a little slow, frankly. The industry is still recovering [from the strikes that almost happened]. Things were rushed into production and then there was nothing. But I did an episode of *The District*, where I played a judge. I've finally graduated from cop to lawyer to judge. I did the *L.A. Law* reunion movie, which was a big sweeps movie for NBC. They're bringing back a lot of old shows to celebrate their 75th anniversary. I'd done a couple of episodes of the show years ago, and in the reunion movie I played a narcotics dealer on death row for a murder he did not commit. He's been setup and he gets Kuzak to represent him for his final appeal before he's executed.

Before that I did a couple of episodes of *Stargate SG-1*, which were directed by Peter DeLuise, my old *21 Jump Street* co-star. Before that, things were great because I was doing two series, *Linc's* and *Legacy*. And before that I was doing *L.A. Heat* and recurring on *The X-Files*.

The bottom kind of dropped out at the end of 1999. It was one of those periods actors have, where everything got canceled. And it was real slow in 2000 and 2001. Now, thanks to *The X-Files* and *L.A. Law* and a few other things that look like they might happen, it's turning around. They say it's cyclical. I'm in my Morgan Freeman phase. "Get me now, people!"

Steven Williams, thank you very much.

A BLOODY DEATH IN "HERRENVOLK"

EPISODE GUIDE

THE X FILES™

3.15: "PIPER MARU" (PART ONE OF TWO) Episode #3X15
Original US tx 9 February 96 Original UK tx 11 June 96

PACIFIC OCEAN
SAN DIEGO and SAN FRANCISCO, CALIFORNIA
HONG KONG

Somewhere in the Pacific, divers from the French salvage ship *Piper Maru* discover the wreckage of a USAF P-51 Mustang fighter aircraft, nicknamed 'Drop Dead Red,' lost since the Second World War. The lead diver, Gauthier, imagines he sees something inside the cockpit of the wrecked plane – an apparent survivor, with a black oily substance moving behind his eyes – and when Gauthier surfaces, his eyes bear the same 'oil slick' anomaly...

In Washington, Skinner informs Scully that, with no new evidence having emerged in five months, her sister's unsolved murder case is about to be effectively closed. Scully hears the news just as word reaches Mulder of the Piper Maru's discovery; he believes that they have found the remains of a submerged UFO, especially as the entire crew – with one exception, Gauthier – are later admitted to a California Naval hospital having apparently suffered exposure to massive, lethal doses of radiation. Curiously, the *Piper Maru* herself showed no signs of radiation.

While Mulder heads out to San Francisco to question Gauthier, Scully decides to visit the Naval base at which she and her family lived as a child, hoping to question an old friend of her father's still living at the base. Neither has much luck: Mulder finds Gauthier lying, unconscious and covered in an oily substance, among his scattered papers, his wife – now carrying the mysterious oily virus – missing; Scully, meanwhile, finds her father's friend less than forthcoming when it comes to the Mustang lying on the ocean floor.

Perhaps the answers lie, instead, with the mysterious individual who appears to be selling secrets to the highest bidder – secrets from a digital tape he stole from Skinner five months earlier...

F.Y.I.

This 'mythology' two-parter began life, as many *X-Files* episodes do, as a single image in the head of Chris Carter. "He just knew he wanted a guy in the cockpit of a World War II plane, banging against the glass," co-producer and co-scripter Frank Spotnitz recalls. "He didn't know how he got there; was this guy alive or dead? was it an illusion? Then he wanted a flashback to World War II aboard a submarine. I was stuck on that story for weeks," he admits.

In-jokes and references abound in this episode: Gauthier is named in tribute to the series' physical effects supervisor, David Gauthier, himself a certified diver; the French salvage ship *Piper Maru* takes her name from Gillian Anderson's daughter, Piper, whose middle name means 'calm and gentle' in Polynesian; finally, Robbie L Maier, who plays the stricken pilot in the flashbacks, is the series' construction co-ordinator.

On its initial US broadcast, "Piper Maru" scored a Nielsen rating of 10.6/18, equating approximately 16.44 million viewers.

Principal Credits

Created by	Chris Carter
Produced by	Ten-Thirteen Productions for 20th Century-Fox TV
Executive Producer	Chris Carter
Co-Executive Producers	Howard Gordon, RW Goodwin
Producers	Joseph Patrick Finn, Kim Manners, Rob Bowman
Co-Producer	Paul Rabwin
Music	Mark Snow

Episode Credits

Written by	Frank Spotnitz & Chris Carter
Directed by	Rob Bowman

Special Agent Fox Mulder	David Duchovny
Special Agent Dr Dana Scully	Gillian Anderson
Assistant Director Walter S Skinner	Mitch Pileggi
Alex Krycek	Nicholas Lea
Chris Johansen	Robert Clothier
Jeraldine Kallenchuk	Jo Bates
Gray-Haired Man	Morris Panych
Wayne Morgan	Stephen E Miller
Gauthier	Ari Solomon
Dr Seizer	Paul Batten
Medic	Russell Ferrier
Hispanic Man	Lenno Britos
Joan Gauthier	Kimberly Unger
Waitress	Rochelle Greenwood
Engineer #1	Joel Silverstone
Navy Base Guard	David Neale
Young (Chris) Johansen	Tom Scholte
WWII Pilot	Robbie L Maier
Young Dana Scully	Tegan Moss
Engineer #2	Darcy Laurie
Capt Kyle Sanford	Richard Hersley
Sick Crewman	Peter Scoular
Young Melissa Scully	Christine Viner

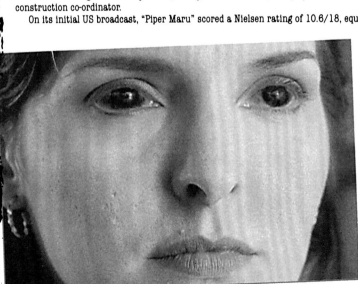

Noteworthy Dialogue Transcript

SCULLY: "You know, it's strange. Men can blow up buildings and they can be nowhere near the crime scene. But we can piece together the evidence and convict them beyond a doubt. Our labs here can recreate – out of the most microscopic detail – the motivation and circumstance to almost any murder, right down to the killer's attitude towards his mother and that he was a bed-wetter. But in the case of a woman – my sister – who was gunned down in cold blood in a well-lit apartment building by a shooter who left the weapon at the crime scene, we can't even put together enough to keep anybody interested."

Unexplained Plot Discrepancies

Four thousand pieces of paper on Gauthier's floor, and Mulder finds the exact two he needs without even a cursory search.

EPISODE GUIDE

3.16: "APOCRYPHA" (PART TWO OF TWO) *Episode #3X16*
Original US tx 16 February 96 Original UK tx 18 June 96

**NEW YORK CITY
WASHINGTON, DC
BLACK CROW, NORTH DAKOTA**

At a Pearl Harbour Naval hospital, a sailor suffering from severe burns explains to three young men from the government the fate that befell the crew of his submarine – that he and his shipmates were on a salvage mission when their captain was apparently possessed by a virus which left a black oily membrane over his eyes. The dying sailor pleads with the G-men to ensure that the truth of his ordeal comes out, but the man with the cigarette looks less than sincere...

After what seemed like an innocent argument in a coffee shop led to Skinner being shot, Scully abandons her investigation and rushes to the Assistant Director's hospital bedside. Mulder, meanwhile drives across country with Krycek, who he met up with in Hong Kong in "Piper Maru," on their way to a rendezvous with the stolen digital tape, which may contain the secrets Mulder has been searching for. En route, however, they are run off the road by two mysterious individuals; Mulder lies dazed in the wrecked rental car while the two men question Krycek about the whereabouts of the tape, but moments later his assailants are seemingly vapourized by a blinding white light. Krycek escapes again.

With Mulder and Skinner both in the hospital, it is up to Scully to pursue the investigation alone – a search that may lead her back to her sister's killer...

F.Y.I.

Visual effects supervisor Mat Beck says that the 'oil slick' effects of the infected victims' eyes were a complex collaboration between he and his Vancouver-based equivalent, Dave Gauthier. "The trick was to track it really well, and make it look as if it was playing on the surface of the cornea," he explains, "so that when the actor moved his or her eyes, squinted or blinked, we tracked it with a slight delay. [That way], the movement had a realistic 'lag' to it, like the sense you get of the floaters in your eye, [where] every time you move your eye you can see it kind of sloshing around in there... It seems to be pretty successful. Chris was delighted with it." Beck adds that, in addition to the human eye being the most complicated image to work on, "It's also an object of primal attention – in any given scene, that's exactly where you're looking. So not only is it really difficult to hook up to because of the complexity of the image, but people are always paying attention to the eyes of the character!"

On its initial US broadcast, "Apocrypha" scored a Nielsen rating of 10.8/18, equating approximately 16.71 million viewers.

Noteworthy Dialogue Transcript

SICK CREWMAN: "That thing – it's still down there. The Navy will deny it, but you've got to make sure the truth gets out. I can trust you to do that, can't I, Mr Mulder?"
YOUNG SMOKING MAN: "You can trust all of us."

Unexplained Plot Discrepancies

Most of this episode's continuity problems did not arise until the Morgan and Wong episodes "The Field Where I Died" and "Musings of a Cigarette-Smoking Man" aired early the following season. The crux of the conflict is that in "The Field Where I Died," Mulder regresses into a past life in which he encounters the Cigarette-Smoking Man's soul present in the form of a Gestapo soldier in the 1940s. But if the Cigarette-Smoking Man had already been born in the 1940s – which he would have to have been to be alive in "Apocrypha" in 1953 – how could his soul be inhabiting an SS Officer?

Incidentally, the young Cigarette-Smoking Man is played here by Craig Warkentin (and re-voiced by William B Davis) rather than Chris Owens who plays him in "Musings... "

Principal Credits
Created by — Chris Carter
Produced by — Ten-Thirteen Productions for 20th Century-Fox TV

Executive Producer — Chris Carter
Co-Executive Producers — Howard Gordon, RW Goodwin
Producers — Joseph Patrick Finn, Kim Manners, Rob Bowman
Co-Producer — Paul Rabwin
Music — Mark Snow

Episode Credits
Written by — Frank Spotnitz & Chris Carter
Directed by — Kim Manners

Special Agent Fox Mulder — David Duchovny
Special Agent Dr Dana Scully — Gillian Anderson
Assistant Director Walter S Skinner — Mitch Pileggi
Well-Manicured Man — John Neville
Smoking Man — William B Davis
Frohike — Tom Braidwood
Langly — Dean Haglund
Byers — Bruce Harwood
Alex Krycek — Nicholas Lea
Agent Fuller — Kevin McNulty
Navy Doctor — Barry Levy
Government Man #1
(Young William Mulder) — Dmitry Chepovetsky
Agent Caleca — Sue Mathew
Elder #1 — Don S Williams
Hispanic Man (Luis Cardinal) — Lenno Britos
Nurse — Frances Flanagan
Agent Pendrell — Brendan Beiser
Sick Crewman — Peter Scoular
Armed Man — Jeff Chivers
Major Domo — Martin Evans
Ambulance Driver — Eric Breker
Government Man #2 — Harrison R Coe
Capt Kyle Sanford — Richard Hersley
Doctor — David Kaye
Elder #2 — Stanley Walsh
Government Man #3
(Young Smoking Man) — Craig Warkentin

Clouding
the Issue

Kate Anderson peers through the smokescreen surrounding
"Musings of a Cigarette-Smoking Man"

O n first impressions, "Musings of a Cigarette Smoking Man" would seem to be a delectable treat: an exposé of the life of this mysterious, shadowy and dangerous individual – 'his background, who he is... and who he wants to be'. But instead of being a significant piece of the overall puzzle and a revealing contribution to *The X-Files* catalogue, on reflection, this episode is precisely what it was intended to be – nothing more than an extravagant concoction of contradictions, uncertainties and self-referencing. In short, tasty-looking, but otherwise unremarkable. More 'hardened jelly and teeth-shattering nuts' than a 'peanut butter cup or an English toffee'.

"Musings" walks a fine line between frustration and downright annoyance – somehow managing not to fall into either trap, thanks in part to James Wong's stylish and refreshing Emmy-nominated direction. Glen Morgan's tongue-in-cheek script is, regardless of its truth or otherwise, a finely-drawn character study: a story of a past told in flashbacks and fragments, which, at times, is both an intriguing and amusing fabrication.

In a tale spanning 30 years of murder, manipulation and deceit, Frohike (one of the paranoid Lone Gunmen) believes he has discovered evidence which could lead Mulder and Scully to the truth behind the Cigarette-Smoking Man's identity. He claims that their nameless nemesis has been responsible for the assassinations of John F. Kennedy and Martin Luther King, as well as manipulating many other pieces of world history. Not to mention fixing Super Bowls and picking the Academy Award winners, whilst harboring a secret desire to be a novelist.

Even by *X-Files* standards, this is a particularly strange episode. Are we to believe that the Cigarette-Smoking Man killed Kennedy and King? Does he really dream of quitting his day job to write adventure stories? Who knows. It's virtually impossible to separate truth from speculation, especially since writer Morgan has carefully covered his tracks by employing an unreliable narrator, here in the shape of Frohike, as the vehicle for telling the story. In addition, Morgan has littered the episode with deliberate inaccuracies; the easiest to spot being the plaque on The Lone Gunmen's headquarters,

Life is like a box of chocolates.

A cheap, thoughtless, perfunctory gift that no one ever asks for. Unreturnable because all you get back is another box of chocolates. So, you're stuck with mostly undefinable whipped mint crap, mindlessly wolfed down when there's nothing else to eat while you're watching the game. Sure, once in a while you get a peanut butter cup or an English toffee, but it's gone too fast and the taste is fleeting. In the end, you're left with nothing but broken bits filled with hardened jelly and teeth-shattering nuts, which if you *are* desperate enough to eat leaves nothing but an empty box of useless brown paper wrappers.
("Musings of a Cigarette-Smoking Man")

proclaiming them to be publishers of *The Magic Bullet Newsletter*, instead of *The Lone Gunman*.

There's no doubt that Morgan and Wong have taken the fourth season in directions it never would have gone without them, with episodes like "Home," "The Field Where I Died" and "Never Again" continuing to demonstrate their phenomenal creativity and sense of adventure. However, "Musings" is altogether something quite different. For a show knee-deep in cover-ups and conspiracies, Morgan and Wong have taken an enormous risk by exposing so much of what may or may not be the truth about this enigmatic character. By doing

so, they have taken that edge of mystery and fear away which established the Cigarette-Smoking Man so successfully. And with the inclusion of a subplot – which reveals that the Cigarette-Smoking Man is, at heart, a frustrated, unpublished writer, this shadowy individual comes across as less threatening and mysterious, more pathetic than dangerous, which is a complete contrast to everything we know about him – albeit, not a great deal.

Of course, no Morgan and Wong episode would be complete without characteristics which make it uniquely theirs, namely humor and the obligatory sports reference – here with the Cigarette-Smoking Man putting Saddam Hussein on hold and rigging the Super Bowl! More recently, since their return, Morgan and Wong have taken to utilizing the cast of their short lived series, *Space: Above and Beyond*. And while Kirsten Cloke ("The Field Where I Died")

Above: Frohike; Right: Morgan Weisser in Space: Above and Beyond

and Rodney Rowland ("Never Again") shone in their guest appearances, Morgan Weisser's lacklustre performance as the infamous Lee Harvey Oswald is instantly forgettable.

"Musings" resulted in part because David Duchovny and Gillian Anderson were tiring of debilitating 15 hours a day/6 days a week production schedules. As James Wong explained: "It's the fourth season, and they're really burned out. So we thought, wouldn't it be great to do a show that they're not even in? It's not something you could do in the first three seasons but we're cool enough as a show to do an episode which the stars aren't even in.

"In *The X-Files*, you have enough interesting supporting characters for you to be able to do this," continued Wong. "And we thought that the Cigarette-Smoking Man was one of the most... I mean, who the hell is he? What has he done?"

Who and what, indeed. One thing is for certain, their unreliable narrative about the Cigarette-Smoking Man's life from 1963 to the present has certainly sparked a certain amount of controversy – and not just among X-philes. Glen Morgan's original ending involved the Cigarette-Smoking Man shooting Frohike dead. But Chris Carter decided to change the ending and let Frohike live because, if he died, it meant that his story was true. To not have that happen, meant it probably wasn't...

"I loved [the episode] except for the ending," said Morgan. "I wanted the Cigarette-Smoking Man to shoot Frohike and Chris Carter wouldn't let me do it."

James Wong agreed: "Absolutely. Chris had us rewrite it so he doesn't kill him at the end – he didn't want to kill Frohike off. But when I was on the set I actually shot it both ways."

While Frohike fans can breathe a sigh of relief, when he first received the script, the Cigarette-Smoking Man's affable alter ego, William B. Davis admitted that he, "had a mixed reaction. I mean, it was a treat to have an episode devoted to my character. [But] some of the ideas in the script seemed a little extreme – you know, that the Cigarette-Smoking Man told Saddam Hussein to call back, and that he fixed hockey games, etc."

Davis also admitted that he was as confused as everyone else, especially since the episode seemed to reveal more than it should: "That was certainly a concern I had," he said. "Are we blowing the

Dean Haglund, Tom Braidwood and Bruce Harwood

"A complex, elaborate joke"

"The promisingly titled "Musings of a Cigarette-Smoking Man" proved only to be an apocryphal tale... and divides fans equally due to the contradictory details revealed about the Cigarette-Smoking Man's past."
Starburst Special #33

"Massive continuity errors have begun to creep in, most notably in Morgan and Wong's brave but bizarre "Musings of a Cigarette-Smoking Man," which prompted hardened X-philes to call for Chris Carter's immediate return [from *Millennium*]."
SFX #26 June 1997

"While at first this episode seems to be a significant addition to the X-Files canon, it eventually turns out to be little more than a complex, elaborate joke. Simultaneously affirming and contradicting what has gone before it, "Musings of a Cigarette-Smoking Man" leaves the viewer with much still shrouded in uncertainty and much still unresolved. Which is as every good X-Files episode should be."
Xpose #6 January 1997

cover of the character, in a sense? Even more, I was concerned that everyone would ask why we were doing it all in one episode. I mean, we could stretch this out over years.

"But my second take on it, after looking at it more and kind of seeing how I lined up to it, was the realization that this is seen through the lens of Frohike. It may or may not be accurate. I'm not quite sure where the fans have finally settled on this – whether people still think that the character was the sole assassin of Kennedy and Martin Luther King and if he really is an unsuccessful writer or not. There certainly were a lot of things in that episode that were inconsistent with other things that had appeared in other episodes, quite consciously so. I think Chris [Carter] intended that there be these contradictions so that you don't know. It may be that the episode is ultimately more an entertainment about the character than a significant piece of the puzzle."

As unique as it is awkward and as memorable as it is negligible, Morgan and Wong's "Musings of a Cigarette–Smoking Man" deserves to be applauded for attempting to keep the show fresh and interesting, by expanding its roots and exploring uncharted territory. Unfortunately, by exposing so much information about the Cigarette-Smoking Man's mysterious

and sinister persona and hidden agenda – regardless of its correctness or tongue in cheek nature – everything that makes him such a successful and captivating villain, built-up over four years, has been torn to shreds in just 45 minutes!

However, like other semi-disappointing episodes, "Musings" does have a fair share of redeeming features. Costume designer Jenni Gullett captures the era to perfection and the overall appearance of the episode – neatly put together, with four segments spanning the Cigarette-Smoking Man's career from the early 60's to the present day – is intriguing and certainly helps to maintain your interest. But obviously, the main attraction is William B. Davis, whose chilling performance lights up the screen, and is quite superb throughout. Particularly outstanding are the striking scenes he shares with Deep Throat (Jerry Hardin) – who is equally impressive as Mulder's late secret source, providing fans with a tasty reminder of the good old days – during an exchange between the two men to determine which one of them will get to make history, by destroying a recovered EBE. Other moments of joy not to be missed include the Cigarette-Smoking Man wearing a nicotine patch and his Forrest Gump-like box of chocolates speech. These ingenious moments – although brief – demonstrate just why the Cigarette-Smoking Man isn't your usual stereotypical, cardboard cut-out bad guy.

"If he lost his position of power, I think he would be a very sad man; that he would be frightened of people," pondered Davis. "Chris Carter talks about him being a destroyer. I don't know if he is a destroyer. I think he's far more dangerous than death!"

EPISODE GUIDE

THE Ⓧ FILES™

4.7: "MUSINGS OF A CIGARETTE-SMOKING MAN"
Episode #4X07
Original US tx 17 November 96 Original UK tx 2 March 97

WASHINGTON, DC; FORT BRAGG, NORTH CAROLINA; DALLAS, TEXAS; MEMPHIS, TENNESSEE and DOGWAY, WEST VIRGINIA

In a dilapidated building in Washington, DC, The Cigarette-Smoking Man opens a briefcase containing audio surveillance equipment, sets up a high-powered rifle and begins to eavesdrop as Frohike relates what he believes to be the details of The Cigarette-Smoking Man's life to a fascinated Mulder and Scully.

Frohike's story begins in 1962, with a classified briefing at which an army Captain is given an extraordinary assignment: the assassination of President John F. Kennedy. The following November in Dallas, Texas, a young Communist named Lee Harvey Oswald is framed as a 'patsy,' while on a grassy knoll across from the book depository, the unnamed Captain sets up his weapon and awaits the President's motorcade. His grisly task completed satisfactorily, the President's assassin goes back to writing his pulp spy novels, and lights his first cigarette...

Five years later, the same man meets in another darkened room, this time to discuss how to deal with the increasingly popular black activist, Martin Luther King. Before long, King lies dead on the steps of the Lorraine Hotel in Memphis, victim of another assassin's bullet. But is the man we see pulling the trigger truly responsible? Or is this chain-smoking, would-be spy novelist merely writing himself into the pages of history?

F.Y.I.

Glen Morgan and James Wong's "Musings of a Cigarette-Smoking Man," which was inspired by DC Comics' *The Unauthorized Biography of Lex Luthor*, can unequivocally be described as the bravest *X-Files* script to date, for reasons outlined below and because it banishes David Duchovny to a voiceover and Gillian Anderson to a flashback! How did the writers get away with it? "We always wait until Chris [Carter] is *reeeally* busy," says Morgan. "Then we know he'll go, 'Yeah, yeah, yeah, okay!'"

Watch out for the appropriation of the briefing scene in *Apocalypse Now* and the 'life is like a box of chocolates' scene from *Forrest Gump*, and a wonderful private joke in which The Cigarette-Smoking Man complains that the ending of one of his stories has been changed – just as Glen Morgan's original ending, in which Frohike *was* killed by the character, was altered by Chris Carter in order to shed further doubt on the authenticity of the story related in the episode (see below).

On its US debut, "Musings of a Cigarette-Smoking Man" scored a Nielsen rating of 10.7/15, equivalent to approximately ten million homes.

Noteworthy Dialogue Transcript

FROHIKE: "If you find the right starting point, and follow it, not even the secrets of the darkest of men are safe."
MULDER: "Cancer man? What did you find?"
FROHIKE: "Possibly everything. Maybe his background. Who he is. And who he wants to be..."

Unexplained Plot Discrepancies

With an episode that seems to contradict almost every known fact about The Cigarette-Smoking Man's background, where do you start? Asked if the story is supposed to be real or apocryphal, director and unaccredited co-writer James Wong admits that he and Morgan "hedged it". "It's called '*Musings* of a Cigarette-Smoking Man'," he explains, "and in the show he's this guy who writes spy novels, so by the end you're thinking, is this real life? Or is this just his imagination of what his real life *could* be – his version of it? It *is* Frohike's interpretation of what [The Cigarette-Smoking Man's] life is, so... Mostly you'll feel that it's history," he adds, "but is it completely accurate?"

Actor William B Davis confesses that he's none the wiser. "When I got the script, I asked Chris [Carter], 'Is this real? Is this the back story of the character?' And he said, 'No.' Then, when I was speaking with Jim Wong, I said, 'Is this the true story of the character?' and he said, 'Yes.'" Ultimately, Carter himself has the last word on the subject: "I loved the ambiguity, where you don't know whether it's true or not," he says, "and that's, I think, the way I'll leave it."

Principal Credits

Created by	Chris Carter
Produced by	Ten-Thirteen Productions for Twentieth Century Fox TV
Executive Producers	Chris Carter, Howard Gordon, RW Goodwin
Producers	Joseph Patrick Finn, Kim Manners, Rob Bowman
Co-Producers	Vince Gilligan, Frank Spotnitz, Paul Rabwin
Consulting Producers	Ken Horton, James Wong & Glen Morgan
Music	Mark Snow

Episode Credits

Written by	Glen Morgan
Directed by	James Wong
Voice of Special Agent Fox Mulder	David Duchovny
Special Agent Dr Dana Scully	Gillian Anderson
Cigarette-Smoking Man	William B Davis
Lee Harvey Oswald	Morgan Weisser
Young Smoking Man/'Hunt'/'Raul Bloodworth'	Chris Owens
General Francis	Donnelly Rhodes
Frohike	Tom Braidwood
Voice of Byers	Bruce Harwood
Deep Throat	Jerry Hardin
Agent	Dan Zukovic
Aide	Peter Hanlon
Young Bill Mulder	Dean Aylesworth
James Earl Ray	Paul Jarrett
(FBI) Director (J Edgar Hoover)	David Fredericks
Lydon	Laurie Murdoch
Section Chief Scott Blevins	Charles Cioffi

THE (X) FILES

PHOTOS BY KEN STANIFORTH © FOX TELEVISION

tungu

MULDER PLAYS RUSSIAN
ROULETTE IN TUNGUSKA
AND TERMA

tion

by mo ryan

The list of collaborators is growing.
In *The X-Files'* last two seasons,
FBI Agent Fox Mulder has revealed that the
United States government is not the only
superpower secretly experimenting on
humans with alien DNA—viewers of the
show have learned that Japanese and
German scientists have also been involved
in these horrific scientific endeavors. This
season, however, Mulder and Scully may
have gotten the biggest shock of all—

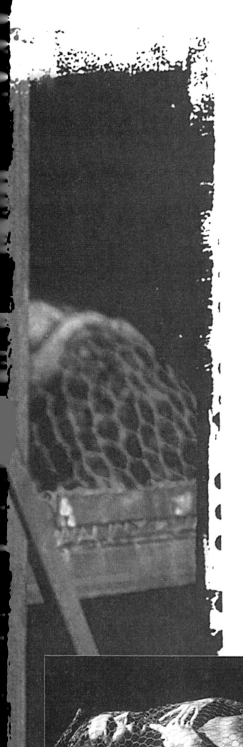

they discovered that when it comes to humanity's close encounters, the Russians have something to hide as well.

According to Chris Carter, who co-wrote Season Four's "Tunguska"/"Terma" two-parter with Frank Spotnitz, it was only a matter of time before America's former Cold War opponent became a player in the show's ongoing mythology arc. "From the very beginning, we've all imagined that if we had X-Files, so did the other superpower," Carter says. "And the Tunguska story [of a possible crashed meteorite] is a real one—it's a turn-of-the-century episode that still has not been explained."

The mythology episodes, in which Mulder and Scully try to piece together the puzzling parts of a global alien-human conspiracy, have become seasonal high points: they can be counted upon to goose the show's ratings and deliver an adrenaline-pumping couple of hours to the show's fans. But X-Philes and network suits aren't the only ones who look forward to mythology cliff-hangers—the show's directors avidly anticipate "sinking their teeth into" these epic episodes, as director-producer Kim Manners puts it. "They're usually bigger episodes, and I find they're a lot more interesting to shoot," says Manners, who directed "Tunguska." "They usually have a terrific script, there are a lot of visual elements that I find exciting, and we have the majority of our mythology cast involved, which is always a pleasure. I got my taste of [directing mythology episodes with last season's] 'Apocrypha,' and then with 'Tunguska,' and I love doing them. We spend a lot of money on them— they really are small feature films."

Director-producer Rob Bowman agrees. "Mythology episodes have all been big favorites of mine," says Bowman, who directed "Terma" as well as past mythology high points like "End Game," "Paper Clip," "731" and "Piper Maru." "'Terma' was fun for me because it was a different kind of [mythology] episode," Bowman offers. "Instead of a lot of high-tech [gear], it was low-tech—a lot of mud and crud and stuff, and we had some great action sequences."

"Tunguska" and "Terma" may have represented a low-tech change of pace, but coordinating all the mud and crud and other headaches that go into the creation of a mythology episode make them endurance tests for all involved. The FBI raid on a right-wing militia group that opens "Tunguska" was particularly stressful, Manners recalls. "I had one night to shoot that, and I had 60-plus [camera] set-ups I had to get, and it was just a nightmare. We had to coordinate 18 good guys, 5 bad guys, automatic weapons fire, squibs, grenades and all the rest of it. Before we began that night, I got together with the crew and gave them a pep talk. The crew always works hard, but sometimes you have to ask for 150 percent, when they usually give you 110. I gathered them around, and I said, 'Hey guys, tonight's the night, we either win or we lose. And if we lose, we're in trouble.' But these guys are amazing, they can dig deep and pull off just about anything."

To get the entire FBI raid completed that night, Manners enlisted three full camera crews, and as one finished filming a segment, the next one would immediately start rolling on a new one. "We literally leapfrogged all night long, and we got every shot but four, which I did later on the lot. It was a nightmare, but [in a way] it was a great night—we got almost everything done."

But that was just the beginning. The next night, the *X-Files* crew filmed all night long at Vancouver's busy airport, shooting some scenes in a recently vacated international terminal and others in the middle of one of the airport's still-functioning terminals. "We've had to fake [shooting in airports] a couple of times," notes co-executive producer Robert Goodwin. "For 'Piper Maru,' we had to create the Hong Kong airport, so we took over what's really a terminal building for the luxury liners that come in to Vancouver and tricked it up with all sorts of set dressing to make it look like an airport. The fact that we could use the actual jetways [for 'Tunguska'] made things a bit easier, but there were still a lot of extras [to coordinate] and a lot of lighting problems and all that sort of thing."

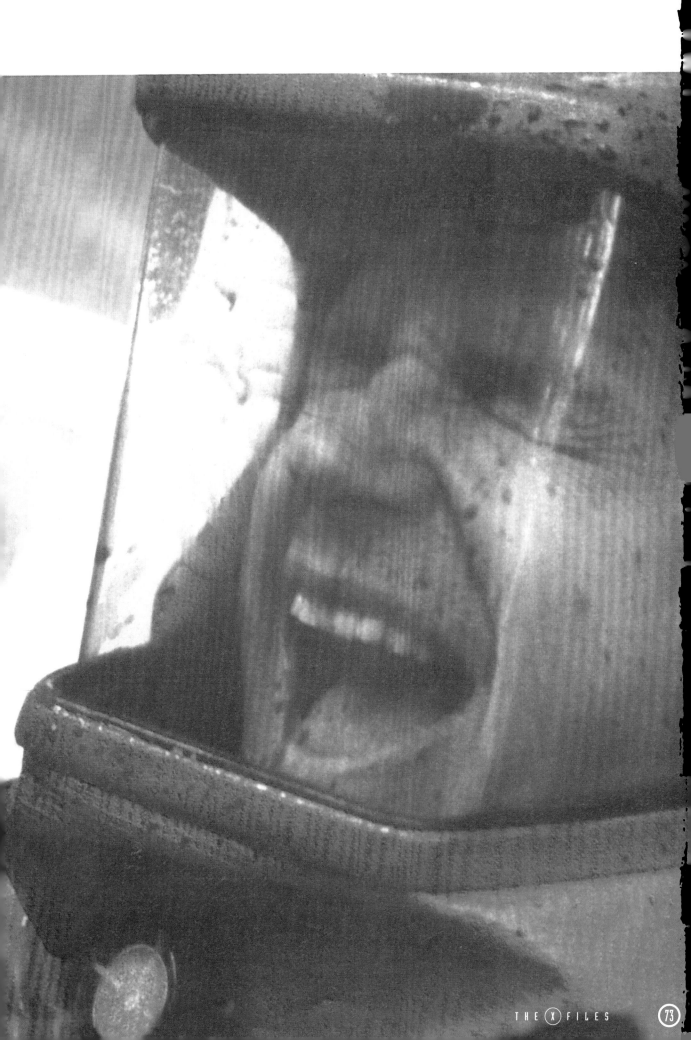

onstruction chief Rob Maier echoes that assessment: Just because an appropriate location is found for a particular scene, that doesn't mean the camera crew and the actors can just walk in and start shooting. "You'd think, 'Oh, well, you were at a real airport, so it must be easy,' but it's not like everything is where you want it to be. We had to create a baggage area, a customs office—there was quite a bit of stuff, even though it was only for a couple of quick scenes. And [the set for a key 'Tunguska' scene]—the lab where a researcher cut into the space rock—that was just an empty room [in downtown Vancouver]. We did a full paint job, we built the glass booth where the saw was and the outer lab, and another long glass wall with lab equipment. Arranging all the lab equipment was a huge job for the set dressers—there was just tons and tons of medical stuff."

Unlike the set decorators, who had to make the lab in "Tunguska" look real, prop master Ken Hawryliw had the task of making the rock slicer appear quite different than such devices really look. "In reality, the equipment is much smaller, and it doesn't do what we wanted it to do, which is cut a cross section out of the rock, which [real devices] don't actually do on that kind of scale," Hawryliw notes. "I designed the table, the saw and the rock, and the high-tech stainless steel arm that held the rock, and the FX guys created the alien goo."

Even the outer space rock used in the episode is a little more exotic than such an object looks in real life, Hawryliw adds. "You look at [NASA's real] Mars rock and there's nothing really interesting about it; it looks like something you found in your backyard. We had to make our rock look a little different," he explains. The final prop "was a composite of masonry and plaster and resin. The thing about this show is, nothing ever comes off the shelf," he laughs. "Everything's customized. We found a rock that we sort of liked—but we ended up redesigning and resculpting it and putting a cool-looking finish on it."

Even the complicated biohazard suits that Scully and Agent Pendrell wear in the episode are more exotic variations on the real thing—courtesy of the Warner Bros. prop department. "I talked to the person who was the technical advisor for *Outbreak*, and they [fabricated] the suits used in that movie because they look cooler than what the Centers for Disease Control really use." The upshot: *The X-Files* borrowed the clunky—but cool—blue biohazard suits used in the 1995 Dustin Hoffman film.

Getting hold of ersatz lab gear is one thing, but how do you re-create a Russian prison camp in the Pacific Northwest? In the past, the show's producers have painted a rock quarry to create the American Southwest in "Anasazi" and have refrigerated an entire sound stage to simulate the frigid Antarctic in "End Game," but creating a gulag was not quite that logistically challenging.

The outdoor prison scenes in "Terma," in which Mulder escapes from his Russian captors, were actually filmed a stone's throw from downtown Vancouver in the city's heavily wooded Stanley Park. The location of the camp, a staging area for maintenance vehicles, "is actually near the mouth of the park, but you can't really see it because it's hidden by the trees," notes Tom Braidwood, the first assistant director on "Terma." "But on some of the angles, you could see beyond the trees and see the skyscrapers of Vancouver. There were a lot of discussions about the fact that if it wasn't a cloudy day, they'd have to paint all those out after the fact to get rid of them."

To make the large parking lot look like the courtyard of a prison camp, the show's producers had to bring in several tons of dirt—but construction chief Rob Maier was worried that the 23 truck loads they had ordered might not be enough. "If we were going to do what was in the script and what the director and the designer wanted to do, we were looking at about $30,000 worth of ground cover—to put it all in, prepare it and take it all back out. But because many people didn't refer to it as ground cover—they referred to it as *dirt*—they thought it was a waste. [Eventually] we scaled it back, and we were just about able to give the director and the designer everything they wanted for considerably less. Still, it ended

up being a couple-acre set."

Once the dirt—er, ground cover—was in place, "Terma" director Rob Bowman and his crew had to film several challenging scenes with a large group of Russian actors, horses, trucks and dozens of dirt-covered extras. "We tried to do it as quickly as we could, but there's a limit to how fast you can go when you're coordinating 100 extras, five or six horses, trucks driving in and out and all that kind of stuff," Tom Braidwood says. "In those kind of situations, the director has to go in really well prepared—he has to know exactly what shots he needs. A lot of times we use two cameras and keep them rolling all the time. That way we get double the amount of footage out of [a day's shooting]."

Many of the actors in the Russian prison sequence were in fact from that nation, but the menacing men on horseback were actually award-winning Canadian riders. "We went to Calgary to get all the world champion riders," says stunt coordinator Tony Morelli. "All of those riders have been in movies before, so whenever I need a cowboy I go to Calgary," which is the capital of Canada's cowboy culture. "The horses were from Vancouver," Morelli adds. "They aren't spooked by cameras, but we also had to find horses that wouldn't be spooked by gunshots. I didn't know how that would go, but they were great."

The horses may have been a dream to work with, but accord-

PHOTO BY ALAN BARTOLIC

ing to director Kim Manners, David Duchovny gave them a run for their money. "As a matter of fact, David damn near outran those horses, he ran so fast" in the chase scene in 'Tunguska,' Manners marvels. "We used to try to dolly with David, or use the Steadicam, but you just can't do it—the man is really fast. So we built a camera rig with bicycle tires that our guys pull in front of David—it's the only way we can keep up with him."

But how do you train for being hung from a tall building? You don't. But you make damn sure you're secured by several strong cables before you try it.

For the scene in "Terma" in which rogue agent Alex Krycek dangles over the balcony of Assistant Director Walter S. Skinner's apartment, actor Nicholas Lea decided that he'd rather perform the stunt himself than have a double do it for him. "When it came time to do the scene, we had built a little platform for him [for him to stand on]," special effects coordinator Dave Gauthier recalls. "He went out there and got used to it, and he did a couple of shots with the platform in place.

"Then at the end of the day, it's raining, it's cold, and now we want to take the platform away and we want him to hang off the balcony, 16 stories high, with nothing underneath him," Gauthier continues. "He was very securely attached to the building by a harness, by cables and by every means we had to hold him up there, but still and all, it doesn't matter. When you take everything away, and you have to step into nothingness and hang from a cable, you're trusting your entire life on that piece of cable. I held Nick's hands as I let him down in the cable, and he said [in a grim whisper], 'Okay, I'm ready.' And I stepped back, and they shot, shot, shot the scene, then I heard Nick's voice saying, 'Get me out of here!' The shot ended up looking fantastic, and I take my hat off to him—I don't know if I could have done that. It took a lot of courage."

Lea wasn't the only one who was potentially in harm's way during the making of the two-parter. In one of the concluding sequences of "Terma," Mulder finally finds the missing interstellar rock, only to find that it's been lodged in the innards of a

gushing oil well. After trying to release the rock, he realizes that a van parked next to the oil well is about to explode, and the FBI agent barely escapes with his life.

"Rob Bowman wanted to have David in the shot, right beside the explosion," Dave Gauthier explains. "So I planned the explosion in such a way that I could get a person very close to it, running away, and make it look a lot bigger than it really was, and still keep it safe.

"To produce that effect, in the van we had about 200 gallons of gasoline prepped in a special way to make it explode, as well as mortars and about 700 meters of explosive cord, in order to completely annihilate the back of the van and create a huge fireball," he continues. "At the same time, we had to make the oil—which was essentially black water—gush 200 feet in the air, so we had a high-pressure pump to make that happen. For the explosion, [what was coming out of the pump] changed from 'oil' to 2,000 gallons of propane and 1,000 gallons of kerosene mixed together, and at that moment, we blew up the van. We did all that in one take."

"When there's [a big action scene] like that, David's great—he listens to instructions very well," he adds. "It was pretty tense. When someone says to you, 'Okay, just walk up to that car, and when you walk away, I'm going to make it explode,' well, you've gotta have some trust there."

As far as Kim Manners is concerned, though, the mythology episodes offer more than just the chance to direct high-impact action scenes. "There's more characterization involved in mythology shows, so Gillian and David and the other players

have more performance to bring to the roles," he offers. "It's not just Mulder and Scully chasing down leads. It's not just a flashlight show where Scully's going, 'Gee Mulder, I don't know if this is possible,' [and Mulder says] 'Believe me, Scully, it's possible.' It's not a mutant-of-the-week show—the actors have more to work with."

Not only do the actors get to add new depth to their characters, the directors also enjoy raising the stakes in their friendly rivalry. "I have to say 'Tunguska' was just an

THE Rat's BACK

On the Internet, he's Ratboy. But actor Nicholas Lea, who plays *The X-Files*, Alex Krycek, has another nickname for himself: the Everlast bag.

He has a point—the double-crossing Krycek seemed to get a serious body blow every few minutes during "Tunguska." "I've never finished a job and felt like I needed a holiday, but I did on this one," says Lea.

And the physical challenges didn't stop there. At one point during the filming of "Tunguska," the actor hung suspended by a cable from the top of a 16-storey building. "I won't try to kid you, it was pretty frightening," he recalls. "When I got there, they had a platform for me to stand on. They were going to shoot me down to the knees, so it would look like I was hanging there, but you wouldn't be able to see my feet. I said, 'You should be able to see my feet there so people know I'm really hanging.' So they took the platform away, and we did it that way."

Soon after that stunt, the actor met John Neville (The Well-Manicured Man) for the first time; according to Lea, Neville said, "'Oh, you're Nick Lea. I heard you'll do anything.'"

Whether or not Lea will do anything is open to question, but it certainly seems that his alter-ego Krycek will stop at nothing to get what he wants. Yet even Lea isn't certain about what motivates the character. "I think that he's driven by a certain degree of vengeance," he offers. "There's a speech I had in 'Tunguska' where I said, 'All I want is to find the man who tried to kill me,' and I think he really believes that."

Whatever Krycek's motivations are these days, he's no longer the fresh-faced agent recruited by Cigarette-Smoking Man to spy on Mulder and Scully. "He started out as a covert agent," Lea notes, "and then became more or less a free agent just trying to keep himself alive. And now it seems that he's possibly working for the Russians. Physically and mentally, he's undergone some big changes.

"When I did my first three [episodes], 'Sleepless,' 'Duane Barry' and 'Ascension,'" the actor continues, "I pretty much just went with the story that was available: he was young guy, fresh out of the [FBI] Academy, who was chosen to infiltrate [the X-Files]. But the story tends to change, so I kind of go with what I have at the time."

Despite his character's duplicitous ways, Lea doesn't think that Krycek is "as cold-hearted as he appears to be. But I do think that he'll do whatever it takes to stay alive and to get done what he has to do."

One of the things that Lea had to do during the making of "Tunguska" was learn a lot of Russian dialogue, a chore he doesn't recall with much pleasure. "It was brutal to learn—it's a language with no connection to English at all. And it takes three or four Russian sentences to say one short English sentence." In the end, he adds ruefully, a lot of that dialogue eventually got axed.

Yet Lea, who will be seen next fall in several countries (but not the U.S.) on the syndicated TV series *Once a Thief*, enjoyed making "Tunguska"— even when things got a little ugly. "I have a great time [on the *X-Files* set,]" he enthuses. "Whenever I hear I'm going to be in an episode, I can't wait to get there. Those people are all my friends, and David [Duchovny] is a very good friend of mine, and Mitch [Pileggi] as well. It's really [a case of] getting beaten up by your friends."—*M.R.*

incredible chapter in the mythology arc— the production and script and the direction were all top-notch," enthuses Rob Bowman. "After seeing 'Tunguska' on the air, I remember thinking, 'I don't know if "Terma" is this good.' Kim and I are good friends, [but] I think we've got a good healthy competition going. It makes us both better." ●

EPISODE GUIDE

4.8: "TUNGUSKA" (PART ONE OF TWO) Episode #4X08
Original US tx 24 November 96 Original UK tx 9 March 97

HONOLULU; QUEENS,
NEW YORK CITY; HERNDON, VIRGINIA;
GODDARD, MARYLAND;
TUNGUSKAN FOREST, RUSSIA and
WASHINGTON, DC

At a hearing of the Senate Select Subcommittee on Intelligence and Terrorism, Scully is questioned over the whereabouts of agent Mulder. She risks her career by refusing to answer on the grounds that she may endanger Mulder's life. She reads instead from a prepared statement in which she damns the "culture of lawlessness" which has made the carrying out of her duties as an FBI agent impossible. "Are you tendering your resignation?" one of the committee members asks her.

Ten days earlier, at Honolulu Airport, a man returning from the Republic of Georgia on "government business" is stopped and searched at customs. When his diplomatic pouch is opened and one of the containers inside exposed, a black substance enters the body of the customs official and appears to paralyse him.

Meanwhile, in the New York suburb of Queens, Mulder and Scully are raiding an industrial area, acting on a tip-off about illegal explosives. The vicious gun battle which ensues ends with the discovery that it was rogue former FBI agent Alex Krycek who tipped Mulder off about the "two thousand kilos of boom-boom" he implies was intended for the next Oklahoma City-style bombing. Krycek claims to have brought him the bust as a peace offering, since he and the agents want the same thing – to take down The Cigarette-Smoking Man. "You're an invertebrate scum-sucker whose moral dipstick is about two drops short of bone dry," Mulder says, but Krycek still has a few tricks up his sleeve.

He takes them to Dulles International Airport in Virginia, where Mulder and Scully attempt to intercept another diplomat on Krycek's advice; the man escapes, dropping a bag containing nothing more than a black rock. At NASA's Goddard Space Flight Center, however, the rock is thought to be a fragment of a meteorite four billion years old – a discovery which leads Mulder to the forests of Tunguska, Northern Siberia, with Krycek in tow...

Principal Credits

Created by	Chris Carter
Produced by	Ten-Thirteen Productions for Twentieth Century Fox TV
Executive Producers	Chris Carter, Howard Gordon, RW Goodwin
Producers	Joseph Patrick Finn, Kim Manners, Rob Bowman
Co-Producers	Vince Gilligan, Frank Spotnitz, Paul Rabwin
Consulting Producers	Ken Horton, James Wong & Glen Morgan
Music	Mark Snow

Episode Credits

Written by	Frank Spotnitz & Chris Carter
Directed by	Kim Manners

Special Agent Fox Mulder	David Duchovny
Special Agent Dr Dana Scully	Gillian Anderson
Assistant Director Walter S Skinner	Mitch Pileggi
Cigarette-Smoking Man	William B Davis
Alex Krycek	Nicholas Lea
Marita Covarrubias	Laurie Holden
Well-Manicured Man	John Neville
Agent Pendrell	Brendan Beiser
Dr Sacks	Malcolm Stewart
Stress Man	David Bloom
Chairman	Campbell Lane
Prisoner	Stefan Arngrim
Timothy Mayhew	Brent Stait

F.Y.I.
"Tunguska," the first part of the fourth season's first mythology story, signalled the triumphant return of Alex Krycek, last seen trapped in a hangar numbered '1013' at the end of last season's "Apocrypha."
"It's something that has been brewing from the end of the second season on," says co-writer Chris Carter, "which is the idea that this conspiracy to keep a secret the existence of extra-terrestrial life is a global and multinational conspiracy, and not just an American one. And there is another Cold War - a race to find the cure for an alien virus which is on the planet."
The first part of the "Tunguska"/"Terma" two-parter scored an unprecedented mid-season rating of 12.2/18 on its US premiere, and its UK video release gave Fox Home Entertainment its second fastest-selling X-Files video title, surpassed only by the very first feature-length release, *The Unopened File.*

Noteworthy Dialogue Transcript
SCULLY: "How'd you get involved with these men?"
KRYCEK: "They found me in North Dakota. They liberated me on a salvage hunt. Hey, you go underground, you've got to learn to live with the rats..."
MULDER: "I'm sure you had no trouble adapting."

Unexplained Plot Discrepancies
It is extremely unlikely, to say the least, that US customs officials would be so foolish as to open a diplomatic pouch being carried by a member of *any* government, let alone their own.

EPISODE GUIDE

4.9: "TERMA" (PART TWO OF TWO) Episode #4X09
Original US tx 1 December 96 Original UK tx 16 March 97

BOCA RATON, FLORIDA; ST PETERSBURG, RUSSIA; TUNGUSKAN FOREST, RUSSIA; GREENBELT, MARYLAND;
RICHMOND and CHARLOTTESVILLE, VIRGINIA; NEW YORK CITY; ALBERTA, CANADA; and WASHINGTON, DC

At a convalescent home in Florida, a terminally ill elderly woman has a voluntary encounter with a surgeon who administers a fatal injection in order to give her a peaceful death. No sooner has she passed away, however, than the 'black cancer' infecting her body emerges... Meanwhile, in St Petersburg, a retired Soviet assassin named Poskaw receives a message from a man calling himself Comrade Arntzen, telling him that the Cold War is not yet over. A few hundred miles north, Mulder languishes in the gulag in which he is being experimented upon, exposed to the extra-terrestrial black cancer at the hands of his mysterious Russian torturers – and their collaborator, Alex Krycek...

Back at NASA's Goddard Space Center in Maryland, Scully continues to examine the scientist 'frozen' by the cancer's infestation. Later, she is questioned by Skinner, who is about to face a Senate Select Subcommittee on Intelligence and Terrorism hearing over the intercepted diplomatic pouch containing the mysterious rock from which the cancer sprung. Skinner is trying to find a connection between the pouch and the murder of the woman it was intended for, a well-known virologist and smallpox expert named Dr Carne-Sayre.

At the ranch where the doctor was murdered, The Cigarette-Smoking Man meets with Well-Manicured Man, advising him to call off the Congressional hearing set for the following day, and informing him that Mulder has escaped his captors in Tunguska. "Wake the Russian bear and he may find we've stolen his honey," he says with a wry smile.

With Mulder looking for a way home, and Scully facing the hearing without him, Krycek encounters a group of one-armed thugs in the Tunguskan forest. Bandits who want to make him one of their own...

F.Y.I.
One only has to look at the vast number of locations and enormous cast list for this episode to have some idea of the scale of the "Tunguska"/"Terma" two-parter. For all the many and varied scenes included, however, actor William B Davis recently told this magazine that at least one scene wound up on the cutting room floor. "We actually shot *three* scenes," he explained. "In the first one, [Well-Manicured Man] had summoned me to his ranch, and we had this spooky scene in which he had found that stuff was going on and told me to fix it. The second scene was me reporting to him on what he had sent me to do, and then the third scene was when he was [about to] take the whole thing public through Sorenson's committee, and I was challenging him that that was a stupid idea. They may just have decided that that was a plot twist they didn't need."

During shooting, an explosion rigged to go off behind the actor at the oil refinery accidentally set the back of his jacket alight. "I'm running from this big explosion," he said just after the incident, "and when [it] happens, I realise there's a fire on my ass! I turned around [and] there was this huge fireball. I was like, 'I could *die* doing this!'"

On its initial US broadcast, "Terma" scored a Nielsen rating of 10.16/15, equating approximately 15 million viewers in ten million homes.

Noteworthy Dialogue Transcript
MULDER: "I'm not going to die."
PRISONER: "No? Why not?"
MULDER: "I have to live long enough to kill that man – Krycek."

Principal Credits
Created by	Chris Carter
Produced by	Ten Thirteen Productions for Twentieth Century Fox TV
Executive Producers	Chris Carter, Howard Gordon, RW Goodwin
Producers	Joseph Patrick Finn, Kim Manners, Rob Bowman
Co-Producers	Vince Gilligan, Frank Spotnitz, Paul Rabwin
Consulting Producers	Ken Horton, James Wong & Glen Morgan
Music	Mark Snow

Episode Credits
Written by	Frank Spotnitz & Chris Carter
Directed by	Rob Bowman

Special Agent Fox Mulder	David Duchovny
Special Agent Dr Dana Scully	Gillian Anderson
Assistant Director Walter S Skinner	Mitch Pileggi
The Cigarette-Smoking Man	William B Davis
Alex Krycek/'Comrade Arntzen'	Nicholas Lea
Well-Manicured Man	John Neville
Prisoner	Stefan Arngrim
Vassily Peskow	Jan Rubes
Senator Sorenson	Fritz Weaver
Terry Edward Mayhew	Brent Stait
Dr Sacks	Malcolm Stewart
Chairman [Senator Romine]	Campbell Lane
Dr Kingsley Looker	Robin Mossley
Auntie Janet	Brenda McDonald
Nurse	Pamela MacDonald
Angie	Eileen Pedde
Dr Bonita Carne-Sayre	Jessica Schreier

THE CONSPIRACY - CLONING

Gene Genies

THE X FILES

We look back on five years of government propaganda, to find the truth behind *The X-Files'* mysterious cloning program.

C ast your mind back. A biogenetics project to create the ultimate soldier stretching back more than 40 years leads Mulder and Scully to investigate one of their most bizarre cases yet – killer clones in the shape of two sweet and innocent-looking eight-year-old girls.

Mulder's mysterious informant, Deep Throat, explains how the Litchfield Project – a top secret program dating back to the 50's – attempted to create prototypes of humans, both physically and mentally superior to normal people. Identical boys known as Adam and identical girls named Eve were 'born.' Their extra chromosomes not only gave them heightened strength and intelligence, but also turned them into psychotic killers.

"Eve" was *The X-Files'* first attempt at a cloning story. It wasn't part of the show's ongoing conspiracy storyline which dominates the series but the episode was nevertheless very much within the bailiwick of *The X-Files* – and a terrific episode to boot.

Cloning evokes age-old science fiction stories and has been as much a part of science fiction lore as time loss and alien implants. While the extraterrestrial theme is undoubtedly the backbone of the show, it is the twists of the government conspiracies and cover-ups that have kept us glued to the show for almost five years.

In seasons one's finale, "The Erlenmeyer Flask" – the first real government paranoia show – writer Chris Carter delivers a shocking first piece of the puzzle. In a project code named 'Purity Control,' we discover that the government has cloned extraterrestrial DNA recovered from alien embryos and are injecting an alien virus into terminally ill humans. As a result, not only do the subjects regain complete good health, but they become stronger than they originally were. The government's aim, it seems, is to create alien-human hybrids.

Mulder's obsession with the paranormal stems from his sister's abduction some 20 years previously. The story develops further in the second season two-parter, "Colony" and "End Game." The Samantha storyline takes a dramatic twist with the reappearance of an adult Samantha (or so we think) and the emergence of a new thread – the secret colonization of Earth by aliens.

BY KATE ANDERSON

Scully meets the women of the MUFON group – her fellow abductees are all suffering from the same cancer as Scully

Events in "Colony" hark back to previous episodes, particularly "The Erlenmeyer Flask." The story begins with Mulder close to death, comatose and suffering from hypothermia, and Scully desperately trying to save him. We learn that two weeks earlier, a strange light hovering above the Arctic Circle crashed into the sea and a survivor was recovered from the craft. Shortly afterwards, Mulder is alerted to a spate of murders of identical-looking men – all of them doctors from abortion clinics across the country. Whilst trying to locate the next victim, a fellow agent dies in the process, his blood having been curdled by some kind of virus.

In the process of their investigation, Mulder and Scully are confronted by an agent from the CIA, Ambrose Chapel. He tells them about a race of clones, developed in the Soviet Union using special DNA properties discovered in identical twins. A program based on that technology, code-named 'Gregor' (which was the name given to each of the clones) was undertaken and several of the Gregors, programmed to serve as spies, managed to obtain strategic positions in the medical establishment. In the event of war, they planned to sabotage blood supplies and pharmaceutical factories, which would effectively cripple the US.

But the abortion doctors are now considered too dangerous to be kept alive. They are being eliminated by a bounty hunter capable of shape-shifting his appearance, who has been sent to destroy the colony. Chapel claims that the government is sanctioning these murders. But little do Mulder and Scully realize that the CIA agent is in fact another shape-shifter – casting doubt on his story.

During their investigation, the story takes a dramatic and intriguing twist. Mulder's father calls, requesting to see his son urgently. It seems that a woman has turned up at the family home, claiming to be his long lost sister, Samantha. And she brings with her a shocking and surprising revelation.

"There are clones living in virtually every

part of the country," explains Samantha. "It's their belief that [human] stewardship of the planet is being forsaken; that by default they will someday become the natural heirs."

She further explains that the attempt to create alien-human hybrids is a move to rid the aliens of their identical appearances. But the experiment wasn't sanctioned by alien authorities. "It was considered dilution of [the] species, a pollution of [the] race."

But in the best X-Files tradition, nothing is as it seems. Mulder's sister is revealed to be an impostor – or rather a 'Gregor,' one of many clones whose physical features were supplied by DNA taken from the real Samantha Mulder during her abduction. At an abortion clinic, Mulder comes face-to-face with the other Samantha clones. They claim to need his help – and that they know where his sister is. But before Mulder can get any more information out of them, the bounty hunter turns up and knocks him unconscious, before turning the laboratory into a blazing inferno.

Mulder becomes more desperate than ever – having come so close to the truth about his sister's abduction. His somewhat reluctant informant, X, tells Mulder that the clones are all dead but that the bounty hunter is still alive. X warns Mulder off the case, telling him it's

Secret cloning labs have been seen twice in the series: "The Erlenmeyer Flask" and "Memento Mori" (pictured)

one battle he cannot win. But undeterred, Mulder pursues the alien bounty hunter to the Arctic, knowing too well that he may have a clue to his sister's whereabouts.

The appearance of Samantha's clones in "Colony" and "End Game" suggests that she is alive, but we do not know where. Still, her return instigates some shocking and disturbing revelations about Mulder's family, particularly his father's involvement in her disappearance. Yet again, Mulder is presented with his Holy Grail, only to lose it for a second and third time.

In "Talitha Cumi" and "Herrenvolk" (the third season finale and the fourth season opener respectively), the shape shifters and the clones return as more cover-ups and conspiracy threads are thrown into the pot. The theme touched upon in the "Colony" and "End Game" two-parter of alien colonization is once again examined.

The story begins when a gunman runs amok at a fast food restaurant. A mysterious man appears and heals the wounds of several shooting victims. By the time Mulder and Scully arrive, he has disappeared. In fact, he turns out to be a shape-shifter, just like the alien bounty hunter, called Jeremiah Smith. Dissatisfied with 'The Project,' he has been living among humans but the incident at the fast food restaurant threatens to expose his existence – to the alien bounty hunter and the Cigarette-Smoking Man – and also risks exposing a conspiracy involving the presence of aliens on Earth. Apparently, the nefarious Cigarette-Smoking Man is working closely with the aliens in preparation for the day of colonization. And the date has been set.

Mulder and Scully discover that Jeremiah Smith – and five other clones – are working in social security offices around the country, collecting genetic information about millions of Americans. They are all linked to the same government secret project involving the cloning of Samantha and a colony of bees engineered to carry the smallpox virus.

Smith leads Mulder to a farm in Canada where fields of strange plants are being grown for their pollen. The farm is tended by a child workforce – clones of a young boy, and of a young girl who looks just like a young Samantha Mulder. "She has no language," Smith tells Mulder. "She is just a drone, a worker." We learn that the clones of Samantha were bred for the first stage of the colonization project – a project which also seems to involve the bees.

Despite Mulder's efforts, his sister (or the clone of her) is taken from him for a second time and all evidence of the colony – and thus proof of the conspiracy – is destroyed. But just as more secrets are revealed, so are more lies... Mulder discovers that his mother knows more about his father's involvement in the project and, perhaps even more shocking, Mrs Mulder and the Cigarette-Smoking Man seem to be much more than just acquaintances. We also

The bounty hunter demonstrates the alien hybrid clones' ability to miraculously heal – saving the life of Mrs Mulder in the process

Another clone of Samantha Mulder is revealed in "Herrenvolk"

ble onto evidence of a top secret breeding experiment and discover that Scully's cancer is also linked to fertility drugs and treatments. They discover her ova – and those from other female abductees – at a facility where the natural order of life is being drastically altered: a laboratory where alien-human clones are being created.

At the clinic, Mulder encounters the presence of multiple, cloned Kurt Crawfords. They tell Mulder that Scully and the MUFON women were used in horrific alien-human hybridisation experiments and that they are in fact the 'sons' of Scully and other female abductees. It soon becomes evident that the embryos from different women were artificially implanted with genetic material.

It isn't until the fifth season two-parter, "Christmas Carol" and "Emily," that the fate of Scully's stolen ova is revealed.

Celebrating Christmas with her family, Scully is summoned by a mysterious phone call – seemingly from her dead sister Melisssa – to a house where a woman has recently committed suicide, leaving behind her husband and a three-year-old daughter, Emily. Suspicious, Scully soon discovers that the suicide was actually a murder; the husband is arrested under suspicion of being the killer, but is himself killed by two unknown men.

Having found out that Emily was adopted, Scully comes to believe that she is Melissa's daughter – only to find to her shock that DNA tests prove Emily to be her own child. She is also distressed to discover that Emily is suffering from a rare disease for which she has been receiving experimental treatment from the sinister Dr Calderon of Transgen Pharmaceuticals – and it seems that her mother's murder occurred when she threatened to cease Emily's treatment.

Emily has a green cyst on the back of her neck which, when pierced, emits a toxic gas very similar in effect to that emitted by the clones from "Colony" and "End Game." Suddenly, it is clear that Emily is not only a product of the ova stolen during Scully's abduction, but also a clone or alien hybrid of some sort – perhaps not dissimilar to the Kurt clones of "Memento Mori," although born a baby rather than a full-grown adult as they were.

When Mulder joins the investigation, the horrible truth begins to emerge. Dr Calderon is himself a clone, who is murdered by two of his fellows – both of whom then use shapeshifting abilities to assume his appearance. Following 'Calderon', Mulder discovers that some of the

ova stolen from women such as Scully have been grown into embryos, then implanted into the bodies of the elderly female residents of a convalescent home – Mulder finds Emily's surrogate mother there, along with a further live embryo that appears to be another product of Scully's ova. But the children born this way aren't physically healthy – they may have been deliberately infected with a terminal disease – hence the 'treatments' that Dr Calderon administers, treatments that seem to actually hasten Emily's death.

Scully chooses to end the painful experimentation, allowing Emily to die peacefully – but the agents are once again left without evidence, as even Emily's body is stolen from its coffin.

After nearly five years of investigation, we are still no closer to a clear truth behind the genetic experimentation we have witnessed in the programme. What seems certain is that both the 'colonists' and the conspiracy have an equal stake in the experiments' outcome, and that the sinister machinations behind them spell serious trouble for the human race.

Additional material by Rebecca Levene and David Bailey.

learn that any clones who question the project are eliminated by the mysterious bounty hunter, and that these hybrid clones may also be part of the plan to introduce alien DNA into the human population.

To a great extent, over the course of four seasons, the story of the abducted Samantha and the apparent involvement of the Mulder family in the increasingly obscure and at times confusing conspiracy, has been pivotal to the plot. But in the gut-wrenching fourth season episode "Memento Mori," Mulder unearths a chilling connection between Scully's abduction and more cloning experiments.

Searching for a cure for Scully's recently diagnosed terminal cancer, the agents investigate the MUFON abductees first encountered in season three's "Nisei." Upon arriving at the home of one of the group's members, they discover that someone is remotely accessing the woman's computer files via a modem. When they track down the hacker, Kurt Crawford, he claims to be retrieving the files to prevent the government from obtaining them. While Scully begins treatment for her illness, Mulder and Crawford find another link between the members of the MUFON group. It appears that all of the women underwent treatment at a fertility clinic. Mulder and the Lone Gunman stum-

Scully discovers the devastating effects of her abduction

EPISODE GUIDE

THE X FILES™

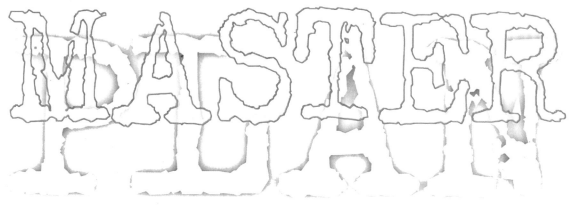

We give you the lowdown on two of the most significant episodes in *The X-Files* mythos. Prepare to have all your preconceptions shattered...

3.24: "TALITHA CUMI" Episode #3X24

Original US tx 17 May 96 Original UK tx 13 August 96

QUONOCHONTUAG, RHODE ISLAND

A troubled gunman goes beserk in a fast-food restaurant, leaving several people dead or dying from gunshot wounds. Yet by the time agents Mulder and Scully arrive on the scene, a mysterious individual has apparently 'healed' the wounds before disappearing into the crowd. The mystery healer turns out to be one of five clones named Jeremiah Smith, each sharing a resemblance and an identity, and each working at social security offices across the country.

Principal Credits

Produced by	Ten-Thirteen Productions for 20th Century Fox TV
Creator and Executive Producer	Chris Carter
Co-Executive Producers	Howard Gordon, R W Goodwin
Producers	Joseph Patrick Finn, Kim Manners, Rob Bowman
	Paul Rabwin
	Mark Snow
Co-Producer	Chris Carter
Music	Chris Carter

Episode Credits

Teleplay by	David Duchovny & Chris Carter
Story by	David Duchovny & Chris Carter
Directed by	R W Goodwin

Special Agent Fox Mulder	David Duchovny
Special Agent Dana Scully	Gillian Anderson
Assistant Director Walter S Skinner	Mitch Pileggi
The Cigarette-Smoking Man	William B Davis
Jeremiah as William Mulder	Peter Donat
Jeremiah as Deep Throat	Jerry Hardin
Jeremiah Smith	Roy Thinnes
The Alien Bounty Hunter	Brian Thompson
Door Man	Angelo Vacco
'X'	Steven Williams
Galen Muntz	Hrothgar Mathews
Mrs Mulder	Rebecca Toolan
Detective	Stephen Dimopoulos
Doctor	John MacLaren
Paramedic	Cam Cronin
Night Nurse	Bonnie Hay

Meanwhile, Mulder is informed by 'X' that his mother has suffered a stroke following an encounter with The Cigarette-Smoking Man at the family's summer house on Rhode Island. Mulder races to her bedside, but is equally desperate to uncover the truth about Smith, who has been captured and incarcerated by the cancerous conspirator. The latter reminds him that he must not use his powers to divert attention from humankind's belief in authority. "They must never believe any differently if the Project is to go forward," he says...

Above: Scenes from "Talitha Cumi"

EPISODE GUIDE

F.Y.I.

While there is much to surprise and delight in "Talitha Cumi," the third season cliffhanger, the highlight is surely the inspired casting of Roy Thinnes – who hunted aliens throughout the 1960s in Quinn Martin's TV classic *The Invaders* – as an alien himself. In addition, his character, Jeremiah Smith, further delighted X-Philes by morphing into the ghosts of those The Cigarette-Smoking Man has had killed for his "higher purpose" – Deep Throat and Bill Mulder. "Morphing is morphing," says visual effects supervisor Mat Beck, for whom "Talitha Cumi" was his final bow for the show. "The trick is to do something different with it. With that shot, it was the same guy in the same suit, and only the face was changing – that makes it harder, of course, because you can't be morphing the suit as well. So basically it was like the old undertaker joke, where we just kept the same suit and swapped heads!" The scene is strongly reminiscent of the 'grand inquisitor' sequence of Fyodor Dostoyevskey's classic novel *The Brothers Karamazov*, and the source was briefly credited in the name of the restaurant, Brothers K.

The Alien Bounty Hunter in "Herrenvolk"

In the New Testament, Jesus uses the phrase "Talitha Cumi" to raise a girl from the dead – it literally translates from ancient Aramaic (the language spoken in Israel during Jesus' time) as "Maiden, I say unto thee, arise!"

X-Phile numerologists will notice that Mulder arrives at the hospital to see his mother at 11:21pm, another reference to Chris Carter's wife's birthday (21 November) in US date format (ie. 11/21).

Noteworthy Dialogue Transcript

JEREMIAH [as DEEP THROAT]: "How many must die at your hand to preserve your stake in the project?"
THE CIGARETTE-SMOKING MAN: "I'm not impressed by your miracles or moved by your trickery. Your justice will be meted out."
JEREMIAH [as DEEP THROAT]: "By whom this time? And by what tool?"
THE CIGARETTE-SMOKING MAN: "By those who possess the tool of your destruction."

Unexplained Plot Discrepancies

The logic leap by which Mulder anagrams his mother's message 'PALM' into 'LAMP' is quite a stretch of the imagination even for him – maybe he reads *Celebrity Skin* for the crossword after all.

4.1: "HERRENVOLK (PART TWO OF TWO)" Episode #4X01

Original US tx 4 October 96 Original UK tx scheduled for Spring 97

RURAL MARYLAND and RHODE ISLAND

A telephone engineer is stung by a bee, shortly before he encounters five identical-looking boys; moments after the boys arrive, he has fallen to his death from a telephone pole.

Elsewhere in Maryland, the Alien Bounty Hunter has come to kill Jeremiah Smith, using the special weapon effective against his kind. Mulder stabs the bounty hunter in the neck with the same device and escapes with Jeremiah, unwittingly leaving Scully with the killer. She manages to escape her abductor, who is clearly more interested in the whereabouts of Jeremiah, and begins to investigate the five social security officers who resemble the mysterious healer.

Meanwhile, Mulder begs Jeremiah to save his mother, who lies comatose in a Rhode Island hospital following her stroke. Together, they drive until they are out of gas, then walk until they discover the body of the telephone engineer, badly decomposed despite possessing a work order that shows he has only been dead a single day. Suddenly, Mulder sees something that makes him question whether the heat has affected his judgement. Down in the valley before them is an extensive network of greenhouses, and tending the crops in one of these is a girl who looks exactly like his sister Samantha did on the day she was abducted. He calls to her, but she cannot answer. "She has no language," Jeremiah tells him. "She is just a drone, a worker." They are interrupted by the arrival of the bounty hunter, who they manage to lure to a stinging encounter with a swarm of bees...

In Washington, 'X' tells Scully that Mulder's mother needs protection. But is he acting – consciously or unwittingly – as a cipher for information from The Cigarette-Smoking Man?

EPISODE GUIDE

Principal Credits

Produced by
Ten-Thirteen Productions for
20th Century Fox TV

Executive Producer	Chris Carter
Executive Producers	Howard Gordon, R W Goodwin
Producers	Joseph Patrick Finn, Kim Manners, Rob Bowman
Consulting Producers	Ken Horton, James Wong and Glen Morgan
Co-Producers	Vince Gilligan, Frank Spotnitz, Paul Rabwin
Music	Mark Snow

Episode Credits

Written by	Chris Carter
Directed by	R W Goodwin

Special Agent Fox Mulder	David Duchovny
Special Agent Dana Scully	Gillian Anderson
Assistant Director Walter S Skinner	Mitch Pileggi
The Cigarette-Smoking Man	William B Davis
Jeremiah Smith	Roy Thinnes
The Alien Bounty Hunter	Brian Thompson
'X'	Steven Williams
Samantha clone	Vanessa Morley
Gray Haired Man	Morris Panych
Mrs Mulder	Rebecca Toolan
Agent Pendrell	Brendan Bleiser
Repairman	Garvin Cross
2nd Senior Agent	Ken Camroux
Elder	Don S Williams
Senior Agent	Michael David Simms

Noteworthy Dialogue Transcript

MULDER: "Samantha? Samantha? Samantha, it's me, Fox, your brother. Do you remember me?"

F.Y.I.

After an extended May to October summer hiatus, ratings for *The X-Files* fourth season premiere broke records for the show and for Fox Television in the US. With 21 million households tuning in, Fox scored its highest Friday night ever, beating the network's previous best – *The X-Files'* third season premiere...

"The season premiere is a big show," David Duchovny told US newspaper *USA Today*. "We shot so much film for it, I'm not sure we haven't already made *The X-Files* film. We've got aliens, bees, clones, bounty hunters and shapeshifters all in the premiere episode. And I get beaten up a number of times, too."

In a surprise move, some of this episode was shot outside Vancouver in a small town an hour's flight away called Kamloops. As Chris Carter explains: "It gives us a nice look that we wouldn't get otherwise. It's something that we, in year four, have the luxury of doing... We can only do things like that at the beginning or the end of the year because it's a very tight schedule. It's really a river valley, golden rolling hills, and it's got a big blue sky. You can get the big blue sky in Vancouver this time of year, but you can't get those rolling hills [and] the spacious panoramas."

Once again, the opening credo is changed, this time to read 'EVERYTHING DIES.'

Among the new names on the credits are Associate Producer Lori Jo Nemhauser and Production Manager George Chapman; another newcomer, Ron Stannett, is credited as Director of Photography. However, as reported elsewhere this issue, he left a short way into filming and was replaced by Jon Joffin.

Roy Thinnes can be seen reprising his most famous role, alien hunter David Vincent, co-starring with *Quantum Leap* star Scott Bakula, in a new telemovie based on the 1960s series *The Invaders*. Brian Thompson, who has so effectively portrayed The Alien Bounty Hunter since the second season story "Colony," can be seen opposite Dennis Quaid and David Thewlis in Rob Cohen's fantasy frolic *Dragonheart*.

Mulder with the clone of his sister Samantha (above and above right) and with Jeremiah Smith (right)

THE (X) FILES

The Diau Fru

By Mo Ryan

Mulder and Scully are haunted by old friends and new mysteries in an epic two-parter

SCENE 1

SETTING: *The black, black night sky*

"Moonless, but with a billion stars a twinkle; no greater antiquity exists... Suddenly, a commercial jet enters frame. It is at an altitude high above us, moving with deceiving slowness and leaving two thin, white contrails behind it. The faint, distorted sound of its engines trailing it, too; sub-freezing temperatures amplifying it into a kind of lonely roar... Making us think that 30,000 feet above us there are passengers who have made a death-defying gamble, who have taken a leap of faith in man and machine... while denying the horrible fact that one slight malfunction in its thousands of moving parts, or one small human error might cause them to plummet to earth at a rate of speed so great that the impact would reduce them and their aircraft into a billion pieces no more comprehensible than the stars above."

tempus fugit
max

episode spotlight

Most X-Philes never get the chance to read passages like that — those are the words on the opening page of "Tempus Fugit," the first segment of a two-part episode that re-introduced fans to UFO follower Max Fenig. Reading the evocative passage that opens the two-part drama, one realizes that "Tempus Fugit" and "Max" are not just new chapters in the show's mythology. Like all great episodes of *The X-Files*, the two-parter makes us ponder the startling ways in which the fragility of human life can be suddenly brought into sharp relief; it makes us realize that even the most misbegotten and wayward lives are precious.

For those reasons, Frank Spotnitz, who co-wrote both episodes with Chris Carter, finds it difficult to classify "Tempus Fugit" and "Max" as pure mythology episodes, which usually involve revelations regarding government knowledge of an alien presence on earth. "I think this two-parter was very unusual for us because it was the first one we've done that was really not a mythology show at all [in the sense that] there's no Cigarette-Smoking Man, there's no syndicate or any of those characters, like **Marita** Covarrubias or X or Deep Throat," Spotnitz says.

Indeed, though the two-parter showcased **some** of the most intense action seen

so far in the series, "Max" director Kim Manners felt that the show's emotional resonance outweighed its sinister elements. The scripts were "very eerie, especially because we fly so much back and forth to L.A. on 737s," Manners says.

And that's the reason the show hit so close to home, says *X-Files* writer and story editor John Shiban. "An airplane trip is so universal," he notes. "Everybody's been in that position—you can empathize with the fear [of a crash], and that's getting people where they live, which I think makes for a much scarier show. You could have set that episode on a military transport and it would have been a much different episode. I think Frank and Chris were right on the nose when they made it [a commercial flight]. If [a setting is] familiar, then the paranormal element is 10 times more effective."

At the beginning of the writing process, Spotnitz says, he and Chris Carter "knew we wanted something with Max and an airplane crash, and that was all." One of Spotnitz and Carter's first decisions involved the method of re-introducing Max, who had made his first appearance in Season One's "Fallen Angel." "I actually thought I was pretty brave—or foolish—to kill Max [right away]," muses Spotnitz. "One thing I don't want the show to do as it gets mature is to rest on its laurels, or start saying to the audience, 'You remember how much you liked this guy back in Season One? Well, here he is again.' I don't want to start recycling our past strengths.

"I thought an interesting and daring way to use Max would be to bring him back and kill him," the writer continues. "You found out he was definitely dead by the end of Act One of 'Tempus Fugit,' which was an unexpected move, I would hope. It was [a case of] using the audience's good feelings toward that character. For those members of the audience that have been with us that long, we were using [Max's death] to dramatize what it feels like to lose somebody in a plane crash; [we also] made that a personal event for Mulder, and invested him in the story in that way."

Spotnitz's main concern was to update Max's story and follow the investigation of the plane crash without revealing too much too soon. As Mulder and Scully looked into the crash of Flight 549, Max receded into the background but remained a prime motivator for the investigators, who were genuinely shaken by the flighty UFO buff's death. "It wasn't until Act Two of 'Max' that we reconstructed what you saw in the teaser of 'Tempus Fugit,' and then we moved the story on from there," Spotnitz explains. "We always try and come up with different ways

of telling these stories—we did it in a different way in "Tunguska" and "Terma," where we started the teaser with Scully before a Senate subcommittee and spun back in time and worked forward to that same moment in "Terma.'"

Once the writers decided on how to tell their story, the production personnel had to figure out how to build an outdoor plane crash site, an indoor crash-investigation area, an underwater alien ship and a few other odds and ends—like a fully movable Boeing 737 airliner. "This was the biggest damn thing I've ever shot in my life," says an incredulous Kim Manners. "Between ['Tempus Fugit' director] Rob Bowman and I, we shot for 28 full days. On *The X-Files*, you get that opportunity. Working on *The X-Files* is like going to Disneyland—you get the best rides in town."

When Manners talks about rides, he's not kidding. For the crucial Fenig abduction scene in "Max," and also for another airborne UFO encounter scene in that same episode, *X-Files* construction crews and special-effects personnel spent weeks constructing a large section of a plane, which sat atop movable, mechanized scaffolding. "The effects department built the hydraulic rig that went under the plane, and [construction] built the plane," explains construction chief Rob Maier.

Originally used for a sequence in "Teliko," the plane was emptied of all its interior decor and raised up to the ceiling of the sound stage while FX workers built computer-controlled, movable scaffolding that would control the plane's movement. After the plane segment was lowered onto the metal structure and rigged to look like a commercial aircraft again, Maier made sure the structure was strong enough to take a lot of shaking, rattling and rolling.

"We had to make it able to withstand the tremendous amount of use that it had to suffer during the next couple of weeks of filming," he notes. "There's actually a fine line between making it sturdy and allowing the plane to move. If it was too rigid, they'd really have to turn up the juice on the rig in order to get any movement out of it, but then [there's the danger] of the plane snapping."

Kim Manners will attest to the vigor with which the plane shook its passengers during the crash sequences. "I put helmets on the camera operators because the plane was so violent," the director says.

For three days, Manners and his crew shook, shimmied and shot passengers out of the ill-fated Boeing. "We strapped the extras

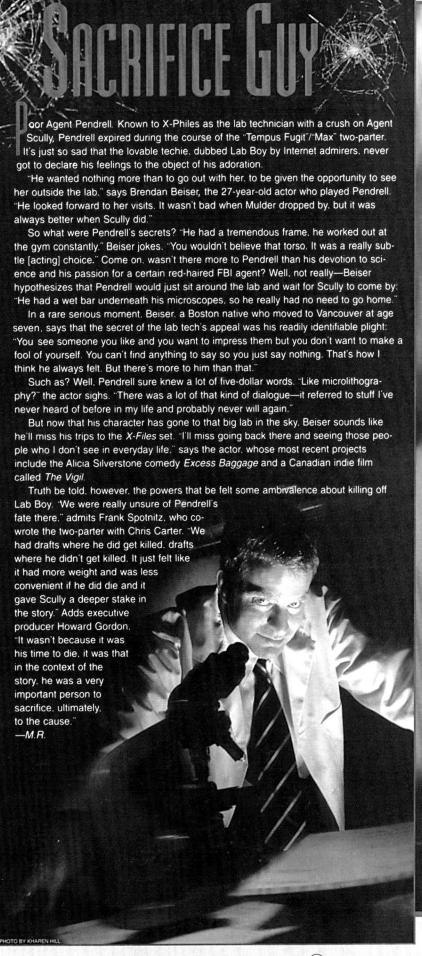

SACRIFICE GUY

Poor Agent Pendrell. Known to X-Philes as the lab technician with a crush on Agent Scully, Pendrell expired during the course of the "Tempus Fugit"/"Max" two-parter. It's just so sad that the lovable techie, dubbed Lab Boy by Internet admirers, never got to declare his feelings to the object of his adoration.

"He wanted nothing more than to go out with her, to be given the opportunity to see her outside the lab," says Brendan Beiser, the 27-year-old actor who played Pendrell. "He looked forward to her visits. It wasn't bad when Mulder dropped by, but it was always better when Scully did."

So what were Pendrell's secrets? "He had a tremendous frame, he worked out at the gym constantly," Beiser jokes. "You wouldn't believe that torso. It was a really subtle [acting] choice." Come on, wasn't there more to Pendrell than his devotion to science and his passion for a certain red-haired FBI agent? Well, not really—Beiser hypothesizes that Pendrell would just sit around the lab and wait for Scully to come by: "He had a wet bar underneath his microscopes, so he really had no need to go home."

In a rare serious moment, Beiser, a Boston native who moved to Vancouver at age seven, says that the secret of the lab tech's appeal was his readily identifiable plight: "You see someone you like and you want to impress them but you don't want to make a fool of yourself. You can't find anything to say so you just say nothing. That's how I think he always felt. But there's more to him than that."

Such as? Well, Pendrell sure knew a lot of five-dollar words. "Like microlithography?" the actor sighs. "There was a lot of that kind of dialogue—it referred to stuff I've never heard of before in my life and probably never will again."

But now that his character has gone to that big lab in the sky, Beiser sounds like he'll miss his trips to the *X-Files* set. "I'll miss going back there and seeing those people who I don't see in everyday life," says the actor, whose most recent projects include the Alicia Silverstone comedy *Excess Baggage* and a Canadian indie film called *The Vigil*.

Truth be told, however, the powers that be felt some ambivalence about killing off Lab Boy. "We were really unsure of Pendrell's fate there," admits Frank Spotnitz, who co-wrote the two-parter with Chris Carter. "We had drafts where he did get killed, drafts where he didn't get killed. It just felt like it had more weight and was less convenient if he did die and it gave Scully a deeper stake in the story." Adds executive producer Howard Gordon, "It wasn't because it was his time to die, it was that in the context of the story, he was a very important person to sacrifice, ultimately, to the cause."
—M.R.

in and jerked stunt people out the door—a lot of people thought that [people falling out of the plane] was done with CGI, but we actually did that [on the set]. They were in what we call a rachet system—it's a harness with a steel cable attached. We counted down, 3-2-1, and hit the switch and bang, they were gone. We just rocketed them out of there. And when we jerked them out of the plane, I put a [special] lens on the camera, so that they went about 40 feet, but because the lens was so wide, it looked like they got very small and then disappeared into the smoke."

There was also the matter of getting Max Fenig out of the plane—in a crucial Flight 549 sequence, he's mysteriously lifted out of the craft and conveyed to and from an alien ship. To get Fenig out of the plane, special effects coordinator Dave Gauthier came up with a rig involving a seat attached to a large crane. "We had Max sitting on a seat and we picked him up and floated him out. We had just the right amount of wind on him, and he ascended up to the lights," director Manners recalls. "The stage was all blacked out, and there was just enough smoke so that it looked like the [Earth's] atmosphere."

Max's unexpected journey went off without a hitch during filming, but Manners admits that prior to the episode's shoot, he had a few concerns about the extras who would be sharing the cabin with Fenig. "When you talk about extras, they're not actors by any stretch of the imagination. I needed 80 actors," he notes. "We had to put them on an airplane, strap them in and shake them for three days. If you suffer from motion sickness, you're in trouble, because it was a very violent ride. Then I needed to believe, when I shot the close-ups, that these were the last moments of their lives. A lot of actors can't make you believe that. They were great though. Lisa Ratke, our extras casting person, brought me 80 of the best extras I've ever worked with in my life. I think they were just really into it. They saw the effects that Dave Gauthier was creating and the effort the crew was making, and I think everybody just rose to the occasion—they were very caught up in the excitement of creating a totally believable film."

What Manners ended up with was an incredibly realistic crash sequence, one that skillfully and empathically conveyed both the terror and the violence of the passengers last moments. The director is justifiably proud of the last shot in the plane sequence: as the craft makes its doomed final descent, two passengers clasp their hands together across the plane's aisle.

Despite the poignance of that moment, Manners, ever the perfectionist, wasn't completely happy with how the shot turned out. "I don't know that it actually read the way I wanted it to read," he explains. "It was two mens' hands, a black man and a white man. I wanted to make a little social comment [but] I don't know if the public realized it was a black man holding a white man's hand."

Once the plane went down, however, its final resting place—or rather places—had to be depicted as well. Three crews in particular worked very hard to construct the widely scattered remains of Flight 459: Construction crews built portions of wreckage from crumpled aluminum sheeting; set decorators supplied most of the personal items and debris scattered through the crash site, and also imported an entire 737 tail section from

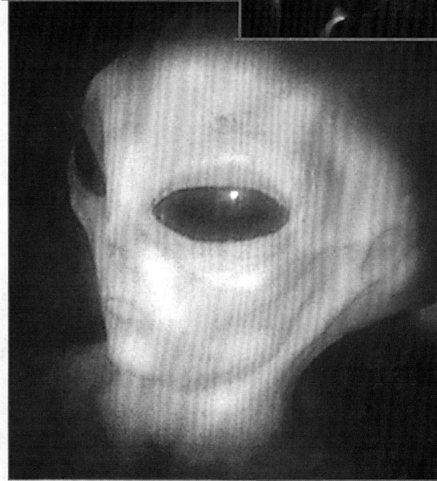

the United States; and greens crews burned portions of the site to give it that war-zone look. "We got all kinds of research photos from actual crash sites, and photos of when [rescue crews] first get there and start tagging it," Rob Maier says. "[We saw how] they mark it all off and collect body parts and put all the right body parts with the right person. We didn't want to gross people out, but we did depict some arms and legs up in trees, and there was a lot of luggage and clothing scattered around."

Creating the crash site was a huge job, but "Tempus Fugit's" demanding shooting schedule meant that it was done more than once. The day after the crash-site footage was shot, filming began at the airplane hangar in which the various parts of the craft were reconstructed by federal investigators. As Maier explains, "we took as many of the big pieces as we could, but we couldn't get every little piece over there quick enough, so we basically had to create two crashed planes."

Well, actually, three. Construction and FX crews also came up with the otherworldly wreckage that Mulder encounters in Great Sacandaga Lake. The alien-crash sequence was actually shot over several days, in a variety of different circumstances. First, the downed UFO was sunk into a tank, where close-ups of an alien's face and of the bizarre wreckage were shot. On another day, David Duchovny was shot diving down to the UFO and encountering bits of the alien ship as he got deeper into the lake (which was actually just the same tank again). Eventually, Duchovny—or rather his stunt double—was filmed encountering members of a Navy SEAL team, who aren't too pleased too see Mulder, since he's intruding on a hushhush recovery of the E.T.'s ship.

That last sequence, shot on a lake near Vancouver, was tough to film because, "it was cold, very cold," director Kim Manners remembers. "The two SEAL team guys were in drysuits, so they were pretty warm, but Mulder's stunt double was just in a [thin] wetsuit, and he was freezing. It was so cold we had to use two doubles—one guy did half a night, and the other guy did the other half. Then [on another day] we had to put David in the tank, and that was not easy. You're trying to communicate, he's underwater, he's got to swim into camera [frame], you've got to stay close enough to him to recognize him, but you've also got to get shots where he swims up [to the wreckage], and during all this, he's got lights in his eyes. It was very difficult."

If "Tempus Fugit" and "Max" had consisted of nothing but heart-pounding action and revelations about a nefarious government coverup... well, that wouldn't have been enough for X-Philes. They've come to expect resonant personal moments between characters—even if they come amidst mayhem and supernatural violence.

And the emotional center of this two-parter, according to Kim Manners, was the slightly goofy character who gave the second episode its name. "I think [Max] gave it a real heartfelt dimension," Manners says. "Max was such a favorite character, and when they showed 'Fallen Angel' the week before the two-parter, it reintroduced him to fans, and I just think there's just a real connection with this kid. And there's a real connection with Mulder—[Max] was kind of a soulmate. He and Mulder are really similar kinds of people. I think we touched ever so slightly on how Mulder was hurt by losing that soulmate."

For Frank Spotnitz, the episodes were fulfilling because they pleased both rabid X-Philes and newer fans of the show. "I did see a lot of the postings on AOL in response to 'Tempus Fugit' and 'Max,' and they were very positive, and the word of mouth I've gotten from people who are not *X-Files* fanatics was very positive too," Spotnitz says. "I think one thing [the latter group] liked about 'Tempus Fugit' and 'Max' was that they didn't require any knowledge of the ongoing storyline, and it seemed very reality-based. Despite the fact that there was a UFO and an abduction, investigations of plane crashes are very much of this world and I think people could connect to that." ●

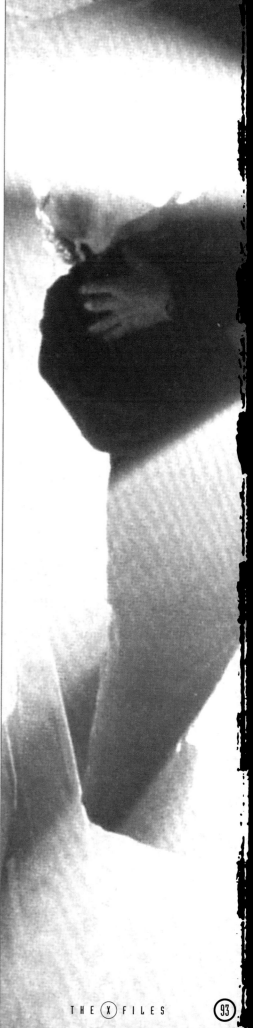

THE TAKING OF FLIGHT 549

By Dave Hughes

"Tempus Fugit"

For as long as UFOs have been part of popular culture, all manner of aircraft have had high-altitude close encounters of at least the second kind.

Official reports of encounters with 'ghost aircraft' or 'foo fighters' (as such phenomena were labelled before the term 'UFO' was coined) have been filed since 1933, when the 4th Swedish Flying Corps launched the first military-sanctioned investigation into the phenomenon. Such sightings increased dramatically during the Second World War, and by the early 1950s the air defence departments of both the British and US governments had instigated large-scale investigations into the 'flying saucer' phenomemon, resulting in a clear ten per cent of all sightings which, "support[ed] the contention that some type of flying object has been observed" and concluded that, "the origin of the devices is not ascertainable."

High-altitude UFO encounters involving commercial airliners, although not as numerous as their military counterparts, are every bit as dramatic. One of the earliest incidents involved a British airliner, which observed "a brilliant object" over Rochester in Kent at 7.17am on May 31 1957. The captain and first officer both sighted the object, following which the aircraft, *en route* from Croydon Airport to Holland, suffered "complete radio failure," which prevented them from reporting the incident until the object had vanished. "Our radio equipment became fully serviceable after the UFO had gone," the captain stated later in his report to the Ministry of Transport and Civil Aviation. Ten years later, in March 1967, a similar report was filed by the crew of a Vickers Vanguard airliner operated by British European Airways (later British Airways). First Officer Graham Sheppard recalls seeing two UFOs over the Bay of Biscay, "engaged in a dazzling display of high-speed aerobatics. We asked Bordeaux Radar controlling that sector if they had any traffic. They replied, 'Unidentified traffic ten miles west of you,' which I would say was exactly where the UFOs were."

In the last 30 years, innumerable similar encounters have been recorded. In 1985 alone, more than a dozen separate but distinctly similar incidents were officially reported from as far afield as China, the Soviet Union and the Italian/Swiss border, culminating in a sighting of a number of UFOs by the crew and *all forty-five passengers* of a Boeing 737 *en route* to Buenos Aires. As recently as July 1995, Aerolineas Argentinas Flight 734 had a dramatic near-miss with an 'OVNI' (*objeto volante no identificado*) described by Captain Jorge Polanco as "nothing that responded to the physical laws as we know them, [but] something similar to an inverted flying saucer, as large as a Boeing 727, and with a very powerful light that was blinding us." The widely-reported encounter was immediately followed by

a blackout of the control tower, forcing Polanco's aircraft to abort its emergency landing.

Such dramatic real-life encounters have now become the inspiration for one of the most epic – and certainly the most elaborate and costly – X-Files two-parter to date. "Although I don't know this as a fact," executive producer Howard Gordon says, "it may very well be the most expensive two hours of episodic television – that wasn't a pilot – that have ever been produced. I wouldn't be surprised if it were." The story opens as celebrations for Scully's birthday are interrupted by a visit from Sharon Graffia, who claims to be the sister of Max Fenig, a repetitive alien abductee Mulder and Scully first encountered during one of their earliest investigations. Graffia tells the agents that Fenig had been killed only hours earlier, in a plane crash in upstate New York. Visiting the crash site, the agents meet Mike Millar, the man in charge of the National Transportation Safety Board's investigation into the disaster, and discover a discrepancy between the official time of the crash and the passengers' watches of nine minutes – precisely the amount of time the agents 'lost' in the pilot episode.

Do you see any need to adjust?
Negative, 549. Steady air speed at 296 knots.
Maintain heading 100, 29,000 feet. Go ahead 549.
What the Hell is this?
549, do you read?
There's something on intercept! My God, My God!
Mayday! Mayday –
– from 549's flight recorder

When the last recorded exchange between the aircraft's crew and the control tower in Albany makes reference to an "intercept," and Scully discovers that the crash's sole survivor is suffering from severe radiation burns, Mulder becomes convinced that Fenig's latest abduction took place *during* the flight – a theory apparently challenged by the discovery of Fenig's body with those of the other passengers. The agents interview military air traffic controller Louis Frish who insists that there was no radio contact with the doomed plane, but when sinister government agencies attempt to silence him for good, he admits to Mulder, Scully and Millar that he *was* the voice on the tape, that he saw an unidentified radar blip enter Flight 549's airspace, and that a mid-air explosion preceded the crash by moments. Was Fenig in the course of being abducted from the aircraft when the UFO containing his abductors was shot down by the military?

MULDER: I think we all share the same goal here, sir, and that's to find out what caused that plane to crash.
MILLAR: And if any of the capable men and women in this room find Dr Spock's phaser or any green goo, we'll be sure to give you all the credit.

Despite the plane crashes, alien encounters, military cover-ups and a dramatic near-miss on the runway, one of "Tempus Fugit"'s most welcome elements is the return of Max Fenig, a character created by Howard Gordon and Alex Gansa for the first season story, "Fallen Angel." "Fenig was an interesting character," Gordon says of Fenig's first appearance. "[He is] a neurotic, paranoid conspiracy theorist who's almost a precursor to the Lone Gunmen. So whatever story we told around him would be secondary to that individual. In an ideal world, you make these stories work on another level by taking the story you want to tell and a character that's interesting and connecting them." Max Fenig was portrayed in that episode by Canadian actor Scott Bellis, whom Gordon describes as, "one of those discoveries we get sometimes in casting. It was a major role and normally we cast our major roles [in] the States. But he was just a fine, fine actor. He read for us, and we said, 'He's the guy.'"

"I knew that I had made an impression," says Bellis, "but the writing was really great and the director, Larry Shaw, let me go with things a little bit, in terms of fleshing out moments here and there. And I know that I helped move the episode along."

Bellis' turn as Max Fenig was equally popular with the show's early fans, and long-term X-philes have often discussed the possible return of the character. "I ran into David Duchovny a couple of times in Vancouver, and he said he'd been throwing some suggestions toward Chris Carter [about] wanting to get me back. I waited around for about a year and a half and nothing happened, so I kind of forgot about it. And I was down here in Los Angeles last November and my Vancouver agent phoned me and said, 'I just got a call – they want to know your availability in February.' And I said, 'Well, three months away, I'm not doing anything as far as I know yet, so go ahead and tell them it's clear.' And I waited and waited to hear back from them, and came back down to LA after Christmas, and then they phoned and said, 'Can we have you next week?' So it was kind of last minute."

MULDER: These men are trained to identify moving parts: hydraulics; electronics. They're trained to reconstruct those parts in the past and arrive at the present, but they can't do that because somebody has stolen the past from them – nine minutes of it. Nine minutes that became a lifetime for those passengers and now their families.

Bellis says that he did not receive a script until he arrived in Vancouver for the shoot. What were his first impressions of the screenplay? "Well, my first impression was that I was disappointed that I didn't have any dialogue," he laughs. "I know my own preference would have been to have maybe a bit of dialogue between Mulder and Max about what had happened to him. But I saw that it was a two-part story, and that it was going to be somehow centered around what my character was doing, and I saw that it was a good story with a lot of twists in it and a big mystery at the core of it. And I was just really happy to be a part of it. It's a great show, and one of the most positive experiences I've ever had working on a set."

Although Fenig does not have any dialogue until the second part, "Max," Bellis says that the scenes replaying his abduction in "Tempus Fugit" were complicated to film. "I spent three days on the airplane, shooting that whole sequence, and taking the time to get all the angles." How was the scene in which Fenig is physically lifted out of his airplane seat and carried out of the aircraft door actually accomplished? "That was an interesting little contraption," he says. "They built a little fibreglass seat for me to sit in, made for the contours of my body. It actually went inside my pants. So I'm sitting in this little chair, and there was a hole in the right side of my pants by my hip, with an arm attached to a crane. They just sat me in the seat and put my pants on in the airplane. Then all they had to do was move the crane arm and lift me up and rotate me. It was quite well done." So, having seen the finished result when it was aired in March, how did he feel about it? "I thought it was great. I think they really pulled out the stops for it."

Bellis adds that, although his character survived the events of "Fallen Angel" only to turn up dead in "Tempus Fugit," there is still the possibility that he may be invited back at a future stage – this is, after all, science fiction. "There's always the possibility that I could show up in a home video. Who knows, I mean anything's possible on *The X-Files*."

For further reading on real-life encounters between airliners and UFOs, see Beyond Top Secret *by Timothy Good.*

This Page: "Fallen Angel"

TEMPUS FUGIT

Truth and C

"Patient X" and "The Red and the Black" paves the way for The X-Files feature film and beyond

onsequences

The truth is still out there. But after years of being as hazy as the fumes wafting from the Cigarette-Smoking Man's Morleys, the elusive explanations behind *The X-Files*' deepest mysteries finally seem within reach.

Well, kind of.

"After four seasons of developing this mythology, we really felt it was time to show how these pieces interlock and give some big answers so we could pose some new big questions," says *X-Files* writer/producer Frank Spotnitz. "It felt like it was time not to keep introducing new elements as much as exploring established elements more deeply, so that people start to get a sense of the bigger picture."

That goal is at the core of the recent two-parter "Patient X"/"The Red and the Black," in which countless mythology threads are spun into a discernible pattern, weaving the fabric eventually setting up *The X-Files* feature film. Past episode themes and references densely pack the two hours; allusions to the pilot, "Duane Barry," "Nisei," "Tunguska"/"Terma," "Zero Sum" and "Redux"/ "Redux II," among others, are strewn among new characters and plot twists. The Well-Manicured Man, UN operative Marita Covarrubias and one-armed loose cannon Alex Krycek all return for long-awaited encores, while Skyland Mountain's spooky magnetism gets revived, too.

"It's an interesting thing," says Spotnitz, who wrote the episodes along with his usual mythology writing partner, Chris Carter. "We're not the new kid on the block anymore. We're a mature show, and we want to stay fresh and vital and surprise and challenge ourselves while still respecting our youth and carrying through ideas introduced some time ago."

The show's brain trust also needed to develop those ideas with an eye toward the feature's summer release date. With that storyline already sealed in celluloid, Carter and Spotnitz found themselves in the unusual position of working backward, carefully laying the foundation for the future big-screen denouement. But while they have the luxury of knowing where they're going, "Patient X" provided the knotty challenge of revealing enough without giving away too much.

"I think we anticipated that it would be an advantage knowing where the characters and the mythology had to be come summer," Spotnitz explains. "It

uncharacteristic foray into some XXX-Files—the Ratboy/Uniblonder love-lock, a twisted manifestation of Spotnitz' much-discussed promise that two characters would hook up this season.

"I know people had been equal parts dreading and hoping to see Mulder in some romantic entanglement, and I think Covarrubias was someone they thought he might be involved with," he says merrily. "But [Krycek and Covarrubias] seemed so natural to me because we revealed in 'Zero-Sum' that she has some association with the Syndicate, and Krycek clearly has had an association with them, so it seemed like a hidden connection in the already-established mythology. It just felt right that these two people would have

> There were things, having seen the movie now, that we knew we wanted to explain more clearly. We wanted these two episodes to do that.
> —Frank Spotnitz

was hard to know what to say and what to withhold. On the other hand, there were things, having seen the movie now, that we knew we wanted to explain more clearly before it came out, and we knew we wanted these two episodes to do that. The role of certain characters, like Well-Manicured Man, was really important to reveal here, [as was] the role that the black oil plays in relation to other aliens. And our human ability to combat it was an important question."

Spotnitz calls "Patient X"/"The Red and the Black" an "enormously important two-parter for the series," so much so that he and Carter constantly discussed the storyline even while attending to other producing and writing duties. "Patient X" director Kim Manners is even more blunt: "This is a great story of epic proportions," he says. Aside from setting up the film, the episodes widen the show's future landscape with new characters like Jeffrey Spender (played by Chris Owens, the actor who portrayed the young CSM in "Musings of a Cigarette-Smoking Man") and the faceless alien fire-starters. They also notably let the bad guys diabolically run rampant—the story's driven by Krycek, Covarrubias and the shadowy Syndicate as much as it is by Scully or Mulder. Oh yeah, and there's also the

some backstory together. It's also interesting because they're not in the movie, and yet we knew we wanted these shows to be big episodes for those characters. It was like a big jigsaw puzzle, taking all of these pieces we knew we wanted to use and trying to find a natural and seamless way of piecing them all together."

Creating a believable love scene was more of a challenge, especially because the series so rarely shows romance. "I don't want it to be a typical scene that you've seen in a hundred movies where they're just groping at each other and passionately kissing," Manners says. "It's something we [needed to be] very careful about."

Accordingly, actors Nicholas Lea and Laurie Holden (Krycek and Covarrubias, respectively) both closely consulted with Manners, Carter and Spotnitz about the proper approach. "It's a big step because it's something we haven't seen any of the characters do," Lea says. "One has to do this with some taste and character."

While the two-parter's return to familiar themes helps fans unravel the conspiracy, it also brought the X-Files crew back to habitual territory. The Greater Vancouver Regional District (GVRD), a watershed and demonstration forest that doubled as the "Tunguska" work camp, was converted into a gulag for "Patient X," while the GVRD's oft-used gravel pit served as one of the episode's

Kim Manners
DIRECTOR

visitation sites, full of burned-out automobiles and people.

"We set about 15 cars on fire and there aren't too many places you can do that in the [British Columbia] lower mainland and get away with it," says location manager Todd Pittson.

Additionally, a 12-kilometer stretch of road near the pit triples as the road to Starlight Mountain, the path to another visitation site *and* the Khazikstan forest. And years before the episode's Russian freighter boiler room became the stage for Krycek's nefarious crimes, it was home to another slimy creature—Flukeman.

Shirley Inget & Brad McMurray
SET DECORATORS

"The engine room scene is in the same facility that we used in 'The Host,' actually an old power substation," Pittson adds. "We go back there because it looks great, works well for us and obviously you're not going to go on a real freighter just to shoot an engine room. Even if we could, I used to work on ships and one engine room looks like another engine room, whether it be a Russian or American freighter. I challenge anybody, short of someone who works on a ship, to contest that."

Even though landlubbers probably can't tell the difference, set decorator Shirley Inget was in charge of making sure everything did look authentic. "Basically it involves building walls of pipe and pressure gauges," she says. "Over the years we've done research, and we've also had a number of scenes set on boats."

The series' Vancouver casting director, Coreen Mayrs, also felt prepared for the two-parter because of experience gleaned from past episodes. "I've probably auditioned every Russian in the city," she says with a laugh. "We had a number of Russian roles to cast in this episode, which isn't as hard for me to do now as it was when we first started exploring that part of the mythology. I was able to pull in most of the characters with people I already knew."

The two exceptions were the most critical Russian roles—the teenager Dmitri and his doomed, nameless friend. "I got a sense that Russian boys tend to mature a little quicker than American boys. When they reach 17 they look like men," Mayrs explains. "Basically we wanted boys that were old enough where it wasn't too cruel to have their lives taken, but young enough so they were believable as teenagers."

A 15-year-old was cast as the teen killed in the "Patient X" opening teaser, while the more physically demanding (and emotionally disturbing) role of Dmitri went to 16-year-old Alex Shostak.

Dmitri's horrifying facial prosthetics—necessary to show the effects of the savage beating the character receives from Krycek—were designed by *The X-Files'* resident makeup guru, Toby Lindala, who particularly appreciates the opportunity to revisit effects. "It's exciting to be furthering the mythology, but a lot of times these episodes are nice because we get a chance to go back to effects we've done before," he says. "Sometimes we've done them in different ways and other times they were really similar, but we've got that experience behind us and have already done the research and development, so we get a chance to really hone things."

One effect Lindala's crew was able to tweak during the two-parter's filming was the gooey black oil slipping into the helpless Dmitri's head. To create the illusion of the splattered oil rejoining its mass and seeping into the boy's face, Lindala created a rig that pumped the substance from a prosthetic nostril and the actor's mouth; afterward, the post-production crew ran the film in reverse. One flat tube sat underneath a swollen-eye prosthetic, while another was nestled within a fake broken nose; the lines ran from the sides of the actor's face and through a "horse's bit" in his mouth.

While the "gag" itself was straightforward, Lindala found that perfecting the oil's viscosity was harder. "It's tricky because we need to have a thick enough mixture to work against the laws of gravity," he says. "We had thinner substance and then really thick substance [before going] somewhere in-between. We also need to get the pressure high enough without blowing through [the rig]."

Sex
and the single arm

Within all the conspiratorial twists and dynamic special effects found in "Patient X," it takes only three words for actor Nicholas Lea to sum up the episode's most memorable moment: "Krycek gets some."

Ah, yes. The return of one-armed menace Alex Krycek would have sent X-philes into a tizzy in and of itself, but his passionate embrace with Marita Covarrubias (Laurie Holden) surely assures that Ratboy's reappearance becomes one of the most-discussed scenes in *The X-Files* canon. But Lea sounds relatively controlled about the steamy situation.

"[Laurie Holden] and I talked about it for a couple of hours," Lea says. "When I first read the script I was like, 'Oh, my goodness'." [But] I love the idea of the contradiction of the heated sex scene and the [artificial] hand."

In fact, it was Krycek's prosthetic hand (a result of an "accident" in "Terma") and the character's Russian dialogue that gave the actor more trouble than the love scene. "These are tough episodes for me," he says. "I'm speaking a fair bit of Russian, I can't move the hand—it's like a golf swing. I have to remember about 12 things at the same time."

The actor had a week to practice the difficult Russian lines, which he learned phonetically. "Speaking a language you don't know and trying to act at the same time is brutally hard," he explains. "It's a classic exercise of left-brain, right-brain. If you get three or four lines into the scene and you're still speaking Russian, it's very hard to remember what you're actually saying."

Language aside, Lea affirms that he still likes Krycek's dubious moral character, even in an episode where he beats up a young teenager and then orders the boy's orifices to be sewn shut.

"[We] don't know whether to hate him or feel sorry for him," he says. "I wanted to keep that going, although it's hard when you're doing such outwardly

evil things. But I've never seen this character as being evil. At this point he's pretty much doing what he has to do to survive and also get some revenge and get back some power."

In fact, the actor likes thinking of Krycek as an anti-Mulder. "He's still trying to get to the truth, but he's not on the bright side of things. There is a certain heroism to the guy in terms of that he's a complete and utter survivor."

While Krycek's exploits keep the character up in arm(s), Lea's richly benefited from the part and was thrilled to return to *The X-Files* set while on hiatus from his Canadian series, *Once a Thief*.

"It's great to see everybody again," he says. "Working here is an absolute treat. This show has done so much for me personally and professionally that I'll be utterly loyal to it until they don't want me anymore."

Of course, more love scenes wouldn't hurt either.

"[That was] a good day in the life of Krycek," he laughs. —A V

Chris Carter requested
"something spectacular,"
for the scenes. And you
can't go much bigger
than a dam.

-Louisa Gradnitzer

Along with the creative "oil rigs," Lindala crafted silicone masks for stuntman Tony Morelli and actor Brian Thompson, the Alien Bounty Hunter who becomes the faceless "firestarter" in the two-parter. "His eyes, nose, mouth and ears are cauterized to seal him—luckily we're only dealing with on-camera orifices," Lindala jokes. The masks, shaped into contorted expressions, covered the stuntman's face along with a fire gel, a protection that allowed Morelli to be in a full-body burn for about 15 seconds.

To get a more authentic Russian look, a collection of 14 Peugeots and other European cars were assembled for the "Patient X" teaser; the automobiles were stripped of their engines, tanks and upholstery before being ignited with a combination of propane and other fuels. But while the dramatic fire scenes literally light up the screen, the two-parter's most awesome effects were left for the dam fire and ascension scenes.

"Chris [Carter] requested, as he put it, 'something spectacular' for the scenes," says location manager Louisa Gradnitzer. "And you can't go much bigger than a dam."

The locations team had their eyes on Ruskin Dam, an industrial-Gothic-style edifice near Mission, British Columbia, for a while, but they never proposed the site as a location because it fell outside of the show's self-imposed geographic radius. "It was designed in the 1930s or something, so it's kind of eerie and Gothic but with a lot of texture," Gradnitzer adds.

Although it rests a half-hour away from the production crew's normal shooting zone, Gradnitzer and Pittson knew the dam would give the scenes an extra visual wonder.

"I think the audience [really gets] a bang for their buck," says Manners. "I'm hoping to get a little Spielberg-esque

Louisa Gradnitzer & Todd Pittson
LOCATIONS MANAGERS

wonderment from the extras and the people. It's big, but as huge as [the scene] is it's really kind of confining because we'll have hundreds of people there."

The task of finding 200 abductees for the epic scene fell to Lisa Ratke, the show's extras casting director. Amazingly, though, Ratke says finding so many bit actors for such a crucial moment wasn't daunting. "It's actually easier sometimes to cast more people, especially because this script needs average-looking Americans," she says. "So it's easier to do than if you have just four or five people—then you have to pay attention to whether they're good actors or not, because they're closer up to the action."

A tougher task for Ratke was coordinating the 100 cars also necessary for the scene. "We go through our files of [extras] and ask them if they have cars and then try to arrange car pools and things like that."

Meanwhile, special-effects coordinator

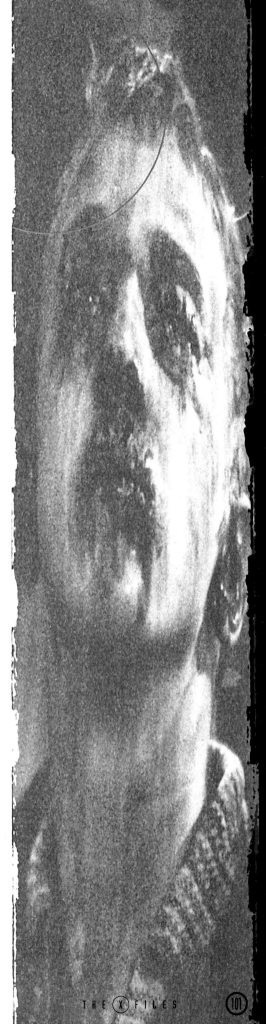

David Gauthier had his own problems with the ascension scene in "The Red and the Black." "When we have that bright light hover over the top of the bridge, it's difficult because we [had to] hang lights where there wasn't any place to put them," Gauthier says.

Because there was no room for cranes, the crews had to build a support system extending off the bridge on which to hold the lights. For the ascension itself the film again was run in reverse, so that the actress appears to be flying up, the ship's force sucking in the water from the river, when in reality she was lowered down in a shower of rain.

Yet although the effects in "Patient X" and "The Red and the Black" were dazzling, it was ultimately the characters' interior journeys that gave the episodes their monumental weight. Spotnitz and Carter wanted to illustrate the shockingly bitter change in Mulder's perspective that had grown in "Demons," "Gethsemane" and "Redux II," when he began believing that the X-Files and his sister's abduction could be all-too-logically explained.

"We thought it was really important to dramatize Mulder's disillusionment," Spotnitz says. "We'd established it by the end of 'Redux II' and had only winked at it since then. There's a joke in 'The Post-Modern Prometheus' when he says, 'I don't know if I believe in that stuff any more,' and the woman responds, 'Oh come on, really?' But we felt we really needed to explain what that's about.

"It's interesting to play because it's a reversal of the traditional roles of [Mulder and Scully]. But by the end of the two-parter, they've undergone huge journeys and you can't have reversals and double-reversals without having your characters learn something," Spotnitz continues. "Otherwise it's just a manipulation and a clever twist. So that was a big topic of conversation for me and Chris and [writer] John Shiban, who also worked on the episode. What do Mulder and Scully learn and how are they changed by these experiences? By the end of the second part you understand why Mulder wasn't himself, but I think it was important to take him that far in order to bring him back where we wanted to have him by the end of the episodes."

And while the feature film provides a concrete end to the writers' means, Spotnitz quickly points out that "Patient X" /"The Red and the Black" is crucial in expanding the show's landscape in future seasons. "It really adds a whole new dimension to the interpersonal dynamics at work," Spotnitz says. "It's something we realized we could do when we were coming up with this story, and it seemed natural and beautiful and organic to everything we had done before. I was telling Chris recently that every once in a while we come up with something that fits so perfectly with what he's set up before that it feels like it was meant to be. This was one of those things." ●

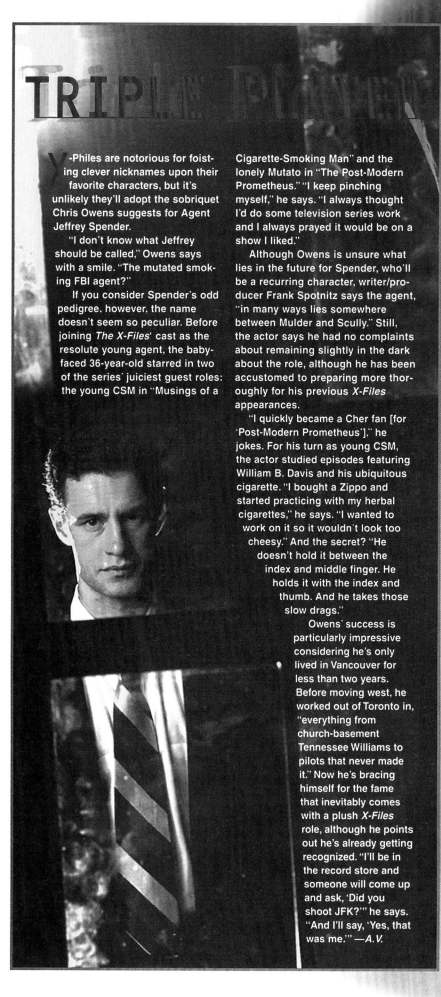

TRIPLE PLAYER

X-Philes are notorious for foisting clever nicknames upon their favorite characters, but it's unlikely they'll adopt the sobriquet Chris Owens suggests for Agent Jeffrey Spender.

"I don't know what Jeffrey should be called," Owens says with a smile. "The mutated smoking FBI agent?"

If you consider Spender's odd pedigree, however, the name doesn't seem so peculiar. Before joining *The X-Files'* cast as the resolute young agent, the baby-faced 36-year-old starred in two of the series' juiciest guest roles: the young CSM in "Musings of a Cigarette-Smoking Man" and the lonely Mutato in "The Post-Modern Prometheus." "I keep pinching myself," he says. "I always thought I'd do some television series work and I always prayed it would be on a show I liked."

Although Owens is unsure what lies in the future for Spender, who'll be a recurring character, writer/producer Frank Spotnitz says the agent, "in many ways lies somewhere between Mulder and Scully." Still, the actor says he had no complaints about remaining slightly in the dark about the role, although he has been accustomed to preparing more thoroughly for his previous *X-Files* appearances.

"I quickly became a Cher fan [for 'Post-Modern Prometheus']," he jokes. For his turn as young CSM, the actor studied episodes featuring William B. Davis and his ubiquitous cigarette. "I bought a Zippo and started practicing with my herbal cigarettes," he says. "I wanted to work on it so it wouldn't look too cheesy." And the secret? "He doesn't hold it between the index and middle finger. He holds it with the index and thumb. And he takes those slow drags."

Owens' success is particularly impressive considering he's only lived in Vancouver for less than two years. Before moving west, he worked out of Toronto in, "everything from church-basement Tennessee Williams to pilots that never made it." Now he's bracing himself for the fame that inevitably comes with a plush *X-Files* role, although he points out he's already getting recognized. "I'll be in the record store and someone will come up and ask, 'Did you shoot JFK?'" he says. "And I'll say, 'Yes, that was me.'" —*A.V.*

EPISODES: 5x13/5x14

CASSANDRA SPENDER

"Patient X"/"The Red and the Black"

 fter three decades in the acting business, Veronica Cartwright was more than ready for *The X-Files*. The paranormal was nothing new to the veteran actress, who played Cassandra Spender in "Patient X" and "The Red and the Black." She was swarmed by 15,000 finches in Alfred Hitchcock's *The Birds*,

VERONICA CARTWRIGHT

menaced by soulless alien doppelgängers in *Invasion of the Body Snatchers*, chased by a more slime-intensive extraterrestrial in *Alien* and forced to projectile vomit gallon upon gallon of cherries in *The Witches of Eastwick*.

"God, it's so weird what you have to react to," sighs the former child actress (whose sister, Angela, played Penny Robinson in the original *Lost in Space*).

Though her *X-Files* episodes featured plenty of weird sights and sounds—spaceships, sentient black goo and people being burned alive—Cartwright says what she'll remember best about the experience was how much fun she had. "The hours were long, but the people were terrific," she says. "I had a great time."

Cartwright says she expects Cassandra Spender to return sometime next season. In the meantime, Cartwright plans to stay involved with the show—as a loyal viewer. "When I got the part, Chris [Carter] wanted me to see the episode with Steve Railsback ['Duane Barry']," she says. "So I watched that, and at the end it says, 'To Be Continued.' I really wanted to know what happened. So I called them up and asked them to send me part two. I really got into it and I've watched it ever since."—*Steve Hockensmith*

ALSO KNOWN AS:

1964-1966: "Jemima Boone" on *Daniel Boone*
1986: "Margaret Flanagan" on *L.A. Law*
1994: "Mrs. Huston" on *E/R*
1995: "Angela" on *American Gothic*

1958: "Allie O'Neil" in *In Love and War*
1961: "Rosalie" in *The Children's Hour*
1978: "Hermine" in *Goin' South*
1986: "Helen Freeman" in *Flight of the Navigator*
1995: "Octavia" in *Candyman 2*
1997: "Connie Cipriani" in *Money Talks*

GUEST X GALLERY

The X-Files Movie

Northern Texas, circa 35,000 B.C.:
two primitive hunters kill a
savage creature in a cave, but
the creature's body oozes a black
substance which infects one of
the hunters...

Present day, Northern Texas:
A group of young boys are playing
outside until one of them falls
through the ground into a cave.
He discovers skeletal remains and
is infected by the mysterious
black 'oil'...

A week later, Mulder and Scully -
currently off the X-Files - investigate a bomb threat at a federal
building in Dallas. They're too
late to stop the bomb going off.
Mulder eventually learns, with
the help of an old friend of his
father's, Dr Kurtzweil, that the
bomb blast was part of a government cover-up to destroy evidence
of a lethal virus being spread by
infected bees.

As the agents get closer to the
truth, Mulder and Scully almost
kiss - until Scully is stung by a
deadly bee, hidden in her
clothing. As Scully is put into an
ambulance, Mulder identifies one
of the paramedics as someone at
the scene of the earlier bomb
blast. The man shoots Mulder and
takes Scully away.

Mulder survives, escapes the
hospital where he is being watched
by shady characters and heads off
to rescue Scully in the Antarctic,
unaware that he is set for a
rendez-vous with the Cigarette-
Smoking Man and a buried U.F.O.
Mulder locates Scully in the U.F.O.
and, chased by deadly aliens,
manages to get them outside - just
as the spacecraft erupts from the
ground.

Back in Washington, D.C., Scully
fails to convince an F.B.I. board
of the recent developments, mainly
because of lack of evidence. Scully
points out that the F.B.I. needs an
investigative unit to pursue such
evidence. Shortly afterwards, the
X-Files department is reopened...

KEEPIN

G Mum

She's played Mrs. Margaret Scully from the very early days of Season One of *The X-Files*, and now Sheila Larken talks to Paul Simpson and Ruth Thomas about her experiences on the show.

When Dana Scully revealed her pregnancy at the end of the seventh season of *The X-Files*, it struck some as strange that she had not confided in her mother, and that Sheila Larken was not seen in the early episodes of the next season. "There was a time when I did a voiceover for the show," Larken points out, "when Dana is having another nervous breakdown, and she gives Margaret a call. She gets my answering machine, and that's it – but it let the audience know that Margaret Scully was still out there."

Larken was not surprised that she had not been invited to return earlier. As she explains, *The X-Files* was going through a period of major upheaval after Chris Carter and co upped sticks from their Vancouver home at the end of the fifth year. "They had to deal with all the different issues," she says. "Changing the light, changing the location and the ambience of the show. They had to deal with knowing that David [Duchovny]'s contract was running out. Chris had to figure all that out and make it work for the storyline. They really had a lot of work to do in those two years."

The actress simply assumed that Margaret Scully was getting on with her life, and indeed, when she did return for Mulder's funeral in "DeadAlive," she wasn't given any other explanation. "They don't do that," she laughs. "You have to fill in the blanks yourself as an actor."

Larken didn't believe that she was

finished with the part. "It did come as a surprise when they called me back," she admits, "but I knew eventually that the mythology of the family line would come back. When I came back, I had no lines. They wanted the family montage at the funeral of all the characters that were still living. I was kind of like a glorified extra!"

With a few exceptions – notably Gillian Anderson and Mitch Pileggi – everyone was new to Larken. "The crew was new, and I had no scene to play," she says. "But then I went down again and did the episode that involved Dana's baby shower, and then another and another – and now

it feels that they know me and I know them. Once again I'm part of the family."

Although she points out that she can't really comment on any changes during the sixth and seventh year, Larken believes that the energy on *The X-Files* set has hardly differed between its Vancouver and Los Angeles homes. "Robert Patrick comes in with such incredible energy," she says. "Kim Manners and the people that are there plugging it out are all fighting as hard to get all the quality that they can in the time allowed. I don't see any of that feeling of, 'oh, it's the ninth year, let's not care as much!' Gillian is still as much of a perfectionist as she ever was."

Margaret Scully was left literally holding the baby in "Nothing Important Happened Today," the opening episode of the ninth season, when Lucy Lawless' character Shannon McMahon comes to call at Scully's apartment, and it seems that she will be involved with young William for some time to come. "I was down in Los Angeles in mid-December for a two-parter that Chris and Frank Spotnitz had written about Dana's baby," she says. "The baby was in danger, and it was just a wonderful show. The mother gets beaten up, Gillian gets beaten up – everybody gets beaten up! It was great to play the 'mom in jeopardy' and it was almost like mom was saving Dana… I wasn't involved in the second part of that show, which I think Chris was directing."

When Larken was first approached to appear on *The X-Files* (almost nine years ago!), some of the staff had reservations. "There was talk about my looking too young for the role," she recalls, "although I'm the exact age of Gillian's mother!"

Larken's husband, R.W. Goodwin, was one of the show's producers, and she broke her usual rule of not appearing in her husband's shows during their formative season. "David Nutter was directing that first episode, and he had been a fan of mine," she explains. "So he and Chris took a leap of faith and cast me. Of course, at that point, they didn't know if it was going to go beyond that one show or not. You never know with that series. The Smoking-Man was essentially a man with no lines the first time they cast him – and then boom! Look at that. That was certainly catching the gold ring on the carousel."

Over the years, Larken has been able to bring some of her own experiences as a mother to the role of Margaret Scully. In "Memento Mori," she added a moment of anger where Chris Carter had scripted for Margaret to cry. "In another one, which my husband directed, we're going to pull the plug on Dana, and Mulder is arguing against it," she remembers. "I stop him short by just saying his name. David was so funny – it just caught him. He looked around the room and said, 'Where is my mother?' I used a tone that only comes with age and having children. One of the nice things about ageing is that you realize that life has given you experience, and I said, 'Fox!' the way I would never had said it 30 years ago. I

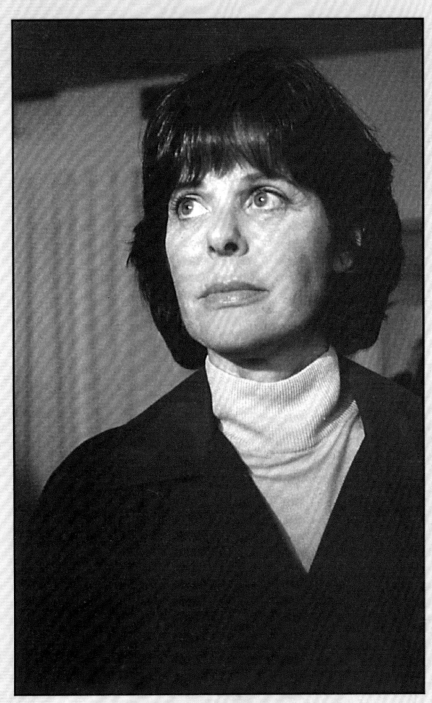

would never have known then how to affect a young person like that."

The relationship between Dana and Margaret Scully has never been easy, and that still continues to be the case. "When I went back to do the show with Gillian, we were once again doing battle," she says. "Dana has to get the answers, and I tell her, what good are the answers? You still have to deal with what this child is, whether it's an extra-terrestrial or the real thing. I think as mother and daughter there are many clouded layers, just as there are with any parent or child."

Larken is full of admiration and praise for *The X-Files'* creator, Chris Carter. "I think he's brilliant," she enthuses. "He has his writing hand around the heart of his audience. I think he knows that there is a part of us, particularly since the 1960s, that will always doubt political authority, and will always believe in some form of conspiracy. We're children, and the parents aren't telling us the truth. That's one pulse of his audience, and the other is that everybody loves to be scared. Everybody loves wondering what's around the next corner, and I think he has a great balance between our paranoia and our love of being scared."

The team around Carter has also played an essential role. "From the get-go he had a wonderful writing staff supporting him," she says. "Vince Gilligan and Darin Morgan, Glen Morgan and James Wong, some wonderful young writers. He's at the helm, leading the way. Nothing seems to stop him. He'll just come up with this idea and that idea! I think that's why it just keeps going. He also has a wonderful eye for casting – if you look at the shows that people love, so much of it has to do with the cast. Gillian and David were just a wonderful pair, and he plucked them out of nowhere, and made a wonderful blend – and now there are these wonderful additions to the cast."

"[Chris Carter] has a wonderful eye for casting. Gillian and David were just a wonderful pair, and now there are the wonderful additions to the cast."

The American actress now lives in Bellingham, Washington, and generally works on movies-of-the-week in the thriving Vancouver film and television community. "I did a wonderful movie with Donald Sutherland called *Behind the Mask*, and a miniseries where I got to play the Prime Minister of British Columbia," she says. "It's been hard: the older I get, the less work there is. I'm so envious of British television and film – you get to see people the way they really look. Even when we age in this country, we're only represented as thin and beautiful. But I've been lucky – I've been able to continue to work." ●

"There was talk about my looking too young for the role (of Mrs Scully), although I'm the exact age of Gillian's mother!"

A REVEALING INTERVIEW, BRIAN THOMPSON GIVES X-PHILES A

MORP

When Brian Thompson guest-starred as "the Pilot" in Season Two two-parter "Colony"/"End Game," he thought it was a one-shot deal. He'd come in, pose as a downed Russian fighter pilot, annihilate some alien clones and move on to his next project. But two simple lines of dialogue suggested by David Duchovny on the day of the shoot managed to weave Thompson irrevocably into the show's tangled mythology.

"I was only slated to work those two episodes," Thompson recalls. "That one line – [Mulder] asked me, 'Where's my sister?' and I said,

…LIMPSE AT THE MAN BEHIND THE MENACING ALIEN BOUNTY HUNTER

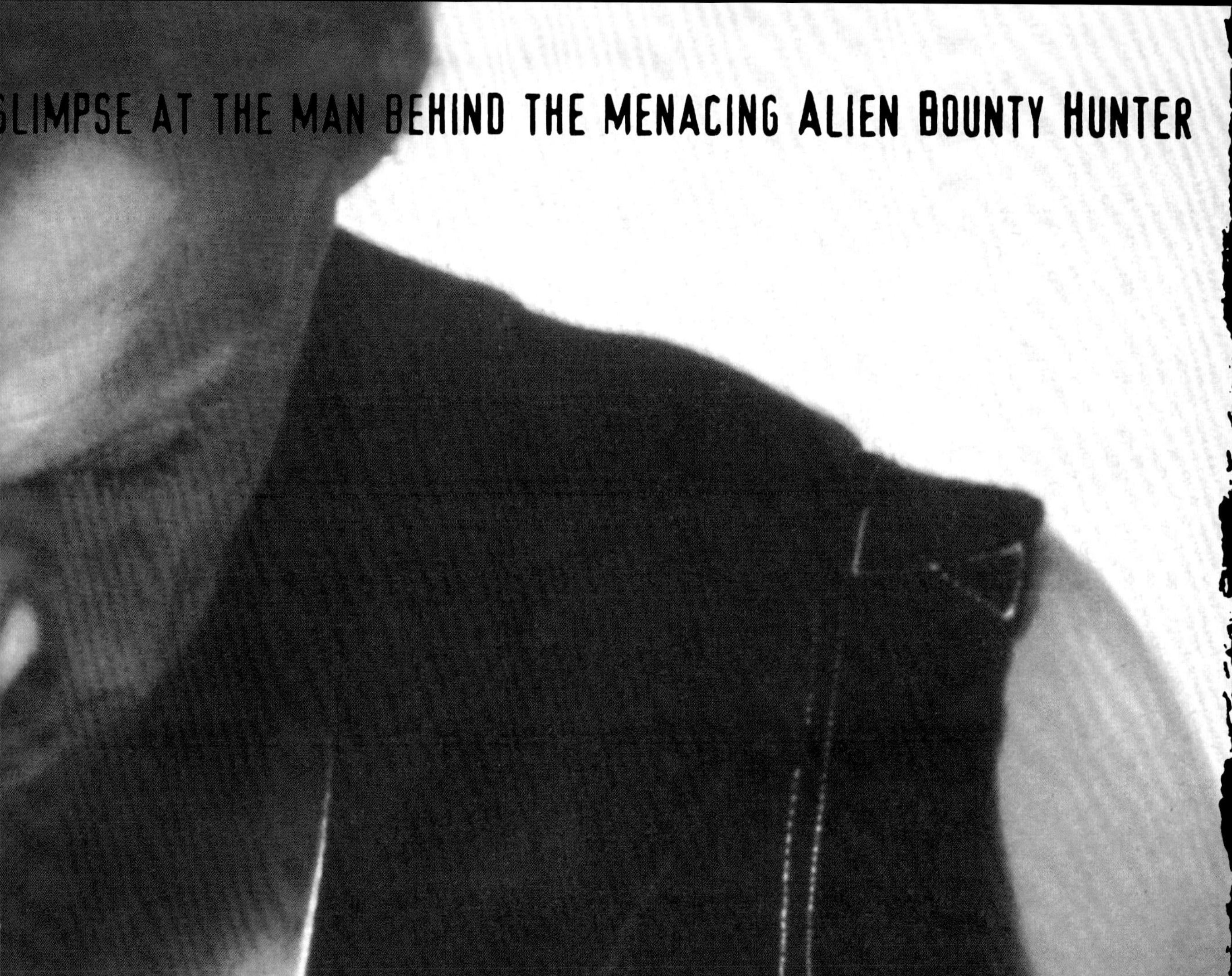

BY JOSH SCHOLLMEYER

…HING GLORY

'She's alive' – tied me to the mythology of the show. I didn't know it at the time, but six months later they said, 'Why don't you come in and shoot another two-part episode,' which was the [Season Three] closer ['Talitha Cumi'] and the following season opener ['Herrenvolk']."

Like Alex Krycek and Marita Covarrubias, Thompson's Bounty Hunter has now become a staple of the series' ongoing mythology arc, resurfacing now and again to cover up hints of the alien colonizers' plans while hiding behind his metamorphosed mask and deadly stiletto.

Like his recurring role on *The X-Files*, Thompson's acting debut came about accidentally. During his final semester in high school, a friend encouraged him to try out for a role in a school production.

"I ended up being in the high school play and getting the supporting actor award for the year," Thompson says. "Plus, I had a really great time doing it. It was more fun than anything I'd ever done, and I'd done an awful lot of things at that point – scholastics, sports, all these activities."

MORTAL KOMBAT:
ANNIHILATION

Acting remained a hobby, however, while Thompson attended Central Washington University. There, Thompson walked onto the football team as a defensive tackle and majored in business management. But no matter what other activities he pursued, his passion for performing still lured him to the theatre whenever he could find time in his hectic schedule.

"I still kept acting almost every quarter," Thompson says. "I would try out for a play, and sometimes I wouldn't even do that much – a walk-on, two-bit part. I would do anything just to hang out in the theatre."

When he graduated, a Portland, Oregon, construction company he worked for the previous summer offered him a cushy management job. "It was a very lucrative job and the best thing to ever happen to me because then my future in that chosen career was waiting there for me," Thompson says. "Here it was, 1984, and it was a $40,000-a-year job. I'm helping run this construction company. It made me feel a bit suffocated because it was all there – here's your life, now what? You live in Portland and have a nice car and a nice house?"

Thompson wasn't ready to end his education or abandon his dreams of becoming a professional actor, so he turned down the management job and began applying to master's programs in theatre. The University of California at Irvine not only accepted Thompson, but offered him a fellowship and scholarship. He was ecstatic. The program was well-respected and in

close proximity to Hollywood, where he could seek film and television roles while still continuing his education.

When the US soap opera *General Hospital* conducted a nationwide talent search his second year at Irvine, Thompson sent in a head shot and résumé. He was shocked when the show's casting directors arranged to meet with him at the Colorado Shakespeare Festival where he was performing. "I met them and that kind of took me into Hollywood for my first real studio audition," Thompson remembers. "I wasn't given the big part, but they ended up offering me a part later on that I actually couldn't do because of my school commitments."

That encouragement was all Thompson needed to boost his career ambitions. During his final year at Irvine, he secured five professional jobs – including three lines in *The Terminator*.

"That was just a bunch of kids making a movie," Thompson says. "Nobody had any idea that movie was going to be so big. No one. The only person who knew what that film was going to be like was James Cameron. That was it. Everyone else was just along for the ride. I was thrilled because it was a feature film, and I was working with a big star."

After *The Terminator*, Thompson played opposite Sylvester Stallone in the action film *Cobra*, and he hasn't stopped working

since. His résumé boasts an array of film and television roles spanning every genre imaginable. For example, having wrapped shooting on Adam Sandler's vehicle, *The Adventures of Joe Dirt*, Thompson flew to Israel to work on Jean-Claude Van Damme's next project.

"There isn't a genre I haven't worked in," Thompson says. "From period dramas to action-adventures to sci-fi/fantasy, I've done it all."

Although the lurking menace of the Alien Bounty Hunter is always felt when he appears on *The X-Files*, his face is rarely seen. Because of the character's shape-shifting capabilities, most of Thompson's dialogue and screentime falls to other actors. In some episodes, he appears for only a few seconds and spouts a mere three or four words of dialogue. And he's been given little guidance as to the Bounty Hunter's origins or motivations.

None of this bothers Thompson. He's provided his own backstory and offered suggestions on how to develop the character to

© PARAMOUNT

JACK OF ALL TRADES: [opposite, from left] Thompson in *Mortal Kombat: Annihilation*; as The Judge in Season Two of *Buffy the Vampire Slayer*; [this page, from top] as Lt. Klag in *Star Trek: The Next Generation*; as the Alien Bounty Hunter in *The X-Files* episodes "End Game," "Herrenvolk" and "Colony"

series creator Chris Carter and the show's writers. Not that they always take this advice.

"I surmise what this character does and what he's been doing based on the same information that [the fans] have," Thompson says. "I suggested that the Alien Bounty Hunter should be the father of the child that's in Scully's belly right now, and that we shoot some flashback scenes to show what happened. But they didn't take that suggestion, which I still think is a good one."

The one writer who did offer Thompson insight into the Bounty Hunter was none other than Duchovny, who added some depth and a bit of history to the character in the script for his directorial debut, "The Unnatural."

"I think ['The Unnatural'] was the episode where I was the most featured and gave my best performance," Thompson says. "It also added a whole dimension to the Bounty Hunter because he was doing stuff on Earth 50 years ago – the same guy. That was way cool."

Thompson and Duchovny have also forged a relationship off the set. "It's a professional friendship," Thompson says. "I certainly respect him. I certainly have enjoyed working with him on the set. I really appreciate his humor, and he recently said he was interested in kite surfing, which I do a lot of."

Though his actual on-screen time is brief, Thompson remains on set for the duration of an episode's shoot. The technical aspects of the process by which he morphs into other characters have evolved since Thompson's 1995 debut on the series – today, a blue screen is used for a more seamless transition – but it's still a fairly tedious process.

END GAME

COLONY

REQUIE

"I THINK ['THE UNNATURAL'] WAS THE EPISODE WHERE I WAS THE MOST FEATURED AND GAVE MY BEST PERFORMANCE... IT ADDED A WHOLE DIMENSION TO THE BOUNTY HUNTER BECAUSE HE WAS DOING STUFF ON EARTH 50 YEARS AGO — THE SAME GUY. THAT WAS WAY COOL."

CHANGE IS GOOD: [left] the Alien Bounty Hunter returns in "Requiem"; [above] he shows his true colors in "The Unnatural"

"They'll lock the [first person who appears as the Bounty Hunter] in place," Thompson explains. "They'll go, 'Freeze frame! Hold it!' Then they'll actually lock down that camera. They'll put clamps on it so it's locked down from underneath and from the sides so it can't move, and then they also have the video playback. They have you step into the video image of the person who was there before. Like David's head isn't as large as mine, so I will have to

be a little farther off the mark than he was to try to get our heads closer to the same size. Some of the shorter people they've actually had stand there on six-inch apple boxes, or they have me spread my legs wider to get the head height the same."

The intricate process certainly beats its archaic, hit-or-miss antecedent. "They would literally draw with a crayon on the television screen where the first guy had stood," Thompson remembers. "Then they

would try to get the other guy to stand inside the first guy's outline."

After tackling a fairly large role in Season Eight's opening two-parter, Thompson can now hang up his stiletto at least until Season Nine. Strangely enough, despite all his film work, his work on *The X-Files* has never conflicted with a movie shoot.

"They call me up every six months," Thompson says. "It's always subject to my availability. It's amazing that I've been out of the country for five months, they call me up and I'm available. We did one episode in August, and now I'm working on the Van Damme movie. Well, they just called me up again and said they're going to be starting up again when this movie finishes. So again, I'm probably going to be available when they call."

Not too shabby for a supposed one-shot deal. ◆

THE (X) FILES

Two

In blockbuster mythology two-parter "Two Fathers"/"One Son," Mulder finally learns the truth about aliens, family allegiances and the conspiracy that could change the world

FATHER'

ONE

S DAY

version

by Gina McIntyre

set photos by Kharen Hill

It's only 4:30 p.m., but the Los Angeles sun, for some reason, has already set behind the uninterrupted field of rain clouds that have dominated the sky for the majority of the early December day. Along Wilshire Boulevard, Nicholas Lea sits in the driver's seat of a non-descript black sedan, his passengers, a well-dressed William B. Davis and fictional son Chris Owens. Davis turns to Owens with an air of solemnity and hands him a shiny, cylindrical object, the lethal stiletto used for dispatching aliens. Owens accepts a weighty assignment from his Cigarette-Smoking father and turns to exit the car; the car door sticks, however, and from an adjacent awning where the crew stands sheltered from the unseasonable drizzle, director Kim Manners shouts, "Cut."

The actors stay in their places, perhaps to avoid the brisk weather—strikingly reminiscent of a Vancouver fall—or simply in readiness to repeat their actions for the camera. Make-up is re-touched and lights are adjusted before Manners, clad in a warm, yellow coat and cap, again calls

HIT AND MYTHS: [clockwise from top] Gillian Anderson and Veronica Cartwright in "Two Fathers"; executive producer Frank Spotnitz; director Kim Manners

from his post, and activity commences. Even when the shot runs smoothly, multiple takes are required to ensure that the director captures every subtle nuance of the scene, not only because it deals with grim business but also because it is one of many emotionally charged moments in what just might be the be-all/end-all of *X-Files'* mythology.

"Two Fathers"/"One Son" is the most epic of any two-parter yet penned by the Chris Carter/Frank Spotnitz writing team. With a cast of characters that reads like a who's who list of the entire show, the episode sets the stage for revelations about the real nature of the truth Mulder's been seeking all these years and actually offers concrete explanations about a multitude of the series' mysteries. After five-and-a-half years of carefully constructing such a complex cover-up, Spotnitz says it was time to deliver some definitive answers to faithful viewers, but capturing the essence of the show's tangled conspiracy in only two 60-minute increments proved a sizeable undertaking.

"After the movie, we all felt the need to shake things up and take the audience some place they don't expect to go," Spotnitz says. "Once we hit on the idea of reprising some of the fundamental aspects of the show, going back to the first season with 'The Erlenmeyer Flask,' the rest of it came very quickly. There are parts of the story we knew we wanted to do for well over a year, almost two years, and other parts that it just seemed now was the time to do. Now, it was really, 'OK, we're going to make a lot of this explicit—what do you say, what do you not say, and what do you do to the future of the TV series?' I think what's interesting and exciting and frightening about this two-parter is the bigness of it.

"It also felt good to us to pull together all of these strands that so many people have been having a hard time keeping up with and say, 'Bang, here it is,'" he continues. "Actually, I think it's shocking. That's what's exciting about it to me. It changes everything."

That it does—more so than Mulder discovering an extraterrestrial lifeform in "Gethsemane" or the faceless alien rebels torching UFO abductees in "Patient X" or

to execute this person," Manners says. "Here's a man whose father is sending him to commit a murder, obviously putting him in a very dangerous position. And Spender, who's an FBI agent, is going to accept this assignment from his father, who he knows is of a criminal element. He's going to go and carry out this execu-

" I think what's interesting and exciting and **frightening** about this two-parter is the bigness of it."

—Frank Spotnitz, executive producer

even the Cigarette-Smoking Man destroying Mulder's office and revealing his identity to estranged son Jeffrey Spender in "The End." As one of the titular "Two Fathers," the slippery CSM does play a crucial role in the events showcased in the episode; in particular, his relationship with his son is called to the fore. Tonight sporting a navy blue wool overcoat, Davis waits to bring the character to life before the camera, all the while coolly exuding the kind of commanding presence one would expect from a lifelong conspirator. Nearby, Manners explains the scene.

"[Spender's] father actually sends him

tion without asking any questions. That's a tremendously heavy scene."

Intense though it might be, the atmosphere on the set is professional, not strained. At this advanced stage in the X-Files' mythology, all of its players, including Manners, share a strong rapport, which is necessary to survive the often rigorous shooting schedules the historic outings require. Every now and then, the director will remind his actors of their place in the story, answering any questions they might raise. More often than not, however, all the elements—actors, dialogue, camera—coalesce into a seamless whole.

"I rely on the actors around me," says Owens, explaining how he approaches such grave scenarios as this. "All I have to do is look at Bill and Nick and I know I'm into something important, heavy, and serious. So that helps a lot. And I think, too, there's something about [the fact that] you know what's going on, so once you hear, 'Action,' or just before you hear that, your mindset just kind of clicks over."

Handling ominous props like the stiletto doesn't hurt, either. "Oh my God, that thing is frightening! It really is frightening, no acting required," Owens exclaims, a trace of his natural sense of humour surfacing. "Dad's giving me that weapon to use. That's a father, eh? Could have sent me to university, but no, here's a weapon. It's the school of hard knocks."

The CSM, of course, is a graduate of that school himself, and the second part of the mythology outing, "One Son," actually takes viewers back in time to 1973 to reveal some of his most difficult lessons. Along with Mr. and Mrs. Mulder (Peter Donat and Rebecca Toolan) and Cassandra Spender (Veronica Cartwright), Cigarette-Smoking Man anchors a '70s-era flashback sequence that helps explicate some of the more bewildering twists of the conspiracy.

Rather than risk confusing the audience by casting younger look-alike actors to play the established characters, the *X-Files'* team instead opted to make Donat, Toolan, Cartwright and Davis look 25 years younger. To that end, make-up department head Cheri Montesanto-Medcalf and artist Kevin Westmore used prosthetic lifts to pull up the actors' skin, effectively making wrinkles disappear. They also filled in their lips and highlighted their cheekbones to give them a more youthful appearance. Although each actor spent roughly two hours in the make-up chair, the effect was astonishing.

"It was kind of interesting because the actors are playing themselves," Manners says. "The make-up people did a hell of a job, making them look as young as possible. They should be very proud because the whole cast looks terrific, especially Bill Davis. He looked like Jack Lord in [Sixties television series] *Stoney Burke*. He's so studly. He looks like a bad Elvis impersonator. Bill loved it. Bill's still got that good young physique because he waterskis all the time. He pulled it off well."

Davis' co-star Cartwright, who donned a strawberry blond wig and bell-bottoms for the scenes, agrees. "Bill was very funny with his Elvis Presley hair, the sideburns," she says. "It was fun. You find yourself walking a little differently and being a little more perky, remembering back all those years."

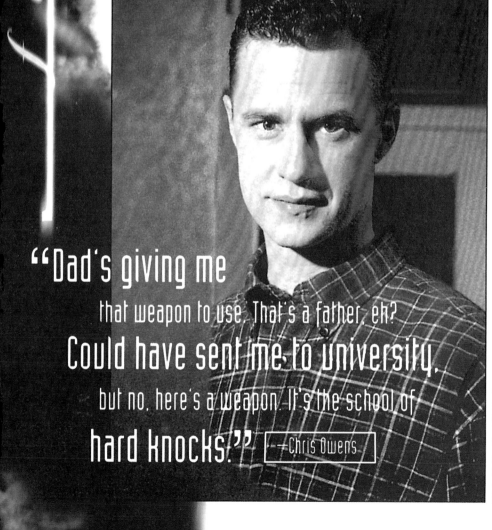

"**Dad's giving me** that weapon to use. That's a father, eh? **Could have sent me to university,** but no, here's a weapon. It's the school of **hard knocks.**" —Chris Owens

first part, now would go to work second unit for the first part of the episode. Also, they may want that to work on the first unit of the second part. When you do the two-parters, there's a lot of just blind running. [You have to say], 'Okay, you're going to be done with the prop by 3pm. I'll be there about 3:30pm to pick it up because

While the actors were reliving earlier days, prop master Tom Day was furiously creating all the necessary elements to convincingly recreate 1973, including Morley cigarette boxes minus the surgeon general's ubiquitous warning. Accuracy, he explains, was key.

"The '70s is kind of a tricky, weird period because so much of what we have now, we had in the '70s," Day says. "If you're doing a period thing from the '40s, you've got a whole period of stuff [to choose from]. If you're doing 1947 and you use something from 1942, it's different than doing 1977 and using something from 1972. There's a lot more design changes in things in that five-year period. Also, a lot more people were around in the '70s.

People are going to say, 'No, no, no, I remember I got little Johnny a super-duper watch in 1975 for his birthday, and I know they didn't have it in '73 because it was the latest greatest when I got it for him.'"

The fact that certain props needed to appear in both "Two Fathers" and "One Son" meant Day had to carefully track every item.

"Two-parters are their own particular challenge," he explains. "What will happen is a prop that we would use on the

the other unit needs it at 5pm.' In order not to spend a world of money and make two of everything, you wind up doing a lot of running around."

To further enhance the look of the '70s shots, special filters were employed to soften the images captured on film, which again helped erase signs of the actors' true ages and lent more of a unique, older feel to the scenes. Manners worked closely with director of photography Bill Roe to ensure that the lighting fit the mood of the sequences. Roe says setting up for the flashback was similar to shooting up-to-date scenes.

Mother
from another PLANET

So just what has Cassandra Spender been up to these many months since her apparent abduction in Season Five's "Patient X"? Emmy Award-nominated actress Veronica Cartwright can't really answer as to her character's exact whereabouts, but she has found some welcome changes upon returning from the great beyond in landmark mythology episode "Two Fathers."

"I can walk, that's nice," Cartwright reports from *The X-Files*' set. Dressed in a simple but elegant black suit, she is still hyperventilating from the last scene she shot, in which Cassandra appears at Mulder's door frantically seeking help—and still reeling from all the shake-ups in the already topsy-turvy world of the conspiracy in which she plays an increasingly important part. "There are things that are revealed. Although I did know that I was married to the Cigarette-Smoking Man, who is Jeffrey's father, I just didn't realize what the whole involvement was and what the details were or what happens as a result of being able to walk. I didn't know any of that stuff," she says.

To fans, it might have appeared less than a sure bet that Cassandra would find her way back into the show's tangled mythology; Cartwright explains, however, that she always knew she would return for more episodes. A very reliable source had assured her it was only a matter of time.

"Chris [Carter] had mentioned that I would come back," she says. "I figured that the alien ship that was in the movie was sort of similar to the way they described the alien ship that I was abducted into. When I saw the movie, with Cigarette-Smoking Man being there and everything, I wondered if that's where I had been taken. When it flies off in the end, I wondered if that was my spaceship. I said to Chris, 'I don't want to die!' He said, 'Don't worry, you're not going to die.'"

Even with such a long break between episodes, Cartwright says it was not difficult to slip back into character. "You find little threads," she says. "She's sort of being revealed as we go along, so those are new discoveries to me, too. I just have to make her as real as possible and a total believer in what happened, just sort of go about it the same way as you would go about any character study. I just allow that part of myself to go ahead and believe that [aliens] really do exist. She totally believes that she's been abducted and she has been."

And does Cartwright espouse the same sort of beliefs in the outré as the character she portrays? "Sure, why not? We can't be the only people," she says with a shrug. "We're just one of several planets. I don't know. I was sort of hoping when the Sojourner went up and was walking along Mars that some little guys would pop up. I always thought that would be just terrific. I can't say that I sit there and wait for them to come. It's certainly believable that they would exist. I mean, we can't be the only lifeform. It wouldn't make any sense. I wondered if they all looked like Jeff Bridges in *Starman*. That would be fine by me."

The actress says the outgoing attitude of cast and crew made returning to the set that much easier. "They're great," says Cartwright. "I think David's hysterically funny. He's got such a dry sense of humour. And Gill, I think, is just terrific. I've felt most welcome and I've had a great time."

In between her *X-Files* stints, Cartwright has been juggling a mind-boggling schedule. "I just did a movie in Austin, Texas, called *A Slipping Down Life*, with Guy Pierce and Lili Taylor. We just found out that we've been accepted into Sundance. We're in competition, so that's very exciting. I have a movie [that was released] in January called *Sparkler*. That's with Park Overall and Freddie Prinze Jr. and Jamie Kennedy. I play a bi-sexual stripper. I had a ball. Then I'm going to do a part in a [television movie of the week] called *Adam*. And I have a six-and-a-half-year-old son. I have to be Mom at school and do the lunch program."—*G.M.*

"We watch a rehearsal and then we just figure out what would be good," he says. "I have to think ahead and figure out which way we're going to be looking. I have to think what is the best place [to light] for the whole scene.

"We used a little more diffusion for the '73 [scenes]," Roe continues. "We tried to keep the light off their faces a little bit more. We didn't go real heavy [with the diffusion] because we didn't want it to be like, 'OK, we're in '73.' Just enough to help. We tried to make it a little shadowy. That's how we always think. Make it moody, make it mysterious, make it scary. You can be bolder and let things happen. It's harder to make it difficult, and it's harder to make it darker, too. Everybody says, 'You're not using very

blood that runs through the veins of some of the series' most inexplicable characters.

The recipe is a specialty, culled from the pages of Vancouver FX wizard Toby

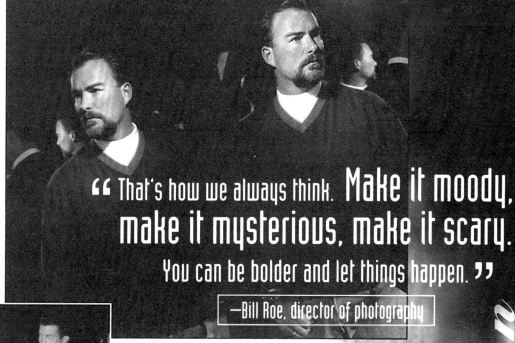

" That's how we always think. Make it moody, make it mysterious, make it scary. You can be bolder and let things happen. "

—Bill Roe, director of photography

many lights,' but you've got to make sure the light is in the right place to make it work. Hopefully, we've been doing that the right way. Everybody seems to think so."

Back in present day,

The X-Files' crew has landed on location in the beautiful Hancock Park neighborhood, where curved streets intersect to fashion a web of stately houses and well-groomed lawns. Inside the kitchen of one of the homes, special effects maven Bryan Blair labors over a sink, filling large syringes with solutions of citric acid and bicarbonate of soda. When the substances, one of which is green, come in contact with each other, they begin to fizz; the resulting mixture is none other than the noxious alien

Lindala's own cookbook. When the script for "Two Fathers" called for the green fluid, Lindala happily shared the formula he first created with *The X-Files'* second generation special effects team.

Now that the secret has been handed down, the real trick is ensuring that no unwanted green stains find their way onto an unlucky homeowner's carpet. Considering the staggering amount of the stuff involved in the day's shoot, it won't be an easy job.

"So far, we've been in two houses like this—big, expensive old houses where we had to [use] either blood or green goo," says John Vulich, whose Optic Nerve Studios crafts the show's FX. "We came up with a blood formula that uses a standard Karo syrup, and instead of dyes we use flocking, which is almost like hair fibres that are chopped up real fine into a powder. But it's not a dye so it can't seep into anything. Once it dries up, it's like dust and you just brush it away. Some of the stuff, we couldn't use that material, so we did have to be careful and put some carpeting down. For the most part, we tried to use stuff that wouldn't stain."

As Blair tends to his chemistry, a man dressed in a casual cardigan and slacks sits

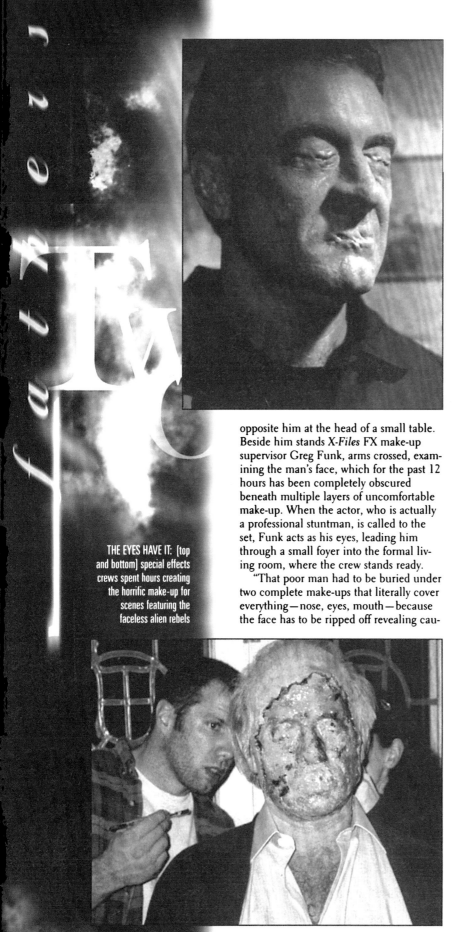

terized features underneath," Funk says. "We had to first make him one of the faceless rebels, so we did a faceless make-up and we put that make-up on him. We also had a likeness of the actor sculpted, molded, foam rubber made. It's almost Halloween mask-like. He's wearing a mask of the other actor that was glued to his face, custom-made for his face, and it gets ripped off. There was goo underneath it, so once it comes off we see some blaah, sort of like an amber gel.

"It's such a hard thing to do. Because every orifice is supposed to be cauterized shut, we have to put very, very small slits between the detail of the scar tissue that appears to be blending over his eyes, his lips, his ears, very small slits he can see through barely," Funk continues. "If you hold a small hole up to your eye, you can actually see a lot. The mouth and the nose are just plain difficult. We put little sections of straws up there just to open those holes up a little wider. It was murder."

THE EYES HAVE IT: [top and bottom] special effects crews spent hours creating the horrific make-up for scenes featuring the faceless alien rebels

opposite him at the head of a small table. Beside him stands *X-Files* FX make-up supervisor Greg Funk, arms crossed, examining the man's face, which for the past 12 hours has been completely obscured beneath multiple layers of uncomfortable make-up. When the actor, who is actually a professional stuntman, is called to the set, Funk acts as his eyes, leading him through a small foyer into the formal living room, where the crew stands ready.

"That poor man had to be buried under two complete make-ups that literally cover everything—nose, eyes, mouth—because the face has to be ripped off revealing cau-

In the coming days, more stuntmen will submit to the torturous process for the episode's dramatic opening sequence in which the faceless men invade a secret medical facility maintained by the Syndicate. As Vulich's crew prepares to transform them, second unit production manager Harry Bring ensures things are in order at the California stockyard where the shots will take place under Manners' watchful eye. It is his job to coordinate all the aspects of second unit filming, which follows the eight to nine days of principal photography for every episode and usually includes the more elaborate scenes of a given show.

For "Two Fathers," Bring's team will set a van—and several people—on fire in a fully operational train yard. Properly executing the complicated shot requires Bring to solve problems before they occur, such as predicting if noise from the trains will interrupt the shoot or determining if the color temperature of the lights illuminating the yard match that of the lights used for the series. Bring must ensure not only that the shot goes off without a hitch, but also that it goes off safely.

"We have made sure that nothing flammable will be near us," Bring says. "We'll make it look like it's closer to the train cars by the use of longer lenses. We're hiring a group of extras that are actual firemen. They have their own pumper truck. We'll also have an ambulance on call for four hours. There's a lot of protection that we take for all our camera crew. They all wear these special suits, and then we have some lens protection, too, so that we don't ruin the photography part of it. Safety is always first."

The nature of the shot dictates much planning; when it comes to things like explosions, there is really only one chance to get it right. "By and large, that's a one-take deal. I think we have two vans, so we can have two takes," Bring says. "I'm sure it will be a multiple camera situation so if some things didn't go exactly how the director envisioned it, through the cutting from camera angle to camera angle, he'll be able to get the scene that he wanted."

As for Manners, he remains unfazed. As he has said in the past, he's just about done it all during his *X-Files* tenure, including staging explosions and lighting stuntmen aflame. The stockyard shoot is days away; he must now concentrate on matters more immediately at hand—a heated exchange

episode is different, he admits, in that it brings an end to so many of the storylines that have lain at the heart of the show for so long. But Manners, who has already been tapped to helm the cliffhanger that will conclude Season Six, is quite confident that no matter how many of the shadowy con-

> "The stand-alone episodes are terrific. The comedies are terrific. But this mythology has evolved and I've been part of that evolution. **I'm excited to be a part of where we are now** in this continuing story." —Kim Manners, director

between Krycek and Spender that Lea and Owens rehearse in an adjoining room.

"It is kind of exciting to be continuing the tale," Manners offers. "The stand-alone episodes are terrific. The comedies are terrific. But this mythology has evolved and I've been part of that evolution. I'm excited to be a part of where we are now in this continuing story. We have a lot of ourselves invested in this, and we've been strung along as well. Chris [Carter] knows what's happening as he goes along, so these shows, they always hold a certain amount of surprise for me."

For all its complicated intrigue, this

spiracy's secrets are revealed, more surprises will remain just around the bend. "I have a feeling there will be a new direction in the mythology where we'll explore, not necessarily new territory, but maybe wrap up a couple of loose ends that aren't wrapped up here," Manners says. "There are still several things after this that need to be answered. I think our quest will be to answer those in the future." ●

DAVID DUCHOVNY CHATS TO IAN SPELLING ABOUT EIGHT YEARS OF TOP-NOTCH ACTING AND ENTERTAINMENT IN *THE X-FILES*, AS WELL AS HIS MOVIE *EVOLUTION*

ALL GOODT

DAVID DUCHOVNY IS IN A MOVIE WITH MARAUDING ALIENS
AND A SMART REDHEAD. DEJÀ VU, ANYONE?

Proving once and for all that the truth is not only very much out there, but that it's far stranger than fiction, *X-Files* star David Duchovny took to the big screen this in a film that indeed involved extra-terrestrial beings and a co-star with red hair. The film wasn't the next *X-Files* feature, however, but rather the Ivan Reitman-directed comedy *Evolution*. The aliens on view in *Evolution* weren't like anything ever seen on *The X-Files* and the lady with the red hair was Julianne Moore of *Hannibal*, *The End of the Affair* and *The Lost World: Jurassic Park II*, not Duchovny's usual partner in crime-solving, Gillian Anderson.

"That was weird," Duchovny says of the similarities between *The X-Files* and *Evolution*. "It was just a coincidence. Ivan called me and said, 'Come have a meeting.' I'd worked with Ivan on *Beethoven*. I'm a fan of the genre that he created, the kind of movie he created with *Animal House* and the *Ghostbusters* films. I don't think people give Ivan enough credit for having created a tone of movie that pretty much everybody works in these days in comedies. Bill Murray benefitted from it, as did Dan Aykroyd and Harold Ramis. These are very influential comic voices of our time. I wanted to work in Ivan's house, so to speak.

"I've always wanted to do what he does in his movies. And it's not necessarily what I do in my work. It's different. So I wanted to be pushed and I wanted to be funny in a way that was different from what comes naturally to me, which is closer to what I did in the funny moments on *The X-Files*.

"So Ivan said, 'I've got a script called *Evolution* and I want you to do it.' I was like, 'OK, cool! I want to work with you. I'll go home, read the script and I'll call you.' I go home and I'm thinking, 'Great, this is exactly what I want. I've got four months before I have to be back on *The X-Files* and Ivan Reitman wants me to be in a comedy.' I start reading the script. 'OK, that's a funny scene. And I'm playing that guy. Cool.' 20 pages later there are aliens. I was like, 'OK, cruel joke. Now I can't do it. That's just horrible. Why?' So I sat down with my wife [Tea Leoni, who guest-starred in the Duchovny-directed episode "Hollywood, AD" and

HINGS....

SPOOKY MOMENTS!

So that's it for Mulder on *The X-Files*. After eight amazing years, David Duchovny has left the regular series, as has Special Agent Fox Mulder. So in honor of a long and highly memorable stint, we thought it was time to celebrate his landmark moments:

First line: "Sorry, nobody down here but the FBI's most unwanted."

Most bizarre moment:
Aging prematurely in "Dod Kalm."
Also nominated: Being cocooned by weird bugs in "Darkness Falls"; bursting in on himself as he's about to kiss Scully in "Small Potatoes"; being time-warped into a different era in "Triangle"; all of "Dreamland"; him and Scully shooting each other continuously in "How the Ghosts Stole Christmas"; getting caught in a time warp in "Monday"; all of "Field Trip"; being granted three wishes by a genie in "Je Souhaite."

Most romantic moment:
The ending of "Existence."
Also nominated: The near-kiss with Scully in the *X-Files* movie; the sleeping bag scene in "Detour"; the New Year's kiss in Season Five's "Millennium"; offering to help Scully conceive in "Per Manum."

Funniest moment:
Being dragged along (yelling and screaming) by a runaway RV in "Bad Blood".
Also nominated: Almost getting jiggy with Detective White in "Syzygy"; pencils on the roof in "Chinga"; singing the *Shaft* theme in "Bad Blood"; the mirror dance in "Dreamland"; cherry pie in "Jose Chung's 'From Outer Space.'"

Most horrible moment:
Being tortured by aliens in Season Eight.
Also nominated: Facing the dark side in "Grotesque"; being experimented on in "Tunguska"; being an amputee faced by beautiful, buxom nurses in "Kill Switch"; facing insanity in "Folie a Deux" and "Sixth Extinction"; having the 'X'-Files office burned down in "The End"; getting it on with Fowley in "Sixth Extinction II: Amor Fati"; being buried in "DeadAlive."

Scariest moment:
Almost being executed in "The Pine Bluff Variant."
Also nominated:
Being trapped in a box car with a timebomb in "731"; facing the prospect that he may be a murderer in "Demons"; trying to escape a UFO while being chased by predatory aliens in the movie; being trapped in a basement full of zombies with an empty gun in "Millennium"; being infected by the monster in "Agua Mala"; almost dying in "Brand X."

Nastiest enemy:
Alex Krycek.
Also nominated: Robert 'Pusher' Modell; the Cigarette-Smoking Man; Tooms; Alien Bounty Hunter; the Peacock Brothers.

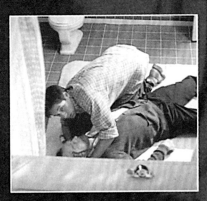

Saddest moment:
Tie: Discovering that his mother is dead in "Sein Und Zeit" and discovering his father's murdered body in "Anasazi."
Also nominated:
Contemplating suicide in "Gethsemane"; seeing his mom wired up to a machine in "Talitha Cumi"/"Herrenvolk"; saying goodbye to his sister in "Closure"; worrying over Scully in "One Breath"/"Memento Mori"/"Redux" etc.

Last line: "I think what we feared were the possibilities. The truth we both know." (*Kisses Scully...*)

Compiled by Martin Eden. Thanks to Kate Anderson

---

stars in big screen dinosaur epic, *Jurassic Park III*], and I said, 'Here's the script. I want to work with Ivan. I want to do this script, but there are aliens in it.' But Ivan didn't know *The X-Files*. I don't think that he'd ever seen an episode of the show. He didn't care about me being with aliens. He wasn't going to play off or against the baggage that I was bringing. So I just decided that the kind of acting I would do in *Evolution* would be so different from any acting I'd ever done that the alien connection would just be a superficial coincidence."

Evolution teams Duchovny not only with Reitman and Moore, but also with Orlando (*Double Take* and the upcoming remake of *The Time Machine*) Jones and Seann William Scott of *American Pie* and *Dude, Where's My Car?* Duchovny plays Dr Ira Kane, a professor at a community college in Arizona who also happens to be a disgraced government scientist. His best pal is Harry (Jones), a fellow professor who coaches the school's women's volleyball team. Ira and Harry's lives change forever when a meteor crashes nearby and they discover that rapidly evolving alien life forms hitched a ride on the meteor. The government plans to deploy military might to blow the aliens to smithereens, but Ira and Harry realize that will only exacerbate the problem, making the alien creatures grow even faster and ultimately leading to mankind's demise. And with the help of a goofy would-be fireman (Scott) and a klutzy epidemiologist (Moore), Ira and Harry set out to save the world as we know it. Along the way, Duchovny gets to moon a general (an ad-lib that Reitman kept in the film) and romance Moore (which was scripted).

One of the film's biggest laughs comes when Ira remarks that he "knows the government." The line in and of itself isn't that funny, but it elicits plenty of knowing chuckles from fans of *The X-Files* who watched Duchovny's alter-ego, Fox Mulder, butt heads with the government every week for eight years. "Ivan actually called me from a screening of *Evolution* and he was angry," recalls Duchovny, whose previous films include *Return to Me, Playing God, The Rapture, Kalifornia, Chaplin* and *Ruby*. "'They're laughing and they're not supposed to be laughing.' Ivan didn't understand it. I was oblivious, too. I don't walk around thinking about Mulder. I'm glad that I didn't realize it when I delivered the line. I don't like self-referential humor. I think it's kind of cheap. But because the line arose spontaneously, and because we'll take a laugh anywhere we can get it, I'm okay with it."

Duchovny is also okay with the end of his career-making stint as Fox Mulder. The actor made his final appearance as the character in "Essence" and "Existence," the two-parter that brought to a close the eighth season of *The X-Files*. The final scene of "Existence" witnessed Mulder and Scully (Anderson) kissing passionately on the lips as Scully cradled her baby boy, William, named after Mulder's father. As the credits rolled, audiences were left with questions aplenty, including: is the baby human or alien or both? Is Mulder the baby's father? And if Mulder is the child's father, how was the child conceived? "I don't know," Duchovny says. "Honestly, I don't know. I would tell you if I did. What do I think?

"THE FATHER OF SCULLY'S BABY IS... HONESTLY, I DON'T KNOW. I WOULD TELL YOU IF I DID."

they'd added the "buddy" element earlier, perhaps pairing Mulder with Skinner (Mitch Pileggi) in the field. Typically honest, he has also said that he felt the writers missed an opportunity to close out Mulder's story over his final few episodes. Audiences never really got a feeling for what Mulder went through during his abduction by aliens and they never saw the true impact of what happened to the character subsequent to his resurrection. And, while the kiss was a powerful and poignant moment, not to

ABOVE: David Duchovny in directing mode on the set of "Hollywood AD"

BELOW: Garry Shandling and Tea Leoni, in a scene from "Hollywood AD."

Mulder's a real ass. He just takes off when she has a baby. But I'm not coming back. It was time. It was eight years. If you look at the actors you grew up loving, they maybe made 40 films. That's 80 hours of film. There are almost 200 hours of me acting on *The X-Files*. I did enough. It was enough for me, enough of me acting on *The X-Files*. And I am really proud of the show. I didn't think the levels of the show had dropped. My leaving was just my personal decision to say, 'I need to go out and do some other things.'"

The actor turned up on *The X-Files* about a dozen times during the eighth season, sometimes in brief cameos, other times in full episodes. Duchovny – who, as a favor to Bruce Harwood, Tom Braidwood, Dean Haglund and producer Vince Gilligan, also made a cameo appearance as Mulder in the "All About Yves" episode of *The Lone Gunmen* – reported that he enjoyed working with Robert Patrick, who joined the cast this past season as Special Agent John Doggett.

Working with Patrick on episodes such as "Vienen," Duchovny noted, made him wish that

mention a worthwhile pay-off to eight years of emotional investment, it will leave the show's writers with the awkward task of explaining away Mulder's total absence in Season Nine.

On the whole, however, Duchovny liked his part-time status during Season Eight. "In terms of time, it was fantastic," notes Duchovny, who, for the record, ranks Seasons Four and Six as the show's best years. "I got to do a movie and I got to spend a lot of time at home with my wife and daughter. And I also got to appear in 12 episodes of the show. It was my decision to walk away, but when I came back and felt peripheral to the storyline, that didn't feel right to me. But again, it was my decision and my fault. When I signed on for the episodes this season, I thought that I would have more to do than I actually ended up having to do. So there I was complaining about not having any time to do anything else, and here I am now complaining that I didn't work hard enough on the show. So I'm not the easiest person to satisfy! But that's how things worked out."

Right now, Duchovny is contemplating what to do next. He's not signed for any other films, although he did shoot a cameo role for the comedy *Zoolander* which was directed by Ben Stiller and stars Stiller, Owen Wilson, Christine Taylor and David Bowie. He's spending free moments with Leoni and their daughter, two-year-old Madelaine West, all the while reading scripts and – putting to use the skills he honed penning the teleplays for "The Unnatural" and "Hollywood AD" – even trying to write a script for a feature. And for all those X-philes out there, fear not, you may yet see Fox Mulder again someday. "I would enjoy doing another *X-Files* movie," Duchovny concludes. "I

will miss the character. I will miss the people. And I will miss the show. I think, in two or three years, if another *X-Files* movie came along, I would be very happy to do it."

Duchovny would be more likely to reprise the part of Mulder if his future projects succeeded in distancing him a bit from the character. Even though *Evolution* served up aliens, it was a comedy, something mainstream audiences – except those who watched *The Larry Sanders Show* – weren't accustomed to seeing Duchovny try his hand at. "People say, 'I didn't know that you were funny,'" Duchovny notes, bringing the conversation to an

end… for now. "It was the same thing last year when I did [the romantic comedy-drama] *Return to Me*. I think that's because Mulder made such a deep impression. Because *The X-Files* is such a successful show and such a culturally pervasive show, it's something I have to get out from under. So I think, for the rest of my life, people are going to say, 'I didn't know you were funny.' Hopefully it won't take all of my life.

"I started thinking about, 'How do I get away from being associated with *The X-Files*?' But there's no strategy. I'm just thankful that I'm trying to run away from a success rather than a failure, because you've got to run away from both of them." ●

ABOVE: A scene from Season Six's "The Unnatural," written and directed by Duchovny.

THE ⓍFILES

LONE GUNMAN

Shortly before he left for Los Angeles to appear in the upcoming *X-Files* feature film, 'Lone Gunman' Byers — aka Bruce Harwood — took the time to give Dave Hughes an exclusive interview

Everyone who has worked on *The X-Files* since the show began back in 1993 has a story which relates how they came to be on the highest-profile series on television. Vince Gilligan, for instance, was invited to work on the series, but initially turned it down. Some of *The X-Files'* actors, like Brendan Beiser (Agent Pendrell) were religious viewers of the show before being invited – much to their delight – to play a part in it. Then

there is Bruce Harwood – as the buttoned-down Byers, part of the justifiably paranoid conspiracy theorists known as The Lone Gunmen – who acted on the show without ever having seen it, and later decided he did not care for it at all.

"Someone had told me it was about two FBI agents who look for UFOs," he says, "and I thought it sounded like the *stupidest* idea I had ever heard. So I thought, 'It'll be a one day shoot, [the show]

> I thought [*The X-Files*] sounded like the *stupidest* idea I had ever heard. I thought, 'It'll be a one day shoot, [the show] will be gone in a year – big deal.'

THOSE BYERS EPISODES IN FULL

First Season
"E.B.E."

Second Season
"Blood"
"One Breath"
"Fearful Symmetry"
"Anasazi"

Third Season
"Paper Clip"
"Nisei"
"Apocrypha"
"Wetwired"

Fourth Season
"Musings of a Cigarette Smoking Man" (voice only)
"Memento Mori"

my agent called and said, 'You know, they want you back on *The X-Files*.' And I said, 'As the same guy?' 'Yeah, apparently you were really popular on the internet!'"

So it wasn't all the great word-of-mouth publicity Harwood was giving the show that made the producers want him back? "Exactly!" he says. "So, we were back, and you can't sneeze at another role without auditioning – that's easy street. This was 'Blood,' in season two. And all the crew-members were talking about ['Little Green Men'] and how difficult it had been to fly the girl playing Samantha out the window. They told me it took all day, and they had to use all these ropes and strings and stuff... So I thought, I have to watch [that episode] to see this special effects shot. The shot lasts, like, two seconds or something. But at that point, both my wife and I were hooked." Finally! Thankfully, since then Harwood has had a chance to catch up with some of the episodes he missed – or dismissed – and has grown to love the show as much as the rest of us. "Now that I've seen more of the first season, I begin to think that there's actually a very wide range of episodes. There are some very, very good ones, and some ones that are not so great. I haven't seen the one with the rogue computer ['Ghost in the Machine'], but I hear that's pretty bad. I've seen 'Beyond the Sea,' which is probably one of the best episodes they've ever made."

Bruce Harwood was born April 29 in North Vancouver, grew up in an area of British Columbia called the Okanagan, which the actor describes as, "a very dry, high plateau between the coastal mountains and the Rocky Mountains." He cannot remember how, or why, he ever got into acting in the first place. "It's a complete mystery to me," he says. "My dad told me when I was young, 'Don't become an actor – you won't make any money at all,' and I believed him, and it's true. But I couldn't find anything else I liked as much. I wish I had," he adds, "because then if I had I'd be doing that instead of acting, and probably making more money!"

The usual series of theatre work, roles in Vancouver-based shows such as *The Beachcombers*, *Wiseguy* and *21 Jump Street* followed, as well as a slightly higher-profile part as a computer technician in Mick Garris' *The Fly II* ("It's pretty bad," he says. "It's only funny if you know the people, because they all get slaughtered in the end") and in a TV movie remake of *Bye Bye Birdie*.

During this period, his favorite television part was a recurring role as Willis on *MacGyver*, "a kind of environmentalist/research scientist who would help [the hero]," this being his first 'guest-starring' role. "I got to do the falling-into-quicksand-and-being-rescued cliché," he recalls. "We have a large boggy area just south of Vancouver called Burns' Bog, and it's supposed to be an environmental wasteland because of hazardous material that's been dumped there. So I'm standing around [doing] all these tests there, and I step into a particularly soggy bit and I start sinking and sinking, and MacGyver has to jump in to help me. I remember being actually sunk up to my armpits in freezing cold bog water, and then a week later going into the studio and being sunk over my head in a little vat filled with boggy stuff, with peat moss. It was a lot of fun," he says, though the rest of us may remain unconvinced.

Then came his audition for *The X-Files*, which presumably must have been a memorable occasion. Or not. "People have always asked me what the audition was like, and you know, I *cannot* remember," he says. "The only thing I remember was that I was given the [script] and it said 'Byers is clean-shaven'. And at

will be gone in a year – big deal.' And we did the scene with the two leads in this abandoned building, and it was early in the morning, and they were very subdued, so we sort of stumbled our way through it. The morning went very quickly," he recalls. "I think it was a really good day, because we got the scene done, I felt pretty happy with what I'd done. We were finished before lunch, and went home for the rest of the day. And that was it. I just put it out of my mind."

Later, Harwood says that he watched the episode in order to record his scene for his audition tape, "and I actually thought the episode was kind of dumb." He laughs, rather guiltily. "I didn't think it worked that well, [and although] it's the first Lone Gunmen episode, it's certainly not the best Lone Gunmen episode." Presumably, then, Harwood watched more episodes, and began to develop an interest in it? "Not really," he admits with another guilty chuckle. "I thought, '*X-Files*? Who cares? Some stupid show...' But I also work part-time at the public library, and when people heard that I was an actor, they'd say, 'Oh, what have you done?' And I'd say, 'Well, I was in MacGyver.' 'Hmm-hmm.' 'I was on a local show called *The Beachcombers*.' And they'd go, 'Yeah, yeah.' 'And I just did this show called *The X-Files* –' And suddenly they would sit bolt upright in the chair and say, 'You worked on *The X-Files!? Great show!*' And I thought, 'What is this? I've got to start watching the show! Why are people so excited by it?' So I watched ['Jersey Devil'] and I still wasn't completely convinced! And then

the time I had just grown my beard, so I thought 'Well, I'm not going to get that. It says clean-shaven and well-dressed.' But I put on my old rehearsal suit and tie, and I went in." Other than that, he says, "I honestly don't remember a thing about it."

Harwood does, however, remember trying to give his wafer-thin character – essentially, a man defined by the way he dressed and combed his hair, and whom Harwood once described as, "a low-key, high-wired kind of guy" – some background in order to flesh him out. "When I first [played] him, I thought of him as a kind of university professor type – I imagined him as a kind of mathematics professor kind of guy," he says. "And in my first appearance I had my hands in my pockets and my shoulders were very tense. Since then, he's gotten more relaxed, and I've been rethinking his social position in that I now consider him to be lower down the scale. I think he spends way more time in this basement office on the computer, gathering all this information together, and a lot less time actually earning a living somewhere."

"Apocrypha"

Maybe that's why he dresses the way he does, the antithesis to the slovenliness of his partners (Langly and Frohike) – because he's a wannabe. "I think what I decided is that he works for a company like Xerox," Harwood explains, "and he's one of those guys who shows up to fix the machine. They're always wearing a suit and tie for some reason, like it's company policy. But I also think the reason he's so buttoned-down is that he works all the time with two guys who are slobs, basically. And he gets up every morning, trims his beard and combs his hair and puts on a suit and tie, and goes to a basement and sits at a computer screen all alone. It's something I haven't quite put my finger on yet, but there's something of an obsessiveness about appearance, about the way things are, that is part of what he is. I really haven't had a chance to nail it, because his scenes are about other things, and he always has to worry about helping Mulder." Perhaps all that work he does fixing Xerox machines at government buildings allows him to take some time piecing together classified documents lifted from the shredder machine? "That's a good idea," he says. "Maybe I'll use that."

Harwood says that, in their appearances on the show – one, in "Musings of a Cigarette-Smoking Man," in voiceover only – the Lone Gunmen have evolved. "I'm happy to say that my acting has improved since my first appearance as Byers, [but] the big change for the Lone Gunmen is that in their first few appearances in the first and second season, they thought of Mulder as being one of them, but a bit out there – a bit of a joke. And gradually they start to become his fan club."

Mulder's attitude to them has probably changed, too: he may have originally thought,'There but for the grace of God go I,' but he obviously now has an enormous respect for their work. "I think that's why they work in the show," Harwood says. "They provide a buffer for Mulder, in that he can be odd, but as

long as we're weirder, he won't ever go as far as we go."

More recently, Harwood's character has changed in other, more tangible ways. In the fourth season episode "Memento Mori," Byers becomes an unlikely action hero as he joins Mulder in breaking into a government building in an effort to learn the truth behind a sinister conspiracy instigated by the Cigarette-Smoking Man and carried out by Skinner. "Byers was the link between Mulder and the two other guys," Harwood remembers, "following Mulder around until we got to a point where we had to split up and I had to head back." Was it difficult for Harwood to have Byers taken out of his natural environment of secret locations lit only by the light from computer screens, and placed into a more heroic situation? "What was difficult about that role is that Byers is totally comfortable being in this basement, gathering information," he says. "This is how I think of him, as the guy who enjoys feeling like he knows everything and is sitting at the center of all these conduits of information and putting together the big picture.

"So having him at the center of the action, which he is not at all suited for, was the main challenge – trying to work out how he would deal with any kind of real danger. And I guess, in the end, you could say that his solution was to run as fast as he could!" Could it be that, just as Harwood was discovering this new side of Byers, so Byers was learning more about himself? "I think in this case Byers was nervous, but fine as long as Mulder was there to hold his hand. The problem was when Mulder said, 'You have to go back on your own.' And I think when Mulder left me I had quite a long reaction take – edited down in the final scene – where I was just watching him go down the corridor, and then the door he had gone through slammed in my face, and I had to leave. And I was like a little puppy dog wondering what to do."

How did Harwood, a self-confessed shy person who works part-time in a library, deal with the recognition that came with working on a high-profile show such as *The X-Files*? "I think I was in shock for much of the time," he says with customary candor. "First off, the show was very popular, and it was nice to be part of that. Then this 'Lone Gunmen' thing started happening, and I started getting fan mail, and I went to about four different conventions in the US, and people started making jokes about spin-offs and stuff. I think my first experience of it was when this group on America Online, who had been talking about *The X-Files* for about a year, wanted to meet each other

> My dad told me when I was young, 'Don't become an actor – you won't make any money at all', and I believed him, and it's true.

in Las Vegas. And at the time, Dean Haglund [who plays Langly] was on-line and had made contact with them, and [when] they invited him to Vegas, he asked me if I'd like to go. I thought, 'Sure, why not? It'd be nice to meet some fans.' And then, at the last minute, Dean couldn't go so I ended up going on my own. So the first night in Vegas, I walked upstairs to a room they had commandeered and where everyone was watching the show, and suddenly I saw all these heads turning as I came into the room..." he says, a touch uncomfortably. "That's when I had the first inkling of what popularity meant, I guess."

Since this unofficial gathering, Harwood has attended a number of conventions, from Burbank to Boston, and has begun to warm to the initially terrifying idea of encountering large numbers of people eager to meet him. "The first convention I was at, I was terrified," he says, "because I had no idea what people wanted, [and] I had no idea what to say. So I just went up there and blurted out stuff for half an hour, and then answered questions, and it was okay. The audience was quite sympathetic to the fact

open this book and showed me these Polaroids of what looked like a guy with a bullet wound or something lying on the ground, and then disappeared after getting our signatures. And I couldn't tell if this was someone who was genuinely unbalanced, or whether it was someone who was sort of role-playing a character and had taken it to a convention. I went over to the other guys who were there and said, 'Did you meet a woman who...' and they said, 'Yeah, that was strange.' But no one knew quite what to make of things."

Since "Memento Mori," his most recent episode as Byers, Harwood has completed a guest-starring role on an episode of another science fiction drama series, *The Outer Limits*, in which he plays, "a frightened technician who was revealing the evil secrets of the government on a television programme. It was a lot of fun – I got to actually fire a gun, [and] panic and break down and do all sorts of things. It's actually the last episode of this season," he adds,

> "E.B.E." was a one-shot deal – I thought that was it – and then I just got swept up into this magic carpet ride which is *The X-Files*.

"Nisei"

that I was terrified, because I told them right away, and since then it got better and better." As an actor who began his career in theatre, was he not used to being the focus of attention in a room full of people? "Because I am a shy person," he explains, "when I'm being myself, I'm going to be a shy person. But when I'm acting and playing a part – and I don't want to go too far into this, [because] who knows what it says about me psychologically – I have no problem in front of crowds of people."

Asked if he has ever met anyone who has given him reason to feel as paranoid as the Lone Gunmen, Harwood immediately recalls someone who approached him at a convention in Indianapolis. "We all remember when a woman came up with a whole series of photos in a photo album, and said that her husband had worked for the FBI, and that he had been shot, and then his body switched. She flipped

"and it's what they call a 'clip episode,' where they use clips from previous shows. So part of the trick is working out an interesting way of working them into the show. The premise is that Alan Thicke, a Canadian actor who's made it big in Los Angeles, is the host of this sort of *Hard Copy*-style TV show, and he is going to be revealing the government conspiracy in some sort of secret genetic studies, and I am his prime witness, and I bring with me clips of different researches, and those are the clips from the shows."

Although few people would suggest that *The X-Files* has made Bruce Harwood famous, the actor admits to having lingering feelings of discomfort now that he has a recurring, popular role on such a major show. "I find it odd because I feel as if I'm being given a free ride," he says, struggling to articulate his feelings. "It's not been so much my talent that got me the part, but just sheer luck, and I've just tried to take advantage of that luck as best I can. It's a very odd trip, very strange for me," he adds. "'E.B.E.' was a one-shot deal – I thought that was it – and then I just got swept up into this magic carpet ride which is *The X-Files*, and now I'm going to be doing a motion picture in Los Angeles."

The film to which he is referring is, of course, *The X-Files* movie, in which Harwood and the other Lone Gunmen will reprise their roles for the big screen. "My thought was that we wouldn't be in the movie simply because a motion picture of *The X-Files* is basically two episodes of the TV show, and in a movie you have to make a different kind of impact on the audience than a TV show does," he explains, expressing his surprise that his services would be required for the show's first big-screen outing. "A TV show has lots of leisure time, and it can introduce characters like The Lone Gunmen and pick them up at a later episode. But I thought initially that a two-hour movie would want to go straight for the guts of the thing, [having] the two stars out there dealing with some kind of mystery, and that our characters wouldn't be required [because] they would just get in the way of people who don't watch the show regularly but just decided to see the movie."

Harwood is also looking forward to finding out more about his character early in the fifth series. "I don't know if it's true or not, but I hear that the first episode the Lone Gunmen appear in next season is going to explain how they got together," he says, clearly relishing the prospect of finding out his character's first name after three-and-a-half years on the show.

With special thanks to Maddelena Acconci

Suspect

Ian Spelling finds out how Tom Braidwood managed to fall in with the wrong crowd

Left: The Lone Gunmen imprisoned in "Unusual Suspects."
Above: Tom Braidwood as Frohike.

S omewhere there's got to be an 'X' file devoted to Tom Braidwood.

Really, there just has to be one. How else to explain the fact that Braidwood has achieved a *bona fide* measure of stardom as Frohike, one of The Lone Gunmen, on *The X-Files*? Perhaps it's time to call in Agents Mulder (David Duchovny) and Scully (Gillian Anderson). Not so fast, Braidwood warns. Not so fast. There's no conspiracy at all, he swears. It was dumb luck, serendipity, good fortune, a matter of timing and all that good stuff, he insists, that led to the invitation to join Bruce Harwood (Byers) and Dean Haglund (Langly) as everyone's favorite paranoid conspiracy freaks. "I never imagined I'd do the role," Braidwood says. "Frohike was an accident. I think Bruce, Dean and I thought of it as just an acting gig, a one-time only thing. We showed up once in the first year and three or four times in the second year, and it took off from there. We just went along with the popularity of the show. But in my wildest imagination I never thought all this would happen."

Hmm, the guy sounds serious. Maybe he's legit. But let's dig a little deeper here,

> "FROHIKE WAS AN ACCIDENT... IN MY WILDEST IMAGINATION I NEVER THOUGHT ALL THIS WOULD HAPPEN."

shall we? Braidwood acquiesces. "How I got the role is a classic story," he notes. "I was one of the first assistant directors [A.D.] on the show. I was prepping an episode ["E.B.E."] with a wonderful director named Billy Graham. They were in a casting session and found who they wanted for two of the three Lone Gunmen. They had their Langly and Byers, but couldn't find anyone to play Frohike. Billy basically said, 'We need somebody slimy like Braidwood.' They came out of casting and I was walking down the hall. Billy saw me and said, 'It looks like you're going to do it.' I said, 'Do what?' and he said 'Frohike.' And that was it. I said, 'Sure, whatever.'

"I had graduated from university and worked on theatre for eight to ten years, doing a lot of acting. I left that when I decided to get into the production end of film and television. I did play odd parts here and there, but I never focused on it at all. I did Frohike for Billy because he was a great guy. It was fine. It was just a small scene. It didn't mean anything." Or so Braidwood believed.

Over time, scene after scene found The Lone Gunmen helping out Scully and Mulder, the latter of whom took a bemused liking to the decidedly off-beat trio. After all, he was at least as paranoid as Frohike, Byers and Langly, right? And it made perfect sense that audiences, too, took a liking to the guys. "We're eccentric and out there on the fringe, and people enjoy that. We're not mainstream," Braidwood reasons. "We're kind of scruffy and a little bit crazy. Quite often [our scenes] have a humorous bent that give the show a lighter side. People enjoy that because the show overall is pretty serious."

So, just who is Frohike?

"He's a bit of a loner and he's a little shy and insecure, but he's surely bright and very interested in the whole process of discovering information and figuring out mysteries," Braidwood notes of the character, whose name is pronounced as Fro-hickey. "He enjoys the friendship of Scully and Mulder. He likes being a part of the tapestry that they're involved with. It's intriguing and exciting for him."

Juggling the demands of his tasks as first assistant director and part-time thespian hasn't been easy for Braidwood. It was a bit of an odd mix early on, but he's grown accustomed to working double duty. "When I first started, it would happen that I'd play Frohike during episodes that I was A.D.-ing," says Braidwood, who lives in Vancouver with his wife and two children, not far from The X-Files' production offices. "And that was fine with me. I would just give the floor over to the second assistant director and do the Lone Gunmen scene. Usually, it was just one scene, and that takes about three or four hours of work. Now that we show up more often, it's usually an either/or situation. I just naturally fall out of the A.D. mode and do the acting thing, then it's vice-versa."

Which brings us to another mystery well worth exploring. What is a first A.D. and what does such

a person do on a show like The X-Files? According to Braidwood, a first A.D. is responsible for taking a script that's heading into production, breaking it down to all of its elements – characters, special effects, props and wardrobe – then into individual strips, as Braidwood calls them. "It's done on a computer," he explains. "We take all the strips and, based on everybody's requirements and availability and how complex things are, we figure out the best order to shoot the script over eight days. We assist the director with setting up meetings and co-ordinating information gathering. In the end, we're essentially responsible for putting the show's schedule together and then going out and helping the director to shoot it. There are two first A.D.s and the way it usually works is that one first A.D. will prep a show and while he's shooting I prep a second show, and when he's finished I shoot the second show and he preps a third show."

Braidwood has been with The X-Files since the very first post-pilot episode, "Deep Throat." He was not involved, however, as a first A.D. on The X-Files film. The film was deep into pre-production while Braidwood was busy as both an actor and first A.D. on the series. Braidwood, however, did join Haglund and Harwood for a brief Lone Gunmen scene in the movie. "I was surprised but thrilled

that they decided to include us," he enthuses. "We had heard we were in and then out, then in and then out. It was a surprise when we were finally really in. I was delighted to be a part of it." Braidwood, of course, can't pierce the veil of secrecy surrounding the movie's production, but he does take a stab at explaining how it will differ from the series. "The effects will be bigger," he says. There's a lengthy pause.

"We don't really know how else it will be different. We were only given the scenes we were performing and that was it. We didn't get to see a whole script or find out what the entire story line was. It was very specific. We got the five or six pages that pertained to us, and that was it."

When Braidwood, Haglund and Harwood get together, Braidwood reports, a good time is had by all. And they hit it off right away, while shooting "E.B.E." back in late 1993. "They are great guys," he attests. "Bruce and Dean had known each other because they are both involved in the theatre community in Vancouver. The parts just seemed to fall into place and take on a life of their own, aside from what was in the script. There was a chemistry there that seemed to work for the three of us. It's been that way ever since.

"I think we've also got a good relationship with

David and Gillian. David looks forward to the Gunmen scenes because they are lighter and more enjoyable in the sense of having fun doing a scene. Part of the purpose the Gunmen serve is to help David and Gillian develop their characters' points of view, although we've been doing more with David lately. Originally, we were just a plot device, a group of guys that had certain information that needed to be explained in the script. Since then, even though we still do that, the characters have grown to be a little more real and we're now more a part of the *X-Files* universe."

> "THERE WAS A CHEMISTRY THERE THAT SEEMED TO WORK FOR THE THREE OF US. IT'S BEEN THAT WAY EVER SINCE."

As a part of that *X-Files* universe, Braidwood has seen his face plastered on posters and trading cards, and in books and magazines. He's been interviewed, recognized on the streets and even attended a number of *X-Files* conventions. Along the way, he's encountered a few paranoid folks who made Frohike seem almost tranquil by comparison. "We've gone to a few conventions and there are people out there like the Gunmen, who are pretty paranoid," he says. "We've also had some strange fan mail. Most of the fan mail is from people who are fond of the show and enjoy what we do, but some people get deep into it and get into their own sense of paranoia and what they figure is going on." And has doing *The X-Files* made Braidwood himself more paranoid? He laughs. "That's an interesting question," he responds instantly. "No, I don't think so. Not really. At my age I'm probably as paranoid as I'm ever going to get."

The dossier on Braidwood is just about closed, but a little background about the guy wouldn't hurt. He's a Vancouver native, born there on September 27, 1948, back in its younger days, when the city was far less cosmopolitan. He was raised in a lovely area called the Endowment Lands, right by the University of British Columbia campus. Braidwood ended up studying theatre there, earning a BA in Theatre and, later, an MA in Film Studies.

"While I was at UBC I was involved with a group called the Tamahnous Theatre Workshop Company," he explains. "In the late 1960s, that was an alternate, underground theatre group. I continued to go to school and, with a friend of mine, got a Masters in film. Eventually, by year eight with Tamahnous, most of the original group had moved on. I'd been working on the side making my own short films and decided to commit in the mid-'70s to getting involved with film full-time.

"It was largely my ambition to direct. I did some directing but [a career] never really came to pass. I got involved with production and it went from there. I worked on several films as a production assistant, then several movies of the week and, when television series came to Vancouver, I did that, too. I worked on American and Canadian productions. I eventually moved up the ladder and became a production manager and a producer. When there wasn't anything to produce, I'd go back to assistant directing for such shows as *21 Jump Street*, *The Hat Squad* and *Nightmare Cafe*. I've pretty much been in television for the last ten years."

And nearly five of those last ten years have been devoted to a little show called *The X-Files*. "It's been great," says Tom Braidwood, who admits to a hidden desire to someday direct an *X-Files* episode. "It's been very hard, very demanding. The hours for everybody, particularly the crew, can be pretty horrific. We have 12 to 14 hour days. That's really, really tough. On the whole, though, it's been a very satisfying experience. The producers are a really good group of people. Chris Carter's commitment to the show is never-failing. It's great to be a part of that. He's very demanding. If something's not right and he has to re-shoot to make it right, that's what we'll do. He's got very specific views and he sticks to them. That's what makes the show as good as it is. The Lone Gunmen work has just been a huge bonus. It's really all been quite remarkable."

Above: "Oi! Langly! No!"; Below left: Under investigation by Lt Munsch; Opposite page: Gunmen in trouble! (All photos from "Unusual Suspects")

Gun-shots

To date, The Lone Gunmen have turned up in more than a dozen episodes, ranging from "E.B.E" to "Fearful Symmetry", "Nisei" to "Memento Mori." The early episodes of season five, now showing in the US, have seen the little fellows making quite a few appearances. Not only are they in "Redux" (the first broadcast episode of the season) they are the main focus of "Unusual Suspects," an episode dedicated almost exclusively to revealing the history of The Lone Gunmen, how they met and decided to join forces. Braidwood cites as his favorites "Memento Mori," in which the Gunmen actually spent a fair amount of time away from their office and - surprise, surprise - "Unusual Suspects."

"We were surprised they devoted a whole episode to The Lone Gunmen," Braidwood admits. "We jokingly had talked to the writers for a couple of years about doing a show about how they came together. When it suddenly happened, it was sort of one of those 'Be careful what you ask for' things. I liked that it was set about eight years in the past and that we got together because of a woman."

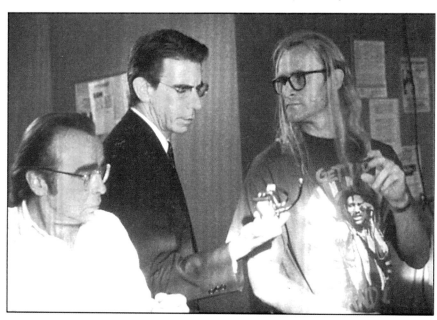

THE CIGARETTE-SMOKING MAN TEMPTS SCULLY WITH THE PROMISE OF A MEDICAL MIRACLE IN THE FIRST MYTHOLOGY EPISODE PENNED BY ACTOR WILLIAM B. DAVIS

TROPIC
CANCE

THERE'S NOTHING LIKE FEBRUARY IN SOUTHERN CALIFORNIA.

BY GINA MCINTYRE
PHOTOGRAPHY BY KHAREN HILL

While a new storm system dumps inches of snow over half the country, the temperature in Topanga Canyon is roughly 75 degrees, warmer if you stand in direct sunlight. Any more than 10 minutes exposure, and you should expect a sunburn – which explains why random bottles of suntan lotion lie scattered around the bleached ground that is serving as the stage for *The X-Files* first unit production for the next three days. Wisely, crew members seek refuge in the shade

R

or under tents to avoid the damaging rays; others don hats to protect their skin from the powerful ultraviolet light.

The precautions are necessary. By the time the day is over, the crew will have toiled for 12-plus hours in the hot sun, working quickly to capture all the scenes they can before evening interrupts their daylight-dependent schedule. On an inlet that lies at the end of a small, out-of-the-way road, several power boats are readied with all varieties of camera equipment, sound devices and plenty of

bottles of mineral water before setting off down the water to film the climax of the 15th episode of Season Seven, a dramatic tale penned by actor William B. Davis – better known to fans as the diabolical Cigarette-Smoking Man – that pairs his character with a reluctant Agent Scully and sends the duo on a mission to recover top-secret information that just might include the power to heal terminal illness.

At present, Davis is clearly not in character. Sporting a pair of new white

sneakers, a T-shirt and a friendly smile, the actor watches from the shoreline as director Rob Bowman readies the shot. "En Ami" marks Bowman's second *X-Files* venture this year – his first being the spooky stand-alone "Orison" – after leaving the series' full-time roster to pursue a feature film career.

But Davis' entry fits well with the director's style; as the man behind the camera for *The X-Files* movie and memorable episodes such as Season Six's finale "Biogenesis" and Season Four's emotional "Memento Mori," Bowman has repeatedly demonstrated his capacity to find the heart of a story, even in the midst of eye-popping action. Davis' episode has plenty of both.

"The essence of the idea was based on a scene from *Richard III* where Richard – who's the ultimate devil – comes across Lady Anne, who's mourning her father-in-law in public. The body's right there, and Richard killed him, and Richard also killed her husband. In the course of a 15-minute scene, he convinces her to be his wife," Davis says. "My original plan was that Mulder was dead. Scully was in the funeral home, and CSM made his first move. Scully being a little smarter than Lady Anne, it didn't happen as quickly. It took a few more meetings."

It's not uncommon for *The X-Files* to draw inspiration from literary sources.

MUSINGS OF A CIGARETTE-SMOKING MAN: [clockwise from top left] a scene from "En Ami"; on location in Thousand Oaks, Calif.; Gillian Anderson in "En Ami"; CSM and Scully in the pilot; director Rob Bowman; [previous page] William B. Davis strikes a casual pose

Chris Carter looked to Mary Shelley's classic *Frankenstein* for his Season Five entry, "The Post-Modern Prometheus." Carter and writing partner David Duchovny patterned "The Sixth Extinction II: Amor Fati" after Nikos Kazantzakis' novel *The Last Temptation of Christ*. So it seems logical that first-time *X-Files* scribe Davis would use Shakespeare's histories as a jumping-off point. But Scully marrying the CSM? It's a plot twist that the Bard himself might have trouble navigating convincingly. However, Davis says the explanation for such a shocking turn of events is simple.

"The idea of the story at that point was really all in her head," Davis explains. "It was kind of her nightmare of the Smoking Man. That's what I submitted. They really liked the dynamic of the CSM and Scully, but they didn't want any more dream shows. They'd kind of done that, so they decided that they wanted it to be real. We started working on a story where CSM would try to win her trust or affection to accomplish a particular goal of his and that's kind of how the story developed."

The final version of the script sees Scully, spurred on by an account of a small boy who was miraculously healed of terminal cancer, embark on a journey to a remote location with her enemy, who assures her that he had a hand in the child's recovery. In order to secure the information promised to her by the CSM, she must keep her temporary alliance secret from Mulder and match wits with the villain, who makes every effort to win her trust. Meanwhile, her partner grows increasingly suspicious about her whereabouts and her safety, turning to Assistant Director Skinner and lovable nerds the Lone Gunmen for help. It's a tricky storyline, to say the least. The episode's dark narrative falls somewhere between standalone and mythology, romance and tragedy, and Scully's deeply rooted animosity and distrust for the CSM must remain at the forefront of the story.

"I think it's very interesting," Bowman says. "I think the idea of getting Scully to go with him is a challenge because Scully can't go with him because the script says so. Scully has to believe that she has reason based on what she sees that there's the possibility that [the CSM might have] a cureall. It's up to me that in each and every scene she remains Scully, that she doesn't sort of acquiesce just because it says in the script that she does, that she has to truly believe, step by step, that she's doing the right thing and that CSM does not earn her trust automatically. It's a very, very hard-earned thing. She's pretty much walled up in several of the scenes. She gives him nothing until she sees more proof."

Davis says he has faith that Bowman will bring the right touch to his script.

"I was thrilled [with Rob Bowman directing]. My feeling was I wanted either Kim [Manners] or Rob to do it. Kim couldn't do it because he was doing the one before. When they said Rob would do it I thought that was terrific. He's been great."

Bowman's task hasn't been easy. It's one thing to successfully execute a plot that takes Scully from FBI headquarters into the CSM's mysterious office and across country on a clandestine road trip to a remote cabin on a lake. But it takes more than expert logistical manoeuvering to keep a story centered on two characters with competing motives moving forward on a believable path.

"She has every reason to believe that he is a liar, that he is a murderer, that he is a betrayer," Bowman says. "She's a very intelligent person who's not easily fooled. Even if he's saying all the right things at all the right times, she gives him nothing until she witnesses with her own eyes things that make her change her mind. She stays in character and stays hard to get almost until the end of the episode. I think that's what the fans expect her to be and that's who Scully is. She is not a person who's convinced easily, as we know."

ALTHOUGH DAVIS' CHARACTER first appeared in *The X-Files* pilot, he has had decidedly few scenes with Scully in the course of his seven years on the show. More often, he lurks in the shadows with fellow conspirators or deals directly with Mulder. But Davis, driven largely by his desire to work more closely with Gillian Anderson, decided it was time for all that to change. And so, he first approached the show's writing team last June with the concept for "En Ami."

"I said, 'If they don't give me some more work to do with Gillian soon, I'm going to write something,'" Davis remembers. "I used to say it facetiously, but then I got serious about it. I think she's so good, and I wasn't doing any work with her."

Of course, the story is also an opportunity to explore another side of the CSM. During the episode, he does his requisite amount of scheming, but he also displays

something of a tender side in one or two contemplative moments.

"If we're lucky, [the audience] will see another side, in a way a better side, a more empathetic side," he explains. "I don't know if they'll like him yet, but that would be

"I SAID, 'IF THEY DON'T GIVE ME SOME MORE WORK TO DO WITH GILLIAN SOON, I'M GOING TO WRITE SOMETHING.' I USED TO SAY IT FACETIOUSLY, BUT THEN I GOT SERIOUS ABOUT IT. I THINK SHE'S SO GOOD, AND I WASN'T DOING ANY WORK WITH HER."
—WILLIAM B. DAVIS

→

FASHION SENSE

DO YOU EVER HAVE THOSE DAYS where you just can't decide what to wear? You stand at your closet holding up first one outfit, then another. Sure, we all do, except perhaps David Duchovny and Gillian Anderson. The two *X-Files* stars don't have to worry about looking their best – that job falls to set costumer Nancy Collini.

Collini first teamed up with Duchovny on *Playing God* and *The X-Files* feature film. When the series relocated to Los Angeles after Season Five, she came on board full time, dressing both Duchovny and Anderson for their weekly appearances as Mulder and Scully and for any public events, from award shows to movie premieres, they attend. She says keeping the actors in character means staying fairly straightforward and sticking with classic styling.

"I just keep their closets really basic," Collini explains. "I keep them kind of tonal, not trendy. I'm really picky about his ties because I think that's the main thing – to keep them really subtle, no loud prints. For me, it's not Mulder. I bought some really great suits for David this year that are simple but fit him really well. My ties are my main thing, and there are some favorite ties that I have."

Of course, there are two sides to Mulder – his professional side and his casual side. And as fans of the series are all aware, he seems to have a favorite outfit for hanging around the apartment.

"Always the gray T-shirt and jeans," Collini says. "It's kind of the Mulder thing. First of all, there's nothing cuter on him than that T-shirt and jeans. It's very key to what he lounges around in. I don't think he has a whole lot of things in his closet. It's a look that we started, and I like to have some sort of continuity. That's why I'm really funny about the tie thing."

This year, Collini says she's been busy with scripts that required more changes for Mulder and Scully and placed the agents in climates ranging from Southern California to Chicago to South Africa.

"David, since I've been with him for so long, he trusts me," Collini says. "[With him], it's, 'What am I wearing?' David will tell me what he wants. If he wants to go casual, we try to go casual. But he's like a clothes hanger. He looks good in everything. Gillian, her wardrobe doesn't really get that casual. She doesn't wear jeans. Because she's a woman, we can bounce around a little bit. It's basically the silhouette I'm interested in on her. She has probably more clothes than him, but she's a girl." —G.M.

asking an awful lot. This is a problem
about writing it, too. I always like him
because he's my character. I may have
been a little soft in how I presented
him. For instance, in the episode,
there's a scene where I shoot someone. In my [original draft], I just shot
him in the arm and wounded him to
prevent him from doing what he was
going to do, and he was mad at me
and yelled at me. When Chris took it
over, I kill him.

"It's interesting because I understand more now how they do things,
how carefully they plot the audience
response," Davis continues. "I tend to –
as a writer, as a director, as an actor –
work more from character. What
would the character do? In some of
our discussions [I would say], 'I think
the character would do blah, blah, blah.'
They'll say, 'The audience will recognize
dah, dah, dah.' Ideally, in any really good
drama these two are married, but sometimes it's a question of which gets the
most emphasis."

Still, it's almost certain that audiences
will gain new insight into the character, or
at the very least, his
wardrobe. Costume
designer Molly
Campbell says she
worked with Davis
to develop some dif-
ferent looks for the
CSM. For the
sequences in the
episode he spends
with Scully at a
secluded cabin on a
Pennsylvania lake,
he dons outdoor
attire. But the char-
acter does appear in
his trademark suit
and tie for the
majority of his
screen time, includ-
ing a dinner scene
with Scully.

"He had a casual
change, but the
casual CSM is still a formal man,"
Campbell says. "It just means that there's
not a tie for instance, and he has on more
of what I would call an Eddie Bauer or L.L.
Bean type of jacket than a dress coat. And

he had a very dressy dinner change. [For
the dinner scene], he's wearing a very nice
navy blue suit. We had originally thought it
might be a black tie place, but they decided
not to go quite that high-end. He's got on a
really great-looking suit, and Gillian's wearing a dress that he has given her. It's a little
departure for us. The idea that the two of

them are carrying so much of the show is a
little unusual."

While "En Ami" does stray from the
usual Mulder/Scully dynamic, it still
required the same kind of spur-of-the-

moment ingenuity from the behind-the-
scenes team. The episode was shot almost
entirely away from the series' permanent
home on the Twentieth Century Fox lot,
meaning that location manager Ilt Jones and
the rest of his department had their work cut
out for them. Among the sites they secured
for the episode were a 42-acre former FBI
training compound that served as the
Cigarette-Smoking Man's top-secret office
headquarters, the remote inlet in Thousand
Oaks and a beautiful cottage across the water
surrounded by lush greenery.

Originally built in the 1920s by a
California attorney, the cabin, complete
with stone fireplace and bearskin rug, boasts
a natural, rustic charm that suited the storyline perfectly. "It's such a unique location
that when they asked for a cabin hideaway
on a lake it was the first thing that popped
into my mind," Jones says. "We looked at a
couple of other cabins which didn't have
views of lakes but were still in creepy, typical
X-Files settings. But when Rob saw that
place, he liked it immediately. That's just
such a spectacularly picturesque setting with
gorgeous foliage around the house, and the
lake views are wonderful, too."

While beautiful, the location does have
its downside. Because of its secluded
nature, there is little in the way of convenient access to the property. Cameras,
lights, catering and cast and crew members
all had to be transported to the house from
an off-site base camp. "You've really got to
have either time or money to film at that
house because the load-in is very difficult,"

EVIL UNDER THE SUN: [above] on location with *The X-Files* crew; [top, right] a scene from "En Ami"

Jones says. "There's a steep driveway. You can't get any trucks down there. You've got to be able to have lots of shuttle vans and things like that to get the equipment down there. It's not for the faint of heart, but I think it's worth it. We couldn't film at locations like that all the time, otherwise the crew would [hurt] me with a rusty bread knife. We'd spend too much time and money on the logistics and not on the actual shooting time. We ask the producers whether or not they want to go for it and they say, 'Well, let's take a look at it.' They go there and say, 'OK, this is a really great location. It's worth the effort to get the stuff down there.'"

With the setting in place, production designer Corey Kaplan spent time studying the romantic aspects of Davis' script to ensure that her work would help underscore the tension between the CSM and Scully. "I really wanted him to seem honestly as if there's a soft side to him," Kaplan says. "We really tried to make him considerate of her and flirtatious and romantic, just like a young woman would expect going out with an older man. He would know how to appreciate her."

Rather than create dynamic sets, Kaplan devoted her time to enhancing the mood at the locations by emphasizing all the right details. "At one point after [Scully] wakes up, Rob wanted to have [the Cigarette-Smoking Man] standing in the kitchen with an apron on, serving her coffee," Kaplan continues. "I said, 'Not on a lakeside house. Have a nice little café table right next to the glass overlooking the lake. It's a romantic morning, and the orange juice mimosa-style is poured for her. Have him do it right.' He did opt for that. I encouraged him to put flowers everywhere that he would have set up for Scully. In the room that was set up for her by the lake, there were flowers, and it was very warm and soft for her. The restaurant had the same feel to it. I think that was my subconscious part of taking the location and making it work for what I think should have been relationship-forming."

So far, the effort has paid off. Despite the flurry of activity as the crew shifts equipment from its original setup outside into the first floor bedroom of the cozy cabin, the location has been transformed into the perfect place to get away from it all – whether that be a day at the office or time spent tracking conspiracies and aliens. The lakeside home seems like the logical place for a romantic tryst, particularly as the setting sun disappears behind the neighboring mountains and the landscape falls into a peaceful darkness.

As Anderson makes her way up the stone steps to shoot her next scene with Davis, the amiable actor finishes his cup of coffee and prepares to slip into his more devious on-screen persona, commenting that his turn as a writer has changed not only his understanding of the series but also of the CSM.

"You always accumulate experience and breadth as you go along, yet you also have to be flexible," Davis says. "I don't know where we're going to go. All the people that CSM normally dealt with are dead. All my actors I liked to work with [are gone], which is very sad for me. I don't get into as much devious plotting with the men as I used to. I'm not quite sure what I'm going to do." ●

THE (X) FILES

After years of searching, Mulder finally learns the fate of his missing sister in THE X-FILES' most emotional mythology two-parter to date

fATE accOmPLI

A NEARLY OPAQUE cloud of manufactured mist fills the wide, open expanse of Stage Eight on the Twentieth Century Fox lot. A strong, circular light cuts through the haze like halogen beams through a night fog, illuminating a rectangular, wooden set that resembles a train car from Santa's workshop on some exaggerated scale. While dozens of people scurry from place to place inside the considerable shadow cast by the box car, director Kim Manners stands on the other side of the stage, walking in circles around production designer Corey Kaplan and visual effects supervisor Bill Millar. Waiting for the final preparations for this morning's scene to be completed, the forward-thinking Manners is already planning the exact choreography of a complicated camera move still days away on the production schedule, with the pair of department heads standing in for Mulder and Scully.

The whole place is a hive of activity. It's the beginning of the second day of shooting on "Closure," the second of a two-part episode that finally reveals what really happened to Agent Mulder's missing sister Samantha. The show,

sein und zeit

12.2.99

by gina mcintyre

photographs by kharen hill

begins with the story of a young California girl, Amber Lynn LaPierre, who disappears one night under peculiar circumstances. The case draws the attention of Mulder, who is struck by its similarities to Samantha's alleged abduction. Driven, the agent and his devoted partner Scully are drawn deeper into the child's case and after much searching, ultimately uncover a life-changing truth.

For years, Chris Carter has indicated that his master plan for *The X-Files* includes the explanation for Samantha's fate, which has been central to the ongoing narrative since the pilot episode. His quest to discover what terrible circumstances befell his beloved sister has spurred Mulder onward through countless adventures, his will resolute and unyielding. But penning the episodes that would once and for all explicate the mystery proved more challenging than Carter and his writing partner, executive producer Frank Spotnitz had anticipated. In breaking the story, the pair directed the storyline onto an entirely new path, borrowing a phrase from German philosopher Martin Heidigger that translates as "being in time" as the title for the first episode.

"I don't think [Chris] thought he would tell a story that said exactly this," Spotnitz

explains. "We're still going to the same place in the end, but I think we found a slightly different way of getting there. We kind of stumbled upon it at the last minute, honestly. We sat down to do this two-parter and these are the post-conspiracy mythology episodes, so they tend to be simpler. We wanted it to be a case that became a mythology episode, rather than just starting out a mythology episode. We found a way into the Samantha story and I think we ended up

going further in explaining what happened to her earlier than we expected to. It was exciting to do. I think it feels very reality based, this-could-be-happening-in-your-city kind of thing, which was very appealing to us about the story. It's always been Chris' maxim of telling stories that seem real, and this seems very real in the beginning and it gets more fantastic."

While the episodes unquestionably belong to *The X-Files'* mythology, they do not involve conspiracies, aliens or Cigarette-Smoking Men – even though the CSM does briefly appear. Instead, the two-parter closely examines Mulder's emotional state, resulting in a gripping tale that afforded leads David Duchovny and Gillian Anderson the opportunity to showcase their acting talents.

"Right before they received the scripts, I called to prepare the actors for what was coming, and I think they've welcomed it," Spotnitz says. "I think they look forward to scripts like this because so many of the episodes are about the cases and that honestly is what's most interesting to us about the mythology shows. They can be about Mulder and

"I THINK [THE ACTORS] LOOK FORWARD to scripts like this because so many of the episodes ARE ABOUT THE CASES AND THAT HONESTly is WHAT'S most INTEResting to us about the MYTHOLOGY SHOWS. THEY CAN BE ABOUt Mulder and Scully as characters MORE than investIGATORs."

— FRANk SPOTNiTZ

FABLES OF THE ABDUCTION: Filming "Closure"; [clockwise from top] Frank Spotnitz, Kim Manners, a scene from "Sein Und Zeit"

Scully as characters more than investigators."

Manners, at least for the time being, is more concerned about logistical issues and exacting camera work – the nuts and bolts of the operation – than how the actors will meet the emotional rigours of such sweeping, important episodes. With dozens of *X-Files* outings under his belt and years of working with Duchovny and Anderson, the director is confident that each scene will take shape naturally under his lens.

"We haven't really discussed it up front," Manners says. "I think this is a story that we're going to have to find together, David and I. As we shoot, I think that it will flesh itself out for both David and myself. It's one of those. David, he's not an actor that likes to plan or predict. He likes to find it on the day, which works well with me, especially in a story like this. It's better to find it as we get there.

"It's a big story," he adds. "I'm kind of excited to answer for everybody, myself included, what happened to Samantha. I'm handling it like I would any other script. I'm just trying to do my best work and tell the story the best I can."

ASSISTING IN THAT mission are the dozens of hard-working members of the series' behind-the-scenes creative team, most of whom are presently toiling on one of three stages on the lot. Today, first unit begins filming at 9am on Stage Eight; then the company will move to the adjacent Stage Five, while second unit work for "Sein

Und Zeit," under the direction of co-executive producer Michael Watkins, is completed on Stage Six. The day will last well into the night.

Rarely does the shooting schedule see three stages in use (generally, *The X-Files* uses only Stages Five and Six); most of the

time, at least one unit is out on location. But this has proven an exceptional year in many ways. Season Seven of *The X-Files* has kicked into artistic overdrive, producing uncompromising, dark outings and quirky, imaginative tales, as well as taking the mythology into unexpected areas. Crafting ➔

Mother
KNOWS BEST

CANADIAN ACTRESS Rebecca Toolan says she was happy to be called back to *The X-Files*' set to reprise her role as Mulder's mother for mythology two-parter "Sein Und Zeit"/"Closure." However, she was not necessarily pleased about the event that signalled her character's return to the show – her tragic suicide.

"Chris [Carter] called me and asked me if I'd read the script," Toolan explains. "I said, 'Yes, but what does it mean? Have I really killed myself?' He said, 'Yes, she did.'"

Well aware of *The X-Files*' penchant for deceiving appearances, Toolan had hoped that her death was only a ruse devised against her emotionally vulnerable son. "The show works on so many different levels of reality you're never quite sure exactly what's happening," she says. "Is it somebody's illusion? Is it a delusion? Is it a drug-induced experience? Has somebody imagined it? I was hoping that it would fall into one of those categories or that I'd been morphed or cloned or something, that the wool was being pulled over Mulder and Scully's eyes."

Sadly, it was not so. Since her debut in Season Two's "Colony," Mrs. Mulder has suffered through the uncertain fate of her daughter, the murder of her husband and a troubled relationship with her son, paving the way for the despair that would ultimately cause her to take her own life. But although her character has now departed the corporeal world, Toolan asserts that Mrs. Mulder still plays an integral part in the show's ongoing storyline.

"There's very definitely a lot of information that the mother holds that she has not yet revealed and that nobody else has revealed," Toolan says. "The paternity [of Mulder] for one thing. Cancer Man has claimed to be Fox's father, but we don't know if this is just his delusion either. As far as we know, there's been no paternal blood test, no matching done. The mother hasn't been asked. She'd have a pretty good idea. Bill Mulder was still alive so there would have been a little conflict of interest there."

Of course, not even Toolan can define with any certainty the nature of Mrs. Mulder's relationship with the CSM, but the actress can say that she and co-star William B. Davis, who portrays the nefarious character, are not of like mind on the issue.

"We have slightly different backstories that we've each created for our individual characters," she says. "We don't feel that they have to match. He does feel that he is Fox's father. I feel and hope that he is not. The way that I play the character is that this is a delusion of his and that he's kind of obsessed with taking over Bill Mulder's position. Of course, his backstory would be that he's, in fact, [Fox's] father. Unless somebody actually tells us point blank,

we'll never know. He could have had some kind of threat that was so big like Armageddon or damaging my existing family, my husband, that I might have yielded. But I prefer to stick with the backstory that this is his own delusion and fantasy."

While Toolan might resurface in future *X-Files* episodes – characters have been known to return from the grave for flashbacks and dream sequences – she can be seen in other projects, including an *They Nest* and *Cold Feet*.

"I'm going to be a regular on *Cold Feet*, which started this season," Toolan reports. "[My character] is the office wife of one of the male leads. She's his office manager, so when he's in the office, she's his second in command." – *G.M.*

such an eclectic mix is sometimes unpredictable.

"It's been different than last year, but actually more hectic," says general foreman Billy Spires. "I don't mean that in a bad way, but we have to have a lot more stuff ready sooner. We haven't had any episode with one main set. It seems like there's eight to 12 different sets every episode that we're getting ready. You don't get to enjoy the fruits of your labor as much when it has to be ready so quickly. Because of the lack of stage space, we have to take [a set] down sometimes the moment they're done shooting either, to revamp it or put something else there.

"We work about 80 per cent of the weekends," he continues. "We'll be working through this weekend on all the changeovers and the sets that have to be ready for Monday and Tuesday. And then we're going to start prepping episode 12. We may have a break for a few hours but that's only because the director hasn't let the production designer know exactly what he wants. As soon as the prints come down to the trailer, it's on."

For "Sein Und Zeit"/"Closure," property master Tom Day's department was required to stage dozens of photographs of young Mulder and Samantha to appear at Mulder's mother's house, which meant finding six children to pose as the siblings at varying ages and inventing memorable poses suitable for framing.

"In this particular case, we had to go back beyond what we usually see of them into even younger and younger [ages]," Day says. "In fact, one of my assistants, he has a son and a daughter who are roughly the same age. We used his children as one of our groups of kids because his daughter is a 1-year-old infant. She's got the chicken pox right now, so it made for these really cute pictures of a big brother holding his little sister who's got the chicken pox."

The photographs, though time-consuming, were not the most challenging item Day was called upon to procure for the episodes. "In ['Closure'], Mulder finds his sister's diary," Day says. "Considering how absolutely central to this entire series that relationship is and how important being able to read what she's written is to that character, that is as huge a prop as we can be responsible for. It's really got to be right on. That's years worth

of storylines and preparation leading up to that. As the prop department, we want that prop to be worthy of the years of build-up something like that gets."

To find the perfect specimen, Day acquired countless diaries and journals, then headed to the show's producers for feedback. "What I'll do is I'll start with Kim and say, 'Kim, what works best for you as far as the logistics of shooting?' Then I'll get multiples of them and have them aged to varying degrees. We'll do maybe one version that

DISAPPEARING ACT: Outside the LaPierre home on Stage Six; [right] Bill Millar; [bottom right] Amber Lynn's room

will have been attacked by mould and mildew, and the other version will be dusty and worn and aged, bleached looking from the elements. Once the director settles on what works for him, size and width and all those parts of it, I'll age a few of them up to show the differences and then I will show them to Chris, Frank and all the guys at Ten Thirteen."

THE SCOPE OF the two-parter – the LaPierre case leads Mulder to other similar cases all with a paranormal bent – is even affecting the workload of effects man Millar. Upon completing a blue screen sequence involving a young boy for the episode directed by Watkins, Millar must begin to procure the equipment necessary for the speciality camerawork featured in the final instalment of the story. He, too, echoes Spires' and Day's sentiments about the frenzied pace of Season Seven.

"['Closure'] is probably the heaviest episode [in terms of visual effects], certainly of the last three seasons," he says. "We probably have four days of motion control shooting to build [some supernatural entities] into moving plates and have them mingle with Mulder and Scully. Integrating all that is an object lesson in choreography and motion control and acting and camera work. [In feature films], certain shots and scenes can take three to five days to set up and photograph, some longer than that. We're being asked to do that kind of quality and essentially get our shots in half a day, which requires an immense amount of pre-planning and a little bit of luck as well."

To ensure that luck is on his side, Millar says it is key to take advantage of the lead

time he has, now nearly eight days. "Kim kind of previsualizes what he wants to do with certain scenes," he says. "We talk and figure out the camera moves largely on paper. Kim wants to be able to move the camera through 360 degrees without giving any evidence that there was any kind of special camera in use. He wants it to look more like a hand-held shot. We figure out what configuration we need of camera track and what kind of motion control camera we need, whether it's a crane, whether it's a crane built on top of a dolly, what axis

of motion the camera needs to describe and how fast the dolly needs to move to get out of its own way so that when the camera turns around to photograph where the dolly was at the beginning of the shot, we've managed to move the dolly around to the other side of the room. All this has to happen over and over again, and the camera has to be positioned for each pass within literally fractions of a millimetre from where

it was, time after time after time in order for us to meld each of those plates together and not see any misregistration, lines or any perspective change that would give away that one of the entities in the scene was shot at a different time or place than everything else."

According to Millar, that particular scene will take two to three hours to set up, roughly six hours to shoot and will require 40 to 50 hours of digital compositing during post-production to complete. It will appear on screen for less than 30 seconds.

The end result, of course, is worth the labor. Week after week, *The X-Files* continues to meet the standard of excellence demanded by Carter and the millions of fans who have embraced the series as a watermark for television. If anything, the unparalleled ambition of episodes like "Sein Und Zeit"/"Closure" is raising the bar higher, challenging the crew to push themselves to reach new creative plateaus.

And viewers can continue to look forward to more of the same. Even though many of the series' carefully guarded secrets have been revealed, some component of the ever elusive truth will remain *out there* and will take shape in even more remarkable forms. "There's something more coming," a confident Spotnitz says with a grin. ●

"WITHIN"

"Nice to meet you, Agent Doggett."

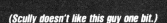

THE BUILD-UP:

After Mulder's shocking abduction, Scully is now partnerless. At work, she arrives to find a team of agents rifling through Mulder's office. It seems that the new deputy director, Alvin Kersh has put together a special task force to investigate Mulder's disappearance.

THE SCENE:

FBI HEADQUARTERS, WASHINGTON D.C.

(Scully waits to give a statement to the agents in charge of the manhunt for the missing Mulder. Another agent is sitting beside her, his FBI badge on his lapel twisted so she cannot make out his name. He engages Scully in conversation about her partner...)

SCULLY: *I think I know Mulder as much as anybody.*

DOGGETT: *Yeah, probably so. I always took the rumors with a grain of salt.*

SCULLY: *What rumors are those?*

DOGGETT: *Well, you know.*

(Scully clearly doesn't know what he's talking about.)

DOGGETT: *Well, that from the beginning he never felt a real trust with you... that you were ambitious.*

SCULLY: *Where'd that come from?*

DOGGETT: *There are women here at the Bureau that he would confide in. I don't know if you knew that or not.*

SCULLY: *No. When was this?*

DOGGETT: *I don't know, it's just talk... So what do you think happened? To Mulder. What's your theory?*

(Scully doesn't like this guy one bit.)

SCULLY: *What's my theory? My theory is you don't know Mulder at all. You never did.*

(She reaches towards him and flips over his badge.)

SCULLY: *John Doggett. Kersh's task force leader. You might have just introduced yourself.*

DOGGETT: *Well, I was getting around to it.*

(Scully is quietly fuming. She stands up and suddenly throws her water in Doggett's face.)

SCULLY: *Nice to meet you, Agent Doggett.*

(She slams the door behind her as she leaves the room. Doggett, water dripping off his face, watches her leave. The other agents in the room – who had been watching the commotion with interest – quickly avert their eyes and get back to work.)

THE SIGNIFICANCE:

The moment Scully and Doggett – her soon-to-be new partner on the 'X'-files – meet. And the old dynamic of sceptic and believer is firmly back in place, albeit with a new twist. Surprisingly, there's a definite chemistry there already between Anderson and Patrick. Things are definitely looking interesting...

TRIVIA:

It was the most coveted role on prime time television. Speculation was rife as to who was going to land the part of Scully's new partner, following David Duchovny's extended hiatus. The rumor mill had linked the likes of Bruce Campbell, Lou Diamond Phillips and Chris North to the show. Then all of a sudden, the wait was over. It was official. Robert Patrick, best known for his portrayal of the T-1000 shape-shifting cyborg in *Terminator 2: Judgment Day*, was the lucky man.

EPISODE CREDITS:

Season Eight, Episode One
First aired 5/11/00 (US)
& 15/02/01 (UK)
Written by:
Chris Carter
Directed by:
Kim Manners
Main actors this scene:
FBI Agent John Doggett:
Robert Patrick
FBI Agent Dana Scully:
Gillian Anderson

Compiled by Kate Anderson

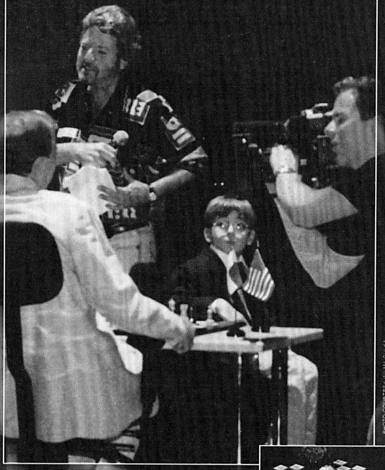

child's PLAY

by Jeff Berkwits

ALIEN ABDUCTIONS *and* BIZARRE EXPERIMENTS *are just fun and games for* The X-Files' YOUNGEST STARS

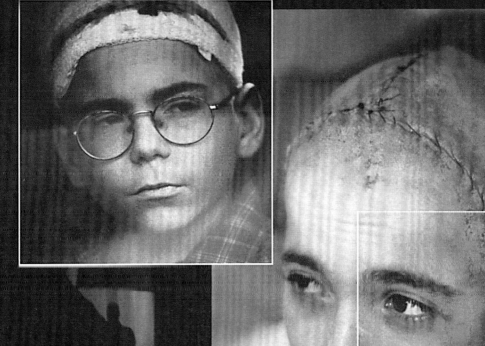

CHILD STARS

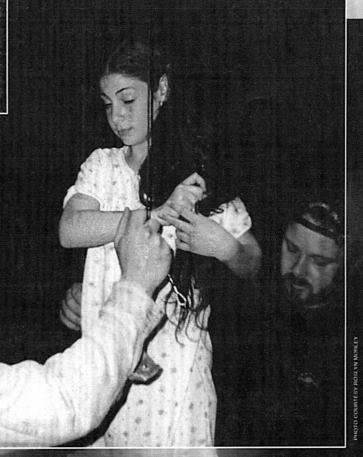

PHOTO COURTESY ROSLYN MORLEY

WHILE IT'S NOT UNUSUAL for the cast and crew of *The X-Files* to receive accolades for their work, it is rare when they take the time to bestow an award upon one of their own. However, a relatively minor but unquestionably painful incident that took place, while shooting Season Four premiere "Herrenvolk" led the show's Vancouver family to do just that – the crew presented a one-of-a-kind honor to Vanessa Morley, the young girl who portrays Mulder's abducted sister Samantha.

The commendation, which Gillian Anderson awarded Morley at an impromptu ceremony, acknowledged the unusual conditions child actors often face when appearing on the series: during one of the scenes at the farm where silent clones cultivate deadly swarms of bees, Vanessa was stung. "David [Duchovny], Vanessa and Roy Thinnes [who portrayed Jeremiah Smith] went in together, and while she was in there one of the bees stung her," explains the girl's mother,

Roslyn. "She shook it off her hand, but it wasn't until after they had finished the whole scene that she let it be known what had happened. They were all quite proud of her!"

Vanessa, in turn, was happy to be recognized. "The director, [R.W.] Goodwin, made a plaque that had a purple heart in the middle," recalls the 12-year-old actress. "It said 'Purple Heart awarded to Vanessa Morley for wounds sustained in the line of duty and courage in the face of adversity.' It was really neat!"

Not that repeat appearances on a high-profile television series aren't neat in their own right. Like their peers, the children who have landed guest-star spots on the show since Season One worry about cleaning their rooms and finishing their homework, but they also have the opportunity to execute feats that would make actors of any age squeamish, such as walking into a building full of bees or undergoing hours of extensive make-up. Accordingly, displaying that legendary

PHOTO COURTESY ROSLYN MORLEY

"courage in the face of adversity" has earned them quite a few feathers to adorn their small caps and brought unique touches to *The X-Files'* eerie world.

"I got brain surgery done to me because they wanted to know why I could read minds," states Jeff Gulka, the 13-year-old boy who plays psychic genius Gibson Praise in Season Five's finale "The End" and Season Six's premiere "The Beginning."

"The operation had to be done rather quickly so it was pretty sloppy...[The special effects crew] had some foam latex and they put it on my head. They stitched it together with stitching stuff, filled it with pretend blood and then painted make-up all over my head to make it look real. It was pretty gruesome."

Such potentially disturbing scenarios create an unusual challenge for the adults charged with finding youngsters to appear on *The X-Files*. "In terms of auditioning young actors for a role, we have to set both the parents and the children up for the nature of the scene," says former Vancouver casting director Coreen Mayrs. "Often parents won't allow their kids to partake in certain storylines, so it can be slim pickings for the casting director. But usually any child who is willing to audition for a role that has some sort of scary element to it is a child that probably has an additional layer to them which helps in these kinds of roles."

"Some of the kids that we have used in the show have been of the alien genre, so there's almost a sort of bewitching and disturbing hidden quality that we look for," continues Rick Millikan, the Los Angeles-based casting director. "In all the parts that we cast, everything is very subtle. Whenever someone is playing, say, a devil or a demon or an alien, it usually comes out as something that is quite indistinct. There's not a slap-in-your-face trait that says, 'Here's a devil.' It's subtle qualities that we look for."

PHOTO COURTESY WILMA GULKA

ALL ABUZZ ON THE SET: [previous pages, clockwise from left] Jeff Gulka ("Gibson Praise") and crew on the set of "The End"; Jeff being stitched for "The Beginning"; Vanessa Morley ("Samantha Mulder") and crew prepare a harness for her abduction in "Demons"; [clockwise from lower left] Vanessa and two clone friends on the set of "Herrenvolk"; a scene from "Herrenvolk"; Gillian Anderson presents Vanessa's Purple Heart; Jenny-Lynn Hutcheson as "Polly Turner" in "Chinga"; Jeff gets a haircut for "The Beginning"

Successfully tapping into these innate attributes is crucial for the young actors, as the characters they portray are generally far removed from their normal personas. "The looks and the feelings come to me naturally," notes nine-year-old Jenny-Lynn Hutcheson, who appeared as Polly Turner in the Stephen King-penned episode "Chinga." "I just get mad and my face starts to heat up and I get this awful glare. It comes to me again and again whenever I have a demanding role... it's just a feeling in my mind." Nevertheless, she is still *acting*; Hutcheson says Polly's disposition is nothing like her own. "It's pretty fun being a demon child and a brat," she admits. "I normally don't get to act like a brat, because if I did I'd probably be grounded for life!"

The *X-Files'* subject matter is unquestionably dark, but both the young actors and their parents insist that playing the spookier characters did not frighten the children. Instead, their roles demystified the filmmaking process and helped the youths more clearly differentiate between reality and fantasy. After all, the monster lurking under the bed isn't so intimidating after you've watched it sitting lifeless on a shelf in a special effects shop.

"When you see your show it's not scary because you've read the whole script," explains eight-year-old Lauren Diewold, best known for her portrayal of Scully's ailing daughter Emily Sim in "Christmas Carol" and "Emily." "I got to see how they did most of the effects."

Her mother explains that although the series was something she had deemed inappropriate for her children, Lauren's guest-star role changed her mind. "When

The X-Files first started she was little and it wasn't a show that we let the kids watch," she says. "But once you know how the effects work, it really does take away from the impact of what you see. When Lauren watches television now, she sees it in a way that is quite different from regular kids. She'll say things like, 'Oh, I know how they did that. The cameras are over here and they did this or they did that.' It really does change her whole perspective about television."

That outlook is also altered through interactions with the various actors, which many of the youngsters, like most fans, find remarkably exciting. "One day I had my yo-yo on the set," remembers Gulka. "I was doing these tricks, and then I gave David a try. He was doing all these other tricks, and he thought he was better than me. So we had a little yo-yo-off, but he beat me." Adds the boy's mother, Wilma: "Jeff didn't think David could yo-yo because he was so much older. But yeah, he could! It was really nice, watching them sitting there yo-yoing."

"David's great," Morley says of her fictional big brother. "He's always asking, 'Are you okay?' or 'Do you want some water?' And he's really funny. He's never done anything really big, but when he messes up lines he'll just kind of laugh."

The children are just as eager to praise Duchovny's leading lady. "Gillian was really

nice," Hutcheson says. "If you screw up your lines she goes, 'Oh, it's okay. You can do better next time.' She's really good at encouraging you."

Both leading actors are apparently good sports when it comes to signing autographs for their diminutive co-stars, too. "I came out to do playground duty one day and Lauren's friends were all gathered around her," recalls Susan Diewold, who at the time also happened to be her daughter's second-grade teacher.

"She was in the process of cutting up 28 pieces of paper to go and ask David Duchovny and Gillian Anderson for their autographs. I told her that I didn't think that they were going to want to sign 28 little pieces of paper, so instead she went to Gillian and explained that her class wanted an autograph. Gillian wrote, 'To St. Mary's Grade Two Class,' added a little blurb and signed it. Then Lauren went to David when he was on the set and got his autograph. He wrote a little blurb too, and what I did was Xerox it so all the kids got a copy. It was fun. They were both really good that way."

The warm demeanour of the stars is also indicative of the overall attitude of the crew toward children. "They treat you like you're not a kid," Morley says. "They don't put you aside. They treat you just like you're one of the big stars like David or Gillian. I was pretty surprised, because I thought I was going to be stuck in a corner or something."

"They were the best crew I ever worked with," adds Hutcheson, who has appeared on other spooky television programs such as *The Outer Limits* and *Poltergeist: The Legacy*. "They were so nice. At times some crews can get bored on the set, or they get kind of cranky because they haven't had a good sleep, and that brings down the attitude of everyone. But this crew was always happy no matter what you did."

The reason for their tireless enthusiasm, Mayrs says, is simple. The crew members extended the same feeling of camaraderie they shared on the set to the children. "We had a great crew in Vancouver that had worked together for a long time," she says. "Many of them were parents themselves or were aunts and uncles who really put the person before the industry. I know our three

CHILDREN OF X: [clockwise from below] Vanessa Morley with on-screen big brother David Duchovny; Lauren Diewold as "Emily Sim" in "Christmas Carol"; Jeff Gulka and Gillian Anderson

mainstay directors – Kim Manners, Rob Bowman and [R.W.] Goodwin – all adore children, and when you've got a director at the helm who adores kids it certainly sets a great tone."

Somehow, according to Millikan, the youthful actors manage to lighten the atmosphere on the set even before arriving to shoot their scenes. "Kids are fun to cast," he says. "They're so innocent, and

they usually don't come in with a lot of baggage. Actors can come in with a lot of shtick and a lot of phonyisms and BS. With kids it's much more fun because of the innocence."

Though that unaffected outlook is definitely refreshing, at least one parent learned that it can occasionally lead to somewhat humorous misunderstandings. "When Jenny-Lynn first read the script for 'Chinga,' she said, 'This Stephen King guy must really like *Goosebumps*,'" laughs Jodi Hutcheson, the mother of the young actress. "Of course I know who he is, but she had no idea. So I said, 'Well, I think he's been writing longer than *Goosebumps* has been around, Jenny.' But she thought he read a lot of *Goosebumps* and that's where he got his ideas."

Regardless of the source of the stories, *The X-Files* and its talented team of child actors are sure to continue to offer goose bumps to fans of all ages.

"Jenny-Lynn once said to me that when Gillian Anderson retires she wants to be Scully," says Hutcheson. "I had to tell her, 'You're going to be waiting a very long time!'" ●

youth gone wild

The *X-Files'* writers don't just take off the kid gloves when writing parts for children, they throw a couple of punches as well. Tortured by demonic twins, hunted by Satan's minions and abducted by serial killers, the children of *The X-Files* have had a rough time of it during the history of the series. Here's just a few of the various torments they have endured.

Names: Cindy Reardon and Teena Simmons
Episode: "Eve"
Ultimate demise: Genetically enhanced clones of the "Eve" DNA, these oddly detached little girls seem like victims until it is revealed that they murdered their fathers. A botched attempt at poisoning Mulder and Scully lands them in jail with an older clone, Eve 6, until Eve 8 comes to their rescue.

Name: Charlie/Michael Holvey
Episode: "The Calusari"
Ultimate demise: After watching his little brother, his father and his grandmother suffer horrific deaths, Charlie is forced to undergo an exorcism at the hands of Romanian holy men. The rite is performed to separate his soul from that of his evil, dead twin, the one who is revealed to be behind the murders.

Name: Kevin Kryder
Episode: "Revelations"
Ultimate demise: The stigmatic-hunting Millennium Man stalks young Kevin, claiming that the boy must die "for the New Age to come." Scully arrives just in time to save Kevin as the killer falls to his death.

Name: Caitlin
Episode: "Paper Hearts"
Ultimate demise: Kidnapped, dragged into an abandoned transit bus and held at gunpoint by child killer John Lee Roche. Caitlin is ultimately saved when Mulder puts a bullet in Roche's head.

Name: Ronnie Strickland
Episode: "Bad Blood"
Ultimate demise: The plastic-fang-wearing trailer park pizza boy is staked in the heart by Mulder. But when the stake is removed by an unknowing coroner, vampiric teen Ronnie returns to his mobile home, only to be trapped inside a coffin by the intrepid agent. *–Chandra Palermo*

KRYCEK PROFILE

You Dirty Rat!

K. STODDARD HAYES EXAMINES THE CHARACTER OF ALEX KRYCEK, ONE OF MULDER AND SCULLY'S NASTIEST, DEADLIEST AND MOST PERSISTENT ENEMIES

Alex Krycek is a liar and a murderer. Everyone says so, usually to his face – everyone being Skinner, Mulder, Scully, and even Doggett, who only met him twice. However, they have left out an important element in their description. More than a liar and murderer, he is also the most cunning player in the game of alien colonization.

Throughout his seven year career as a rogue F.B.I. agent, Syndicate trigger man, and wanted malefactor (by both sides), Krycek is always the wild card, his loyalties doubtful, his purposes hidden, even his actions most often a mystery.

Krycek didn't start out as the king of murder and double dealing. When he reports to his F.B.I. superiors at the end of "Sleepless," he is just an ambitious young man putting his feet on the lowest rungs of power. He's eager to prove his abilities and his loyalties to this shadow bureaucracy, which he senses is the real power in the Bureau. No doubt he's also hoping to become one of them as soon as he can.

When he sets out to stop Mulder from rescuing Scully at Skyland Mountain, his methods are crude – he simply kills the tram operator and strands Mulder in the tram high up the mountain. And the only way he can think to silence Duane Barry is to murder him. These acts accomplish his goals, but they also incriminate him beyond question, since Mulder and others know that he was the only one who could have killed Barry or the operator. He confirms his guilt by disappearing immediately afterward.

Though his crimes in "Ascension" make Krycek an outlaw to Mulder and to Skinner, they apparently make him a trusted agent for the Syndicate. The next time we see Krycek, he's been charged with two assignments that are crucial to protecting the Syndicate's secret conspiracy: the murder of Bill Mulder and the recovery of the digital tape that contains conspiracy records. It's pure bad luck that he botches a third job, the assassination of Scully, when he and his fellow assassin mistake Melissa Scully for her sister in the dark of Scully's apartment ("Anasazi,"

"REQUIEM"

"PIPER MARU"

"The Blessing Way," "Paper Clip").

For Krycek, his possession by the Black Oil entity is a critical turning point. The entity uses Krycek as a host, to get it to the Cigarette-Smoking Man, who has its ship. The Cigarette-Smoking Man lets the Krycek entity get to the missile silo where the ship is stored, knowing the entity will leave Krycek and re-enter its ship. But then, instead of freeing Krycek, his own associate, the CSM leaves Krycek trapped in the silo ("Piper Maru"/"Apocrypha").

"PATIENT X"

Whether it's the possession or the betrayal that changes Krycek is impossible to say. But from then on, Krycek becomes an independent agent. He works with the Syndicate as an ally not a servant – often enough, an unreliable ally, who is just as likely to betray vital information to Mulder, Scully or Skinner, as to try to kill the X-Files agents on the Syndicate's orders.

The two-part story "Tunguska" and "Terma" shows just how far Krycek has gone from the callow, ambitious young agent of "Sleepless." Two years later, Krycek is at the top of his game. He knows exactly how to get Mulder to trust him – not completely, Krycek knows that's impossible – but just enough to do what Krycek needs him to do. He joins a terrorist militia, then secretly betrays their plans to Mulder and allows himself to be arrested. And he allows Mulder to have just enough information about a mysterious diplomatic pouch whose contents, a black meteor fragment, he needs to make disappear. He lures Mulder to Siberia to make him disappear, by telling Mulder the rock was found near the Tunguska impact site – a name he knows Mulder will recognize, but which he himself pretends not to know.

These episodes show how much Krycek will risk when something important is on the line. While the

Cigarette-Smoking Man rarely puts his own person in danger or hardship, Krycek has more guts. He's willing to put himself in Mulder's hands if its necessary to accomplish his purposes, even though he knows that Mulder needs very little excuse to kill him for the murder of his father. He can be certain that at the very least he'll endure some very uncomfortable days as Mulder's prisoner (how uncomfortable he may not have realized until Skinner handcuffs him to an outdoor balcony, and Mulder threatens to leave him handcuffed in a car at the airport).

None of this deters Krycek from his plans, which go off just as he intends – almost. The one thing Krycek doesn't count on is the result of his lie to the local Siberian peasants, that he's a gulag escapee. Believing the lie, they save him from the gulag experiments in the only way they know – by cutting off his left arm, without anesthesia. Yet even this doesn't seem to throw Krycek off his stride. Through all that happens he continues to run the game, engineering the murder of the doctor who might identify the black oil, and the final destruction of the space rock.

As a human being, Krycek is the sort of man you would never want to have as your enemy – nor indeed, to have in

THE KRYCEK FILES

A few of the unresolved and debatable questions surrounding Krycek.

WHY DID THE BLACK OIL ENTITY SEEK OUT KRYCEK AS A HOST? ("PIPER MARU")

The entity possessed Joan Gauthier in San Francisco, then used her to travel all the way to Hong Kong, where it cornered Krycek in an airport men's room to transfer itself to him. Couldn't it find someone in the US to get it to the Cigarette-Smoking Man and its ship?

HOW DID KRYCEK ESCAPE FROM THE MISSILE SILO? ("TUNGUSKA", "TERMA")

Krycek tells Mulder that the terrorist militia found him and freed him when they were scavenging for weapons technology. But the militia leader tells Mulder that Krycek came to him and his group and enlisted them in his plans.

DID KRYCEK KILL BILL MULDER? ("ANASAZI")

He's the only one we see in the bathroom with Mulder's father just before the fatal shot. But Krycek has always denied that he killed Mulder's father and even speaks to Mulder and Scully of "the man who killed your father, and your sister" as the Cigarette-Smoking Man. And if he was the killer, why did he wait until Mulder arrived before pulling the trigger? Why not do the job and escape before Mulder arrives?

HOW DID KRYCEK GET AN ALIEN VACCINE, TWO DIFFERENT TIMES? ("THE RED AND THE BLACK," "DEADALIVE")

Krycek makes a deal with the Well-Manicured Man, for his own freedom in exchange for the Black Oil vaccine. The Well-Manicured Man tells the Syndicate that Krycek got the vaccine from the Russians, who developed it. How did Krycek get such high-up connections in Russia, to have access to the vaccine? More puzzling still, why does Krycek have the replicant vaccine for Mulder? We never learn who made this vaccine, nor how Krycek got it.

WHY DOES KRYCEK DECIDE TO KILL MULDER? ("DEADALIVE")

By his own account, Krycek has protected Mulder for years, feeding him information, always hoping Mulder would win the alien war. Then suddenly, after helping Scully escape the replicants, Krycek ambushes Mulder with the declared intention of killing him. His explanation, that it's too late to stop "them" and that Mulder knows too much, is no different than the circumstances of many past situations, including some when Krycek helps the agents. It's certainly not enough to account for Krycek deciding he has to kill the one man he feels some sort of kinship with.

"S.R. 819"

"THE END"

your life at all. As a character in a complex, conspiracy-driven TV series, he's indispensable. Conspiracy stories derive much of their suspense from complex plotting that keeps the audience guessing about what the characters know, who they are allied with and what they intend. In this dramatic setting, Krycek is the ultimate adversary, a bad guy whose loyalties and motivations are always in question. Sometimes he is clearly an agent of the Syndicate, other times he seems to be working for no one but himself, and at still other times, he seems actually to be trying to help the good guys.

And how does he know what he knows, or get the items that he gets, such as the alien vaccine, or the nanotechnology infesting Skinner's blood? Many of Krycek's actions remain mysterious, creating the kind of plot puzzles that fans can debate endlessly on web sites and message boards [see *The Krycek Files* boxout.] These mysteries, as well as his close association with the alien colonization storyline, create a kind of anticipation surrounding the character. Whenever Krycek appears, we expect surprises.

Krycek also makes an important contribution to the character mythology of *The X-Files*, through his relationships with the Syndicate and with Mulder. Krycek, more than any other character, shows us that the Syndicate is not as omnipotent as it first appears. He double-crosses them, and sometimes even holds power over them; as they in turn double cross him and argue among themselves over what he might be offering. Krycek shows us that the Syndicate's members are just mortal men, after all.

More important, Krycek builds up Mulder's personal mythology. In the world of *The X-Files*, it's a given that Mulder is the one man who can expose the conspiracy and save the world from the alien colonization, just by his determination to find the truth. Krycek consistently treats Mulder as the most important person involved in this war. True to Krycek's ambivalent nature, he does this sometimes by trying to stop Mulder, and sometimes by trying to help him. He underlines this in "The Red and the Black," when he ambushes

Mulder in his apartment. Mulder is in the height of his unbeliever phase, and Krycek's intent is to snap him out of it, and make him join the fight again.

"There is a war raging, and unless you pull your head out of the sand, you and I and about five billion other people are going to go the way of the dinosaur," he says, implying both by his words and by his urgency, that Mulder is essential to victory.

Krycek's relationship with Mulder is one of the most intimate in the whole series. Mulder consistently shows more violence to Krycek, in his language and his words, than to almost anyone else. Aside from the liar and traitor aspects of Krycek's career, Mulder is certain that Krycek murdered his father. And yet when Krycek talks, Mulder can't

help listening, and even, in spite of himself, believing Krycek and going where he leads.

For his part, Krycek usually talks to Mulder as if Mulder is the only person who can handle the game as well as Krycek himself. The success of his scheme in "Tunguska" shows how well he understands Mulder. Their final encounter in "Existence" shows how much Mulder means to him. Krycek would shoot anyone else from ambush. When he decides he has to kill Mulder, he needs to meet him face to face, so he can explain.

"I could have killed you so many times, Mulder, you gotta know that. I'm the one that kept you alive, praying you'd win somehow... You think I'm bad, I'm a killer. We wanted the same

thing," says Krycek, and then he calls Mulder "brother."

"I wanted to stop them. All you wanted was to save your own ass," Mulder retorts, but then he affirms their intimacy by using Krycek's first name. "If you want to kill me, Alex, then kill me. Just don't insult me trying to make me understand."

Krycek, who has killed many people without a second's hesitation, aims his pistol at Mulder, puts his finger on the trigger – and hesitates. He hesitates so long that Skinner has time to get there and stop him. And even though Krycek begs Skinner to kill Mulder, he knows, and we know, that it's not going to happen. Not killing Mulder is the last choice Krycek ever makes. ●

PASSION WITH MARITA IN "PATIENT X"

THE KRYCEK EPISODES

SEASON TWO
"SLEEPLESS"
"DUANE BARRY"
"ASCENSION"
"ANASAZI"

SEASON THREE
"THE BLESSING WAY"
"PAPER CLIP"
"PIPER MARU"
"APOCRYPHA"

SEASON FOUR
"TUNGUSKA"
"TERMA"

SEASON FIVE
"PATIENT X"
"THE RED AND THE BLACK"
"THE END"

SEASON SIX
"S.R. 819"
"TWO FATHERS"
"ONE SON"
"BIOGENESIS"

SEASON SEVEN
"THE SIXTH EXTINCTION II: AMOR FATI"
"REQUIEM"

SEASON EIGHT
"DEADALIVE"
"ESSENCE"
"EXISTENCE"

"REQUIEM"

SUPER SOLDIERS, U.F.O.S AND PLENTY OF EXPLOSIONS – IT'S TIME FOR SEASON NINE'S LATEST MYTHOLOGY INSTALLMENTS, "PROVENANCE" AND "PROVIDENCE." OUR REPORTER BRAD FOLLMER JOINED THE X-FILES CAST AND CREW TO FOLLOW THE BEHIND-THE-SCENES ACTIVITIES.

DESE SO

PHOTOGRAPHY BY BRAD FOLLMER
SPECIAL THANKS TO ROBIN BENTY

R✝
II

It's about 4:45pm on a late-December afternoon and the crew of *The X-Files* is in a race against time. The sun has just dropped below the horizon of the desert, and soon it will be dark; but the most important shot of the day still needs to be done – and in a few short minutes it will be too late.

Shadows reach across the dry dirt bed in this remote section of the California high desert, a constant reminder – if any were needed – that time is of the essence. Chris Carter, directing from a script he co-wrote with fellow executive producer Frank Spotnitz, is hurrying to complete a major stunt before dusk. He takes a quick look through the viewfinder of one of the five cameras ready to roll, and notices that something is wrong: the rear-wall façade of the building they're about to blow up is not tall enough to block out the sky. It will ruin the illusion by making the structure seem fake. Something needs to be done. Fast.

Bill Roe, the show's award-winning director of photography, calls out a solution that seems so simple: raise the wall two feet. Without so much as a beat to acknowledge the difficulty involved, the crew sets about doing just that – all with the sun's rays quickly fading. As it turns out, the 'wall' is actually just a piece of lightweight foam that is effortlessly repositioned. Yet on camera, it looks completely believable.

The location for the past two days is a remote stretch of land located an hour outside of Los Angeles. Looking a bit like Iraqi soil, it is where they will shoot the grand scale teaser sequence of "Providence," taking place during the Gulf War a decade ago. In the scene, a U.S. soldier named "Cpt. Josepho" (played by Denis Forest) observes the miraculous arrival of a group of Super Soldiers. Appearing like a mirage from the sand, they complete their impossible mission, despite taking heavy fire. Josepho is the sole witness to these incredible events.

With an empty director slot, Carter stepped in behind the lens at the last minute. Not only is his script a major undertaking, but the change of plans brought about even more complications, including a short time for preparation. In the desert, they are halfway through the shoot, but the episode pages aren't quite finished.

"I'm *still* writing the script," sighs Carter. "There's just never enough time when you're trying to write, produce and direct."

As the actors portraying the Super Soldiers run through their scene one last time with stunt coordinator Danny Weselis, the special effects team, under foreman Kelly Kerby, puts the finishing touches on the pyrotechnics. The sun has already disappeared, making it too late to do the important shot in direct daylight.

Alleviating the tension, cinematographer Roe and gaffer Jono Kouzouyan, who is in charge of the show's lighting, devise a solution. Although they are stuck in the middle of the desert, the crew just happened to have brought along a piece of equipment to do just the trick. Out comes a massive truck fitted with an enormous hydraulic arm that can raise a bank of lights into the air strong enough to illuminate a parking lot.

"It wasn't even there for (that purpose). It was there for the night shot,"

Roe says, referring to an unrelated scene involving the Lone Gunmen inside a parked van. "Jono and I just looked over there and went, 'Hey, we could use that. In about half an hour we're going to need it.'"

Meanwhile, Weselis prepares his team of actors. They are an impressive-looking bunch.

"Some of my stuntmen were former military. One was a 25-year Navy SEAL instructor," says Weselis, proudly.

Others hail from the Marines, the Rangers, and the Army. During their two days on location, they'd had to do a number of paramilitary drills for the cameras, including a run through the desert with 14-pounds of squibs on them for as many as 30 to 40 simulated bullet hits. Although they are a highly professional crew, there have still been a few missteps that have made for some lightness on the serious set.

"I thought that it was funny that you think of the stuntmen as being these perfect physical specimens, able to do anything," Carter laughs. "But a couple of times, they tripped and fell. Some of their shooting didn't look quite right."

The constant challenge at the desert location is to shoot everything required within a tight schedule. This particular teaser required twice the amount of time to shoot as used on a regular teaser. But it had originally been even more elaborate.

"I'd written a much bigger – probably twice as big – action sequence," says Carter. "So I was already stealing from the time of my other work. But I felt that Frank Spotnitz came in and gave me very good advice, which was to cut the teaser down. I was too ambitious, even in the two days I was doing it in. When I cut it down, I still barely made my work, and even then it was with some tremendous good luck."

Yet as grand as it is, Carter wishes he could have made it even bigger.

"I still would have liked to have gotten more material," he says.

Although finding a location to shoot the Iraqi sequence seemed like it would be the episode's biggest obstacle, co-executive producer Michelle MacLaren was pleasantly surprised at how quickly location manager Ilt Jones accomplished the task.

"Ilt had obviously researched it and was taking us somewhere that he knew about," MacLaren says. "We were way out in the desert and we drove around this corner of these hills and I felt like we had entered another country. It was so desolate, and there were these stone

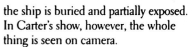

buildings that looked like a bomb had gone off in them. It was perfect."

To make it even more perfect, the episode required that a building actually be blown up. That building, and those around it, was the product of the show's art department and construction crew, who built all the edifices in the teaser from scratch.

"There was one little building that was there, but we had to give it a façade because it wouldn't have been appropriate for the Iraqi setting," explains production designer Corey Kaplan.

Once the Iraqi building was rigged to explode and the lighting crane was positioned when the stuntmen were in place, Carter and crew took cover a safe distance away. Following the "action" command, the front of the building blows up into flames and debris. Several seconds later, the Super Soldiers appear from the dust, burned but remarkably uninjured. The most incredible part of the shot is

that the actors have been near to the explosion the whole time. This ensured that the cameras could run without cutting to allow the Super Soldiers to get into position. It had been one continuous take.

"The explosion occurred in front of them," explains Weselis. "The soldiers were inside a window shooting out. It was cork and dust and dirt mortar that blew up to give the effect."

Another challenge for this two-part mythology series is the spaceship, seen in both episodes, which had to be constructed and dug into a hole, not on the friendly confines of the Fox soundstages, but in a whole different remote location. The set for these scenes is found in the hills near California's Simi Valley. In Kim Manners' episode, "Provenance,"

the ship is buried and partially exposed. In Carter's show, however, the whole thing is seen on camera.

"We literally dug the hole the size of our spaceship, which is very large, outside in the middle of a field and put a tent up over it," explains MacLaren. "The spaceship had to be built in pieces and then assembled in the hole."

"What feature films do in that case," reveals art director Sandy Getzler, is "build the shell of something, and they build a miniature, and they do visual effects. But we didn't do that."

"Chris Carter wanted the *whole* ship," Kaplan emphasizes, "which we're not really used to because we kind of always depend on my favorite man in the art department – John Wash."

Typically, only a small portion of the ship would be built on set, and the rest would be filled in digitally by visual effects supervisor John Wash during post-production. With the exception of the UFO taking off, however, shots of the spacecraft in this episode were done practically.

"It was all nerve-wracking," Kaplan explains, "because you have to build it in sections, you have to get it out to the location and you have to get it together so it doesn't look like it came out in 4x8 sections."

The end result fooled even its designer, as evidenced in the show when the UFO takes off and leaves a charred hole in the ground. After watching footage of the scene, Kaplan confessed, "I was looking at it going, 'Oh God, what a wonderful miniature.' Then all of a sudden Gillian and Annabeth come running (into the shot) and it's like, 'I can't believe *The X-Files*!'"

Despite her surprise, though, Kaplan insists she's learned to take the outrageous requests of the show's creators in her stride.

"This show can't shock me," she proclaims. "I find myself saying, 'Okay, now where do you want your spaceship? And you want a pirate ship – where do you want that one?' It's just another day at work. It's wonderful."

Part of what makes their creations so believable on screen is the incredible detail to which the art department attends. Nearly every surface of the spacecraft, for instance, is covered with

the writing of an intricate alien language, much of which may never be noticed on television but still contributes to the overall effect.

Kaplan reveals this was done by designing individual characters – or letters – for the imagined language and then programming them into a computer. The finished product was output as rub-on lettering, and then applied to the ship. Yet, don't go looking for the hidden meaning in the content; only the art department knows what's actually written on the ship. Besides, you could fill a book with the amount of text that covers the massive ship.

In addition to its sheer size, the craft also housed an elaborate lighting design that included over 100 individual lamps hidden within. Gaffer Kouzouyan offered Carter a range of creative options for bringing the lights to life on the screen. Carter instead opted for a straightforward approach, and jokingly chided Kouzouyan for being so bold in his suggestions.

Kouzouyan humorously replied to Carter, "You're the monster that created it!"

Yet the cool sets and special effects wouldn't work on screen without a story to back them up. Fortunately, this episode unfurls more of the mythology that develops existing characters as well

as introduce new ones. A cult of alien worshippers abducts Scully's baby. An FBI agent near death is magically healed by the powers of an alien artifact. In the Canadian wilderness, a buried UFO comes to life. The Super Soldiers reappear in flashback, as we begin to learn more about the enigmatic "Toothpick Man" in the present day. And Reyes questions her own issues of faith, as she prays for Doggett to come out of a coma.

"Her faith is a kind of catholic – with a small 'c' – faith," Carter clarifies about Reyes in the script. "Doggett's coma forces her to act on that faith, and I think that is the interesting thing – that we can all believe, but how we act on our faith is another thing."

This re-evaluation of faith is consistent with a comment voiced by Scully about the writing on the alien spaceship in the first episode of this two-parter: "Everything mankind believes in is in question." In Scully's case, it is the willingness to remain open-minded about her faith in light of the birth and disappearance of her 'miracle' baby, William.

"What I'm trying to play with," Carter reveals, "is really a kind of fantastic mythology that seems to have some basis in fact, which is what, to me, sort of sums up the whole pursuit of alien life and alien artifacts. So what

happens is that – in relation to Scully – the birth of the miracle child and the need for understanding and answers gets very interesting when it's upset by the introduction of this crazy man from this crazy ship."

Carter is intrigued by the questions it raises in relation to traditional religion and Scully's faith, adding, "I think that particularly when you have a child you are bound to look for answers in the wildest places."

Attempting to thwart Scully from uncovering the truth is the recently introduced FBI character known only as the Toothpick Man, played by Alan Dale. Asked if the Toothpick Man will play a role similar to that of the Cigarette-Smoking Man, Carter is tight-lipped, offering that he would be, "a more dangerous character."

"He has a connection to a more physically dangerous group of people," Carter says, referring to the Super Soldiers.

Exactly how the character's involvement will play out in future episodes Carter isn't saying. But, to be sure, he and the writers at Ten Thirteen have more dilemmas in store for the Toothpick Man and the other characters as the series finale approaches, and we'll be waiting impatiently to see how it unfolds. ●

OTHER GREAT TV TIE-IN COMPANIONS FROM TITAN
ON SALE NOW!

The X-Files - The Official Collection Volume 1
ISBN 9781782763710

The X-Files - The Official Collection Volume 2
ISBN 9781782763727

The X-Files - The Official Collection Volume 3
ISBN 9781782763734

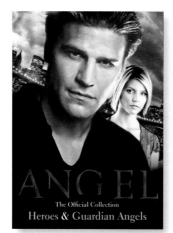

Angel - Heroes & Guardian Angels
ISBN 9781782763680

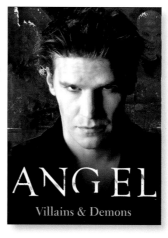

Angel - Villains & Demons
ISBN 9781782763697

COMING SOON

Buffy - The Slayer Collection Volume 1
ISBN 9781782763642

Buffy - The Slayer Collection Volume 2
ISBN 9781782763659

Buffy - The Slayer Collection Volume 3
ISBN 9781782763666

For more information visit www.titan-comics.com

TITANCOMICS